THE GENTLEMAN
PRESS AGENT

Also by Robert Simonson

On Broadway Men Still Wear Hats
Cafe Society (play)
Role of a Lifetime

THE GENTLEMAN PRESS AGENT

FIFTY YEARS IN THE THEATRICAL TRENCHES *with* MERLE DEBUSKEY

ROBERT SIMONSON

APPLAUSE THEATRE & CINEMA BOOKS
An Imprint of Hal Leonard Corporation
New York

Published in 2010 by Applause Theatre & Cinema Books
An Imprint of Hal Leonard Corporation
7777 West Bluemound Road
Milwaukee, WI 53213

Trade Book Division Editorial Offices
19 West 21st Street, New York, NY 10010

Printed in the United States of America

Book design by UB Communications

All photos are from the personal collection of Merle Debuskey

Library of Congress Cataloging-in-Publication Data

Simonson, Robert.
   The gentleman press agent : fifty years in the theatrical trenches with Merle Debuskey / Robert Simonson.
      p. cm.
      ISBN 978-1-55783-765-3 (hardcover)
   1. Debuskey, Merle. 2. Press agents—United States-—Biography. 3. Theater—New York (State)—New York—History—20th century. I. Title.
      PN2287.D352S56 2010
      659.2'9792092—dc22
      [B]
                                                            2010011022

www.applausepub.com

To the unsung

Inscription on the plaque dedicated on November 4, 2009, at the Public Theater.

CONTENTS

FOREWORD

All enterprise, be it the arts, business, or social movements, needs "the oxygen of publicity to survive." In this book, Robert Simonson tells the story of the legendary New York press agent Merle Debuskey. A Jew from Baltimore, he weathered anti-Semitism at the University of Virginia, which he attended on an athletic scholarship. Seasoned by competitive sports and the military—he was an all-American lacrosse player and World War II veteran who saw action in the Pacific—Debuskey knew how to fight. And that gritty spirit, combined with his open-mindedness, intelligence, and honest persuasiveness, guided many major cultural and political figures and earned him the trust and respect of the smartest and most influential journalists.

The typical theatrical press agent was a P. T. Barnum figure, feeding journalists gossip and half-truths about the established stars and big Broadway shows he represented. But Debuskey, a unique blend of City College professor, strategist, and Damon Runyon character, broke that mold. For one thing, he went to graduate school on the G.I. Bill and earned a master's degree in public relations from the New School. His press releases were famous for their breadth of ideas and love of language. His approach was hand tailored to each project, and he was always truthful with his clients. A phenomenal multitasker, Debuskey could represent many shows simultaneously, and he worked with Broadway producers as varied as Mike Todd, the flamboyant showman; Alexander Cohen, who produced the Tony Awards for twenty years; and Philip Rose, who made history when he produced *A Raisin in the Sun*, the first Broadway play by an African American woman. He not only worked on Broadway and with stars like Zero Mostel and Lauren Bacall, but also championed unknown Off-Broadway companies such as the New York Shakespeare Festival and the Circle in the Square, which went on to enormous success.

Debuskey was involved in the civil rights movement, and when Julian Bond went before the Supreme Court to argue his case to be seated by the Georgia legislature, it was Debuskey who represented him. As president of ATPAM, the union for press agents and theater managers, he was respected by labor and management. Debuskey supported artists who were attacked as communists and organized journalists to write against the House Un-American Activities Committee. When Joseph Papp was considering capitulating to Robert Moses over his demand for a twenty-five-cent admission charge to see Shakespeare in Central Park, it was Debuskey who counseled Papp that free Shakespeare was worth fighting for. Papp went on to defeat Moses in court.

I first met Debuskey in 1995. Sixteen years after founding Theatre for a New Audience, a nonprofit organization whose mission is to vitalize the performance and study of Shakespeare and classic drama, I was desperately seeking a press agent who could advocate for fuller coverage in the *New York Times*.

We met in his decidedly unglitzy office in a nondescript building on Eighth Avenue and Fifty-fifth Street. After we talked for a while, he explained with great care that he couldn't help me, but agreed to stay in touch. After many meetings, Debuskey decided to have his associate, Susan Chicoine, represent us. Soon afterward, he joined our board. One year later, we received our first feature in the *Times*.

"What news on the Rialto?" asks a character in Shakespeare's *The Merchant of Venice*. In *The Gentleman Press Agent*, Robert Simonson tells a complex, colorful story of the man who understood New York's Rialto better than anyone. Though his behind-the-scenes profession means that many people have never heard of him, Debuskey played a major role in shaping several of New York's most cherished cultural institutions. New York is what it is today, in part, thanks to Merle Debuskey.

Jeffrey Horowitz
Founder and Artistic Director
Theatre for a New Audience

ACKNOWLEDGMENTS

This book could not have been attempted without the participation of Basil Merle Debuskey, who, as he approaches his eighty-ninth year, retains a sharp memory of the preceding eighty-eight. I thank Merle for the time he donated in the form of numerous interview sessions conducted over a period of two and a half years. I also thank his wife, Pearl Somner, for giving up her husband for those periods of time. Merle also allowed me free rein to rifle through his voluminous files of correspondences, documents, photographs, and press clippings. In support, confirmation, and accreditation of the Debuskeys' testimony and papers, I interviewed dozens of theater professionals whose lives touched on Merle's. These included Mickey Alpert, Emanuel Azenberg, Russell Baker, Clive Barnes, Doris Belack, Larry Belling, Robert Buckley, Susan Chicoine, Bruce Cohen, Chris Cohen, Jason Steven Cohen, Judy Davidson, Ruby Dee, Gemze de Lappe, Bernard Gersten, Madeline Lee Gilford, Shirley Herz, Jeffrey Horowitz, Bob Kamlot, Richard Kornberg, Paul Libin, Don Loze, Herbert Mitgang, Gregory Mosher, Sidney Offit, Gail Papp, Philip Rose, Harvey Sabinson, Gene Saks, Lee Silver, Marilyn Stasio, Leo Stern, Bob Ullman, Zoe Wanamaker, Jon Wilner, Laurel Ann Wilson, and Gene Wolsk. (Since our meetings, Barnes and Gilford have passed away.) Great thanks goes to Phil Birsh, the publisher of Playbill, without whose enthusiasm, encouragement, and generosity this project never would have been instigated; John Cerullo and Marybeth Keating at Applause Books, without whose patience, understanding, mediation, and diplomacy the book would have never reached publication; and my copy editor, Barbara Norton, whose insightful suggestions and sharp eyes led to a tighter and better book. I would also like to thank Playbill.com's editors, Andrew Gans and Kenneth Jones, who took it in stride when I went AWOL from my senior contributor duties for weeks at a time while I worked on this manuscript. Finally, I owe a great debt of gratitude to my lovely wife, Sarah Schmeler, and son, Asher, who had to hear the improbable and phonetically loaded name Merle Debuskey spoken in our home about five thousand times over the past three years. That couldn't have been easy.

THE GENTLEMAN
PRESS AGENT

PROLOGUE

In 1971 the Broadway press agent Merle Debuskey, born a Jew and now a confirmed agnostic, began carrying a paperback copy of the New Testament in his pocket. It wasn't a solace. It was a weapon. The new musical he was representing was being attacked from all corners. Not by critics—it was too early for that; the show hadn't even opened yet. His assailants weren't necessarily theatergoers at all, in fact. They were self-appointed defenders of that holy book in his pocket and its principal protagonist. And they didn't like *Jesus Christ Superstar* one bit.

In the days just before the rock musical's Broadway opening, near-chaos broke out. The musical was assailed by a number of attackers—Catholics, Protestants, and, the most animated of the bunch, Jews. All pious parties considered the rock opera perfectly blasphemous. "The situation was rabid and volatile in a fashion essentially never before seen on Broadway," recalled Debuskey, who had by that point seen three decades of Broadway action. "On the day of the opening, every denomination was getting in on the act, issuing dictums about a show they had never seen."

To the Catholics and the right-wing Protestant groups, *Superstar* was objectionable because it denied his divinity, treating Jesus as a man and not as God. Many also considered that it made Judas something of a hero. "But the topper," recalled the publicist,

> was a letter hand-delivered from the American Jewish Committee to
> each critic, maintaining that the show was "mischievous and possibly
> a backward step on the road toward improved Christian-Jewish

relations." The committee declared that the musical "unambiguously lays the primary responsibility for Jesus' suffering and crucifixion to the Jewish priesthood," which is "portrayed as hideously inhuman and satanically evil: contemptuous, callous and bloodthirsty."

Though Debuskey had represented hundreds of shows, *Superstar* wasn't exactly the kind of thing he was used to handling. And not just because his associates were engulfed in a cloud of marijuana smoke every time they ranged backstage at the Mark Hellinger. For one thing, most of the producers he dealt with—the cream of the profession, including Joe Papp, the team of Cy Feuer and Ernie Martin, and Alexander H. Cohen—could be communed with at a moment's notice. *Superstar* was produced on Broadway by the Australian music tycoon Robert Stigwood, whom Debuskey only knew by name. Stigwood was a master in a field Debuskey considered "a treacherous terrain bristling with duplicity, theft, ingratitude, and riches that would make a piker of Midas." But he lived in the United Kingdom, and he stayed there right up until opening night.

The show's writers—a couple of English wastrels named Tim Rice and Andrew Lloyd Webber—had been cooperative enough, going cheerfully to the interviews Debuskey set up for them. But Stigwood had no experience on Broadway and seemingly no particular curiosity in how it worked. He had amassed an immense fortune in pop and rock music, being among the first to breach all the boundaries between individual managers, booking agents, record producers, concert and theater producers, and music publishers by coalescing all those professionals into one person—himself. His client list included the Beatles, Mick Jagger, Rod Stewart, David Bowie, Eric Clapton, and Cream. "He probably could have challenged the Bank of England," opined Debuskey.

But at least Stigwood was human. *Superstar*'s other producer—equally absent and untested in theatrical waters—was a corporate entity: MCA Inc.

Those protesters outside the theater, however—they were definitely human. As Debuskey looked over the riotous scene, it occurred to him that that his earlier efforts to calm the waters might not have done the trick. The press agent had offered scripts to some religious leaders and had invited others to a run-through of the show, which was being directed by Tom O'Horgan—the same Tom O'Horgan who had been the one-man band for the Second City at the Square East cabaret downtown, which Debuskey had nurtured for several years. "There was no antagonistic response, and it quelled our anxiety in that area," he recalled.

Yet here were those same leaders and their followers, mad as hornets. Christians and Jews were joined in opposition but separated by holding pens: the police set up wooden barriers dividing the different denominations from one another. The din was magnificent. Each group was determined to object more vocally than the last.

Press is good, and certainly the protests were netting *Superstar* a boatload of attention. But Debuskey knew that could boomerang. You could refute your critics—they expect that—but you couldn't safely ignore them. That would only fuel the fire. Some sort of diplomatic statement had to be cast out into the teeth of the howling masses.

Debuskey left an associate to monitor the mob and went in search of the elusive Stigwood. Was he out front? No. Backstage? No. The publicist finally located the blasé producer in the $700,000 town house he had rented, where he was happily working out his opening-night party plans, flying in two hundred guests from England and ten family members from Australia.

Stigwood knew how to head off a crisis, if he could be bothered to do it. *Superstar* was a new breed of show in that it was as much a musical enterprise as a theatrical one, and Stigwood had been faced with multiple pirated concert versions of the musical. So he decided to eliminate them by mounting three "official" touring concert versions that had criss-crossed the country and grossed millions. He deployed an army of lawyers spread around the country to stop the pirated versions and had obtained eighteen restraining orders.

"I convinced him that the situation demanded a response from the production, and he agreed to call the MCA people," remembered

Debuskey. "He said we would meet at an office in the theater in an hour." When Debuskey arrived, he discovered Stigwood in a dressing room writing notes to accompany his opening-night gifts to the company: coffee mugs adorned with the show's logo. The branding of the show had begun. "He made it clear that the matter at hand was interrupting his task."

The suits from MCA arrived. Debuskey pleaded to all that a statement had to be made rebutting the avalanche of criticism. The producers were flummoxed. So Debuskey went into his ventriloquism act. "I pulled out a statement I had written and offered it up as one that could come from them," said Debuskey. "They read it and agreed on its content. I covered my ass by asking them to sign it."

Then the two MCA suits left. After a bit they returned to say that though it was a good statement, they could not have MCA sign on. But they thought Stigwood should. "They left, and I explained to Stigwood that MCA was headed by the most powerful figure in Hollywood, Lew Wasserman, who was very active in top-level Jewish organizations, and that these guys knew their jobs were on the line if Wasserman was of a mind to support the Jewish organizations involved in the controversy." Debuskey then left and distributed the release to the press.

Outside, the audience members encountered near-pandemonium as they tried to enter the theater. "They had to wend their way through the shouting Christians and Jews," Debuskey said, "each group of demonstrators trying to be more truly religious than the other. There were the paparazzi and the onlookers trying to spot the celebrities, the accredited photographers, the reporters, and the TV crews."

The curtain was held as the production waited for celebrities delayed by the demonstrations. But the show finally went on—to wild audience acclaim. The critics were not so kind, but that made little difference. With huge advance sales, it would run for nearly two years.

An article that appeared in the *New York Times* about the Jewish organizations' complaints read:

Robert Stigwood, the British producer of the show, which opened last night, issued a statement through Merle Debuskey, its press representative, which said in part: *"Jesus Christ Superstar* is, in my opinion, an affirmation of life, of humanity. It is not a literal representation of the passion of Christ as revealed by the New Testament. It views, in contemporary style, the timelessness of a legend, a myth, and the confrontations of a reformer and the Establishment which continually recur in the history of man. No man is guilty—not even Judas—no man is innocent. It is my fervent wish that the stage piece effect a communion with the audience that is spiritually exalting."

Such legerdermain, said Debuskey, "is the nature of the beast—for the press agent to create the statement, which is accredited to someone else."

Stigwood and his British associates left a few days after the premiere, and Debuskey never again had a word with any of them. The only acknowledgment he got for handling the opening-night altercation came from O'Horgan, who thanked him for stepping in. The Brits, he said, were "assholes."

INTRODUCTION

On the north side of West Forty-eighth Street, in the middle of the block between Sixth and Seventh Avenues, directly across from where the Cort Theatre still (infrequently) packs them in, there once sat a snug red-brick-and-marble Broadway house with the half-poetic, half-prosaic name of the Playhouse. The top two floors—accessible only by a cramped, three-person elevator manually operated by a syntax-challenged first-generation Slav named George—were carved up into a warren of offices. During the 1960s, until the theater was torn down in 1968, some of these rooms were occupied by arguably the two greatest press agents Broadway ever saw.

Judy Davidson was a budding young publicist during the opening months of the Kennedy administration, and she met both men. She was first interviewed by Richard Maney, a booze-and-blarney-soaked Montana-born Irishman of legendary status. Maney was beloved by pressmen for his barroom camaraderie and his flavorsome, purple-prose press releases, which more often than not improved on actual events. Maney and his longtime client, the louche stage star Tallulah Bankhead, enjoyed each other's company lavishly, but, on that day females did not figure into Maney's plan. He took one look at Davidson, his shock of white hair growing one shade paler, and cried, "Hire a girl?! Not in this office."

Davidson left Maney's cluttered den, its walls decorated with framed cover stories, and walked over to another office housed under the theater's mansard roof—a couple of rooms that had been rented by the youthful firm of Debuskey and Krawitz. The two men hired the young woman on the spot.

At that time the partnership was hot. When the two publicists decided to join forces, Seymour Krawitz brought to the table the long-running comedy hit *Mary, Mary*, while Merle Debuskey had the mammoth musical *How to Succeed in Business Without Really Trying* in his pocket, not to mention the rising New York Shakespeare Festival, led by the impetuous visionary Joseph Papp. The excitable Krawitz was a decent, well-read, middle-class type. Fussy and a little manic, he managed to carve out a living for himself in the business. Debuskey, in contrast, was a tall, handsome, Jewish, Baltimore-bred, All-American lacrosse player. It was he who would become the most successful theater publicist New York would see during the second half of the twentieth century.

Debuskey was an anomaly in his profession in almost every way. He bore himself like a producer, a politician, a pundit—anything but a press agent. One fellow flack, Mickey Alpert, compared him to a City College professor from the 1930s. The critic Clive Barnes thought he comported himself like an ambassador or senator: "He was one of these people who decided what he was going to look like at forty and looked the same when he was seventy." The veteran newsman Harry Haun used to joke that he cut so distinguished a figure and looked so good in a tuxedo, he could model for bourbon ads. During the 1970s that tux was often a suave brown-velvet one— a gift from his longtime companion (and eventually his second wife) Pearl Somner. It was frequently covered by a grand camel's-hair topcoat with wide fur lapels that Pearl called his "Impresario Coat."

Debuskey was well educated in a line of work in which most previous practitioners had learned from the gutter up, working "out of the back of hosiery stores," as Alpert put it, and relying on street sense, barroom deals, and tactics reminiscent of P. T. Barnum. He had received his tutelage under none other than Edward Bernays, whom many consider the father of modern public relations. Debuskey was untempted by the two great vices that plagued men in his trade: he boozed little and gambled not at all. Instead, he used his free time to play tennis, charm the opposite sex, and type lengthy, single-spaced missives, often with no direct practical purpose in mind, to the critics and columnists of the day. Whereas Maney would conjure schemes, feeding false information to the columns to drum up publicity for his clients, Debuskey would instruct his underlings to play it straight with reporters. There would be no bullshit in his arena.

One could say he had an acute case of integrity wholly at odds with his occupation. In direct contrast to the publicist's innate reflex to be a "yes man," he posted a sign on the wall reading "No is also an answer." But instead of working against him, his reputation for candor and morality actually brought him business. The producers Cy Feuer and Ernie Martin, Philip Rose, the Shuberts, and Alexander H. Cohen—the top men in their field—flocked to him, amused by the newest novelty: the thinking, unintimidatable, scrupulous flack. The man's name itself was a kind of catnip for attention. (Debuskey dropped his true first name, Basil, early on.) The *Detroit Free Press* critic Larry DeVine recalled first coming across the loaded moniker on a press release announcing an upcoming Miami Beach visit by the saloon singer Bobby Short. To confirm, he contacted Short, who replied, "Yes, a person named Merle Debuskey definitely does exist."

Larry Belling, who worked in the offices of Krawitz and Debuskey for a time during the Joseph Papp years, vividly recalled his very different duo of bosses.

> Seymour was very much a go-getter. He was always checking and rechecking little details and forgetting the big ones. He was out there hustling all the time and very energetic and gregarious—and never seemed to bring any work into the office. Merle would sit there smoking his pipe; he used Balkan Sobranie tobacco, a Macedonian blend with Turkish Yenidje leaf and Latakia....He sat back and talked very slowly and at great length about a myriad of subjects, and the world would come to him. I just thought Merle was fantastic, because he never appeared to do any work, but he brought all the business into the office.

"He had tremendous respect among the newspaper people, because he didn't lie," recalled Davidson. "He appeared low-key. He was anti–*What Makes Sammy Run.*" Belling once broke into a sweat when fielding a call from a newspaper editor who asked if he should send his first-string critic or a second-stringer to the production of a dog of a play that Debuskey was representing. He put the man on hold and asked Merle. "Never lie," said the boss. "Tell him to send a second-stringer." The show closed on its opening night.

Blacklisted actors such as Jack Gilford, Zero Mostel, and John Randolph saw in Debuskey a sympathetic lefty who had managed to avoid the House Un-American Activities Committee's censure. Debuskey's office became a kind of refuge for them, and there they would sit every day to shoot the breeze, hear the latest scuttlebutt, or simply vent. They trusted the publicist. Hadn't he put up John Henry Faulk in his own house when the radio personality took on Joseph McCarthy and the blacklisters in court? Hadn't he found Joseph Papp a lawyer when the impresario was called before HUAC? Hadn't he dined with Alger Hiss?

The group would send George, the elevator operator, out for sandwiches from the beloved Gaiety Deli on Times Square, and the gabfest would begin. It was a good place for out-of-work actors to be. The hive of studios atop the Playhouse also included the headquarters of the League of American Producers; the office of Richard Barr, then the producer of the era's hottest playwright, Edward Albee; and the office of the old-time producer Max Gordon, who every day would amble into the Debuskey offices with the salutation, "Well, boys, what's new on the Rialto?"

Debuskey, who liked talking perhaps more than anything (except possibly sports), would readily indulge them as well as himself, embroidering long, loping sentences that trailed off endlessly into the air like the smoke from his pipe. "He would seldom say in ten words what could be said in a hundred," said Belling. If no one dropped by, there was always the phone. The cigar-chomping producer Ernie Martin, a pal, would call and tell him to drop everything and get over to his office—there was a chauffeur-driven limo waiting to take them to Belmont. Philip Rose, who made his name with *A Raisin in the Sun*, would draft him for a pool-playing session with Sidney Poitier at a subterranean gaming den on

Broadway. Just about anybody might call to arrange a tennis game. Papp, who had his own direct line in Debuskey's office, would begin with a pun and end shortly after with an order to hustle down to the theater. Papp's demands and needs were the same—enormous and unending—whether he paid Debuskey nothing (as he did for the first ten years or so) or a pittance (as he did thereafter). The relationship was far from smooth—from time to time Papp would fire Debuskey, and at other times Debuskey would quit—but the separation wouldn't last for long. Debuskey believed in the Shakespeare Festival and happily helped explain it and Papp to the press for thirty years.

Alex Cohen would call to talk about anything and everything, from the grosses of his latest show to world affairs and philosophy, in conversations that could last for hours. Cohen knew that in Debuskey he had someone who could expound on matters wide and disparate. Debuskey was good for an opinion, sage but not spiteful, of the prospects of any show on or off Broadway. He would speak on the Student Nonviolent Coordinating Committee, Women Strike for Peace, and César Chávez's United Farm Workers, because he had labored for these organizations, always pro bono, and sometimes with adverse consequences. Debuskey is one of the very few Broadway press agents in history to have an FBI file.

He did it all without seeming to break a sweat. Years later Don Loze, who handled Feuer and Martin's affairs in the 1960s, would marvel: "Merle was able to juggle our business with all the other things he was doing and one never interfered with the other. When I learned the dimensions of the other things, I was kind of overwhelmed."

"That was the stunner," agreed Marilyn Stasio, a theater critic who spent part of her long career at the *New York Times*, and who overcame her professional scruples to become friends with Debuskey. "He was doing what he did for so many different producers—Philip Rose, Joe Papp, Cy Feuer—all at the same time. If theater producers were the princes that they think they are, then Merle Debuskey was their Richelieu."

Chapter 1

BEGINNINGS

The stories of the New York theater press agents who operated before World War II were all the same: land on Broadway and make it there or get out. Debuskey's path was a new one. The man behind hundreds of Broadway shows made a name for himself in Greenwich Village, in a new, amorphous, creative universe labeled Off-Broadway.

After graduating from Johns Hopkins and following three years' service in the navy patrolling the South Pacific, Debuskey thought getting a job in journalism would sate his passion for words. He had always wanted to be a writer and had done some sports writing for his college newspaper. But, as in college and in the armed forces, anti-Semitism hindered him. At an interview at the *Baltimore Sun*, the major newspaper in his hometown, he was told that there were no openings on the paper's news staff and that there were not likely to be any in the near future. Recalled Debuskey: "The interviewer said, though, that he liked my background and thought I had a future in journalism. So to help me get a start, he offered to recommend me for a position with a small newspaper in Cumberland, Maryland. There, he said, I would cover politics, sports, obituaries, marriages, and more. It would be, he said, a great training ground."

Excited, Debuskey told one of his classmates, Russell Baker, who would go on to become a columnist for the *New York Times*. "Don't you know," said Baker, "that sending you to Cumberland is part of the *Baltimore Sun*'s 'final solution' for aspiring Jewish journalists?" H. L. Mencken, the famed *Sun* journalist of the first half of the twentieth century, had had anti-Semitic leanings, Baker pointed out, and things hadn't changed much since his time. And so in 1947 Debuskey packed his bag and headed for New York, where he hoped anti-Semitism would present less of an obstacle.

Merle's eldest brother, Matthew, a pediatrician, had a good friend from his Johns Hopkins Medical School days, Artie Rosenblum, a general practitioner with a combined office and home at 1302 Avenue L in the Midwood section of Brooklyn. Debuskey was offered a trundle bed in Rosenblum's office. The catch was that Merle would have to rise early enough—usually by 8 a.m.—to stash the trundle bed and make the office available to patients.

Debuskey registered under the G.I. Bill for a graduate degree in public relations at the New School for Social Research on West Twelfth Street in Greenwich Village. He wanted to take courses in journalism, but since none were offered at night and he needed to search for work during the day, he signed up for public relations and publicity classes. Teaching it was Edward Bernays, the legendary PR man credited with incorporating psychology in publicity as a sure way to manipulate the American consumer. He called his technique "the engineering of consent."

"He was the nephew of Sigmund Freud," recalled Debuskey,

> a relationship he made known on any and all occasions. In our studies, he admitted that he learned from Freud and utilized some of Freud's principles, such as people's unconscious and psychological motivations. My first impression of him was a man of supreme self-confidence and self-promotion. His demeanor was polite but unquestionable. His appearance was right out of Central Casting for a banker in a black-and-white '30s movie.

In one class, Bernays boasted that he could make any Broadway show a sellout. Debuskey thought this might be true, but Bernays' price tag would cancel out the producer's subsequent profit.

At the New School he met two World War II veterans, also unemployed, who would push him toward what he calls his "unwitting slip into the world of theater." Mel Goldblatt was from a well-to-do family in the Midwest that wanted him to join their hardware business. He had resisted, hoping to become a theater administrator. Irving Stiber had planned to become a director and had studied at the New School in its Dramatic Workshop, founded by Erwin Piscator, the exiled German stage director who, with Bertolt Brecht, had been a leader in the theater of Weimar-era Berlin. His classes featured students who became the core of the golden age of American theater, among them Marlon Brando, Rod Steiger, and Elaine Stritch.

After class, over beers and cheap bowls of soup in neighborhood Italian restaurants on MacDougal or Bleecker Street, Debuskey would avidly listen to Goldblatt and Stiber's plans to create a cooperative theater company in the Village. Debuskey knew almost nothing of the theater. He had studied Shakespeare and Molière but had seen only one significant play, a touring production of Eugene O'Neill's *The Iceman Cometh*. Goldblatt and Stiber, meanwhile, could debate the merits of the important New York theater companies of the first part of the twentieth century—the Provincetown Players, the Washington Square Players, the Civic Repertory Theatre, the Group Theatre, the Theatre Guild, Orson Welles's Mercury Players, and the Federal Theatre.

The new company, in Debuskey's view, was a direct result of the men's wartime experiences.

> In 1947, when I came up, there was an attitude among all these guys of "Look what happened in World War II. What an experience." The whole country got together and did marvelous things. There was a sense that there's a shot at it, if you want to take it, and let's do it. When I ran into these people who were interested in the theater, they were conditioned by this experience of World War II. They felt, "What are you talking about, man? Telling us we can't get this group, can't get this show? Can't get a theater going? Man, if we try we can do it." Joe Papp had that conviction that was really deep, and part of it was that World War II experience. "What do you mean I can't do it?"

Over the months the collective came together. Actors were drafted, money found, designers committed. The original press agent, however, had been fired. They offered the position to

Debuskey, who had recently earned his PR degree. The salary was $25 a week. Sensing an adventure, attracted by the beautiful women involved, and currently unemployed, he agreed, on one condition: that he be made a member of the cooperative. "This, of course, eliminated any financial compensation." For money, he relied on a government program that gave unemployed veterans $20 a week for fifty-two weeks.

The collective hadn't simply taken Debuskey's publicity skills on faith. He actually had experience—Broadway experience. Early in 1947 he had submitted his résumé to the employment bureau of the journalism and entertainment chapter of the American Veterans Committee. Almost immediately he had gotten a phone call from Hans Jan Lengsfelder, a handsome, gentlemanly figure with a carefully shaped head of wavy white hair and a slight Eastern European accent. Lengsfelder worked in some misty, undefined area of jewelry sales but, Debuskey soon learned, had been one of Europe's most popular songwriters and playwrights between the two world wars. The Viennese-born composer had written dozens of plays and operettas that had been produced in Europe. In the United States since 1932, he now proposed a most unusual theater project. Through his new company, called Your Theatre, Inc., he intended to produce *Heads or Tails*, a farce about a roving diplomat's domestic crisis. The venture would be backed by the theatergoers themselves, who, by buying a ticket for $1.20, became angels. A week before the play opened at the Cort Theatre on April 27, 1947, the troupe had sold more than 34,000 tickets, enough to assure a four-week run.

Part of Debuskey's job in this faintly ludicrous enterprise was to greet potential investors who came up to the office to meet with the European master himself. "First there was the tantalizing wait," he remembered. "Mr. Lengsfelder was on the phone with an important actor, journalist, or Wall Street personage. And after a measured moment, into the room swept the impresario, who gallantly led the impressed walk-in money into his private office. Ticket sales soared. The money rolled in."

The tickets entitled the backer to a share of the profits—a problem, since there weren't any. "'Heads or Tails' You Can't Win!" John

Chapman's review in the *New York Daily News* read. But Lengsfelder would not surrender. That December he announced that he would try again, using the same investment method. "Some of that capitalization had been expended—some of it for legitimate expenses," said Debuskey. "All those lovely, happy angels now transformed into angry Lucifers . . . with pitchfork tails."

The slippery and ingenious Lengsfelder quickly slithered out of this new noose. He told everyone that the project had been saved by his own remarkable generosity; he would give his investors a bonanza—the rights to one of his plays, which had been a huge hit in Europe before the war. He would take no royalties as playwright, nor would he accept the producer's share of any profits. Debuskey, suspicious by this point, read the script. Immediately sensing disaster was looming, he left long before the premiere. His assessment proved accurate: there was no show. And in June of 1948, the *Times* announced that Your Theatre, Inc., had dissolved.

"I had now been introduced to Broadway," Debuskey recollects.

—

The young Off-Broadway collective called itself the Interplayers, and secured a playing space. And what a space it was—none other than the original Provincetown Playhouse, on MacDougal Street, just off Washington Square Park. The Provincetown Players, which birthed Eugene O'Neill, worked at the address after moving its headquarters from Cape Cod to Manhattan. What a place to begin! If only it were inhabitable. Said Debuskey, "It was either owned or leased long-term by a raggle-taggle Gilbert and Sullivan troupe. During the summers, the non-cooled theater simulated a blast furnace, and they wisely exited the city to perform somewhere upstate. They had decided to rent it during the heat of this summer."

On the first day at their new home, the entire company, brimming with postwar optimism, was given brooms, mops, pails, paint, and brushes and put in a fifteen-hour shift. The crew set to work, and work it was. "On first moving into our new home, we discovered it was in worse shape than we had anticipated," Debuskey remembered.

It seemed not to have been cleaned since the original Provincetown Players had baptized it. There was the suffocating odor that accompanied the herd of cats that roamed the building. The rest rooms were of a frightening nature. Ventilation was minimal, and the interior simulated a sauna. The stage, with its concrete cyclorama, designed and built for O'Neill's *The Emperor Jones* in 1924, provided a significant obstacle for the players, who soon would accumulate bruises and scrapes that had to be treated at the nearby St. Vincent's Hospital.

Pushing a broom was Gene Saks, who would go on to direct many Neil Simon plays. Michael V. Gazzo, who would write the drug-addiction drama *A Hatful of Rain*, mopped and complained. And swabbing the men's room was a young actress from Texas named Kim Stanley.

"He was very different from the other people," Saks said, recalling the big, athletic jock who was their press agent. "He was like a regular person. He was not a troubled neurotic. I didn't know anybody in the theater who had ever played lacrosse. I was very relieved, because I considered myself an odd person to be in the theater."

Working conditions were abominable. The cyclorama was useful for lighting effects but frustrating for a director, who had to stage crosses, entrances, and exits around it. The dressing rooms were crowded. Actors who exited one side of the stage had to go down the steps to the basement, run under the stage to the other side, and go up the steps to make their reentrance, seemingly unperturbed by their frenetic dash. The temperature on the stage often reached 103 degrees. Costume changes required the flexibility of a contortionist. But the actors, while not exactly pleased by the difficulties, were content.

"Off-Broadway started because we wanted to act," remembered Saks.

> There wasn't much chance to act on Broadway. There was a chance, but it was a long shot. So we gathered together in little bands and began the Off-Broadway movement. It was the only way to go. We had stars in our eyes, but of a different kind. The truth is we all wanted success, like any other young actor. But we also had this

feeling that the theater should be bigger and better than anything that was being done then commercially. We fulfilled a need that the audience was hungry for. And it made us feel that we were artists.

The initial offering of Jean Cocteau's little-known take on the Oedipus myth, *The Infernal Machine*, was followed by Sean O'Casey's *Within the Gates* and E. E. Cummings's *Him*, a success that ran for more than three months. Cummings himself, who lived nearby on Patchin Place, would sometimes stroll by the theater and examine the photos outside and the blowups of reviews, but he rebuffed all entreaties to talk with the company or attend a performance.

In the Interplayers production of *Him*, in a small role as one of three Weird Sisters loosely modeled on the witches in *Macbeth*, was Kim Stanley. Debuskey had partly joined the group to meet girls, and Stanley was the most fascinating one in the bunch. Born Patricia Reid in Tularosa, New Mexico, she had picked up acting experience in Pasadena, California, and Louisville, Kentucky, before she hooked up with the Interplayers.

Debuskey remembered Stanley in photographic detail.

I thought her singularly attractive, both physically and in her personal demeanor. She was lovely, but not beautiful. Her face lacked the bone structure to effect beauty. She had soft, blondish hair, an irresistible smile, and a well-proportioned body atop well-shaped legs. Her...skin had an amber tinge that she would ascribe to her Native American antecedents—an assertion never substantiated.

Other male members of the Interplayers had picked up on that golden hair and well-proportioned body, and Debuskey soon found himself in competition for Stanley's favors. She played off her attractiveness, Debuskey said, in

a somewhat humorous fashion, sensuously teasing in a "You realize, do you not, that I'm only playing the game?" manner. It was a marvelously balanced act that worked splendidly. The males who were attracted but were rejected remained affectionate, and the women admired and enjoyed this carousel. Some even tried to graft it onto their own persona.

Debuskey was not among the rejected. He and Stanley began an affair that lasted for a tumultuous twelve months. Even then, the "female Brando"—who would rise to the top of her profession before retreating into self-imposed obscurity—was beset with demons, among them alcoholism. She had already disposed of one husband, Bruce Hall, who had lasted but a year. But Debuskey developed "a deep attachment to this tantalizing woman. I was not unaware that this was a treacherous, slippery slope, but I decided to enjoy it as it either developed or waned."

Stanley used her magnetic charm just as well onstage as off. "She was marvelously manipulative, behind a mask of self-effacing openness, receptiveness, and innocence," Debuskey recalled.

> It became apparent early on that she was a superior acting talent. She knew it, knew we knew it, never flaunted it. She was smart enough to recognize that it was an advantage that lent weight to her opinions, without ever having to assert it. And she had a superb theater background, with more experience than most of the actors. All the directors were well aware of her acting ability and charm, knowing it would project from the stage.

"Kim was very influential with people," adds Saks. "She put people together and manipulated them. She was a doer."

The two Kims, the personal and the professional, collided one night when she collapsed onstage while performing. An ambulance hurried her over to an East Side hospital, where she remained for several days. Her mother came up from Texas, and she and Debuskey met for the first time. Following the incident, Stanley returned to the production, fending off all inquiries as to what had happened. On another occasion she became overwhelmed with chills and trembling. Debuskey took her to her apartment and called a doctor friend, who gave him instructions, adding that he should get her to a hospital if she didn't improve by early morning.

"I had described all the symptoms, and I think he was certain of the cause—alcohol—but he didn't want to go into it at the time. She lay on a couch, and I covered her with every warm item in the apartment, including myself, forcing her to take liquids. By morning she had recovered." Stanley refused to get medical attention.

The affair came to an end when Debuskey discovered "what I had thought was a marathon was in reality a relay race." Stanley had other lovers; Debuskey knew at least three of them, including Gazzo. He confronted her.

> She insisted that this was who she was, and that I had to accept it. I withdrew from the relationship. I didn't think she was wronging me. This was her innate behavior. Didn't men behave in this fashion? Nevertheless, because of this and other tweaks in her character that were becoming evident, my ardor had diminished. Instead of lovers, we became familiars.

One of Stanley's other lovers, the director Curt Conway, "was a heavier, and consequently a more compatible, imbiber of alcohol," said Debuskey, "who proposed and eventually married the prize." In Saks's opinion, Debuskey was "well out of it."

The Interplayers were getting some attention. The *Star* ran a lengthy article on the Interplayers, quoting a press release in great detail and, oddly, citing Debuskey by name as the author of the piece. But there were problems within the troupe. Said Debuskey, "As the summer wore on, it became obvious . . . that the severe imbalance of talent and personalities among the group as a whole would destroy it. There was too much dead weight to carry." Finally the group adopted a plan: each member was to submit a list of ten people he or she felt should stay. The ten members with the most citations would continue. Those who were to be removed each received a share of the assets. Those who were to continue received nothing. Among the chosen ten were Louis Criss, Gazzo, Harry Guardino, Saks, Stanley, Irv Stiber, Mel Goldblatt, and Debuskey. "I was surprised; I had not voted for myself, and I still had no conviction that the theater was an area within which I wished to continue. And I had no particular talent to enhance and held little regard for the practice of press agentry."

Toward the end of the summer the collective deliberated on what to do next. They had no money, so leasing a theater was not an option. Finally they decided to create a studio environment in which the group could collectively achieve the quality of a real ensemble. The company rented a plain space in the Carnegie Hall tower and, out of public sight, met daily to work. This continued for a couple of months until the group grew impatient to test the result of its efforts before an audience. A new production, *The Dog beneath the Skin*, was mounted, but after a modest run, the group was seized by another bout of self-criticism and splintered further. Debuskey, Gazzo, Guardino, Saks, Stanley, and one new member, Bea Arthur—Saks's future wife—comprised the new unit, which called itself Off Broadway Inc.

The group planned a season for the late spring and summer of 1949, and Saks, Stanley, and Gazzo each put up $1,000 to finance it. Another old-time Village theater rich with history, the Cherry Lane, was rented. The introductory production would be an attention-grabber: *Yes Is for a Very Young Man*, a Gertrude Stein drama about the German occupation of France in the war that had never before been seen in the United States.

"The single impediment," commented Debuskey dryly, "was the need to obtain the rights."

As the only noncreative member in the group, Debuskey was assigned detection duties. The trail led to Carl Van Vechten, who had met Stein and Alice B. Toklas in Paris in 1913 and become their lifelong friend. He controlled the rights to Stein's works in America. Van Vechten was a magazine writer, music and dance critic, photographer, and novelist. He was obsessed with black life and artists and in 1926 wrote the influential but controversial novel *Nigger Heaven*, set during the Harlem Renaissance. Though homosexual, he was married for most of his life to the Russian actress Fania Marinoff.

In 1949 Van Vechten lived on West Seventy-second Street, just off Central Park. Debuskey visited him on a steamy day in late spring. The writer, fat in a rumpled turtleneck sweater, with a ring of pale hair surrounding his bald head, invited the perspiring young press agent in. Just inside the door was a round anteroom with a pedestal standing in its center supporting a tall sculpture that Debuskey considered the biggest phallic symbol he had ever seen.

Van Vechten asked a few questions, but otherwise he let Debuskey make his case by describing the state of the theater group and its ambitions. The interview was brief. Van Vechten rose up, silently led the publicist to the door, took his hand, and said, "Have your lawyer call me tomorrow. I am sure that Ms. Stein would encourage you."

The Stein coup had the desired effect: the news was picked up by all papers. The play went into rehearsal with a cast that included Arthur, Gazzo, Saks, Stanley, and another young member, Anthony Franciosa. Lamont Johnson directed. After opening night, June 6, 1949, the usually quiet Commerce Street was choked with taxis and limousines. The major critics, curious to view a dramatic work by Stein, came downtown for the first time after World War II. Reviews ranged from good to raves. The best notices were reserved for Kim Stanley. "As a young French mother, the Off-Broadway people have a talented actress with temperament, craft and, if there is any justice on Broadway, a future," wrote Brooks Atkinson in the *New York Times*. Stanley became a notable talent. By 1951 she was on Broadway, and by 1955 she had starred in the original productions of William Inge's *Picnic* and *Bus Stop*.*

But success is never simple, and problems ensued. The first, ironically, concerned the fact that the play was selling out and might run all summer. An original agreement between Gazzo, Saks, and Stanley that each would have a major role in a play was in jeopardy. "So, somewhat deluded by our success and the attention

---

* Debuskey encountered Stanley one more time before they lost touch altogether. In 1961, while handling a Stanley vehicle called *A Far Country*, directed by Stanley's husband at the time, Alfred Ryder, he knocked on her dressing room door at the Music Box Theatre to go over some details surrounding a publicity interview. "There was Kim at her makeup table, wearing a light robe, bending over and pulling up her stockings. She greeted me in that same teasing fashion I remembered. But I was shocked almost mute by the sight of the blowsy creature that had uttered the greeting. We bussed, exchanged polite chatter, and resolved the business, and I left." By the time she was forty, Stanley had abandoned the stage altogether.

paid to us, we decided to close the Stein play," said Debuskey, "and put on a new work, *Too Many Thumbs*, by an unknown, Robert Hivnor, a Columbia University professor." The play, a fantasy, began with a struggle at a small college between a professor of religion and the head of the anthropology laboratory, where a chimpanzee that had been brought into the lab had mysteriously started to advance through various stages of evolution up to and beyond mankind.

The disastrous decision to cut the Stein play short had predictable results: the phones stopped ringing, and Commerce Street returned to its tranquil self. Without the cachet of the Stein name, the company was no longer news. A disagreement arose over what the third production would be. Saks prevailed with his choice of Molière's *The Bourgeois Gentleman*, driving away Gazzo and, more critically, the troupe's new star, Stanley. After the play closed, Saks and Arthur left—together. Off Broadway, Inc., was abandoned. And so, it would seem, was Debuskey, the man who had captured the Stein play and the spotlight in the first place.

He soon found a new and larger purpose, however. Off-Broadway successes were accumulating around town. In addition to Off Broadway, Inc., the Interplayers had done well with Sean O'Casey's *The Silver Tassie*, while Studio 7 drew attention with August Strindberg's *The Father*. Those three troupes, along with People's Drama and the Hudson Guild, joined together to form the League of Off-Broadway Theatres. The organization increased the nascent movement's profile, but it also set off an alarm at the actors' union, Actors' Equity Association, which saw a group of theaters with a portfolio but no performer's contract. Equity officials descended on all five theaters and instructed their members to walk out on their shows, effectively closing them down.

"The earlier gathering of the theaters into the Off-Broadway League proved most fortuitous," observed Debuskey. "Since we were a group, we prevented our being picked off one by one. Collectively, we might be able to act effectively." The League fought back by throwing a counterpunch in the press. Off-Broadway press agents being a rarity, Debuskey was selected to lead the attack. He alerted the journals that he was hoping to discuss the problem with Equity and develop a less draconian solution. With the press covering the situation, Equity couldn't avoid him. It helped the League's cause that several Off-Broadway productions had recently received great reviews.

> They were already under pressure from their members, led by Sam Jaffe, who thought the new Off-Broadway movement would provide roles for Equity members and wanted to reach a suitable arrangement. My first goal was to have them withdraw their order for their members to walk from the productions as long as we were in negotiations. They agreed, and the shows resumed.

After several weeks of talks a contract was agreed upon, based on one that had been used successfully in Los Angeles for several decades. Equity's main concerns were that their members be under a contract which provided a minimum base salary, and that protections be built in to prevent exploitation. A token payment of $5 a week was settled on, with an escalation clause based on the number of seats in the theater and the box-office gross. It was the beginning of what would later become the official Off-Broadway contract. And, perversely, it sparked the beginning of Debuskey's Broadway career.

Chapter 2

THE SHOWMEN AND THE ALL-STAR

A lot of press agents flinch when the phone rings. Ninety percent of the time, it's bad news on the other end of the line; that's the nature of a business in which a small percentage of shows succeed, and even those are not guaranteed any press coverage. Debuskey never flinched. He had fought Christian bullies on the segregated streets of Baltimore, hard-charging opponents on the gridirons of the University of Virginia and Johns Hopkins, and the Japanese in the South Pacific. Producers didn't scare him much. He always had an opinion to offer, not always the same one as the person making the call, and he couldn't be bullied out of it. Reporters liked that. So did producers—at least the ones with enough self-confidence to meet someone toe to toe. And so, through quiet confidence and an imperviousness to panic, Debuskey managed to position himself, if not on equal footing with his employers, then just a couple steps down from the throne—a sort of counsel to the king. The writer Don Dunn, in his book on the making of the 1971 Broadway revival of the musical *No, No, Nanette*, observed that Debuskey "successfully [made] producers feel he [was] more of a 'consultant' than a 'flack.'"

Debuskey's tendency to given an unvarnished opinion of plays submitted to him by producers "lost him work," according to Bob Kamlot, who, as general manager at the Public Theater, worked with Debuskey for ten years. Paul Libin, the former Circle in the Square executive who employed Debuskey for twenty-five years, doesn't think his style would work in today's theater because "there are too many people around with an insecurity about their ability to undertake an enterprise. They need to be buoyed up that they're doing the right thing." But during his time Debuskey forged bonds with several of the major producers of his day, and the tie almost always lasted—ten, twenty, thirty years or more. Debuskey and the producers he worked with stayed together through hits and flops.

In the decades following World War II, when there was almost always one producer to each show and relationships along The Street were person to person, this dynamic was possible. The theater world was, as Debuskey's contemporary Harvey Sabinson put it, "a *haimisch* business"—homey, comfortable.

Debuskey's exploits in legitimizing Off-Broadway had gotten his name in the newspaper. He still had no intention of making press agentry his life's work, but he couldn't stop the phone from ringing. Wolfe Kaufman was an unkempt former columnist for the *Chicago Sun-Times* who, after reinventing himself as a big-time press agent, now serviced the Group Theatre veteran and Actors Studio co-founder Cheryl Crawford. He offered to buy Debuskey lunch, but Debuskey begged off. Then Kaufman sucker-punched him. The musical *Regina* was to have its first day of rehearsal soon in the Martin Beck Theatre. Would Debuskey like to attend? Debuskey recognized the names involved: the composer Marc Blitzstein, the playwright Lillian Hellman, and the director Bobby Lewis. He had never seen a Broadway rehearsal before. And it would be the first time the entire company would hear the score. Debuskey couldn't resist the bait. "The cast sat on folding chairs along the back wall, the stage area dimly lit, with Blitzstein seated at a grand piano with a standing work light. By the time Marc had played the last note, I was a goner, a teenager with her first corsage." "I signed on that afternoon."

Debuskey could not fathom how Kaufman got his reputation. Crawford's general manager hated him. Tennessee Williams and Alan Jay Lerner, whose works Crawford produced, refused to speak to him. "He was an absolutely amoral creature," recalled Debuskey. "He was lazy, untrustworthy. He would go in his room and close the door. Seldom heard from him." Kaufman's eternal absence threw

Debuskey up against the formidable, mannish Crawford, who dressed primly, in neat, quiet, expensive suits and comfortable brogans, and spoke to the direct purpose, her only chit-chat being a firm "hello."

Debuskey's first Broadway opening was on October 31, 1949. Sweating, he watched *Regina* from the back of the house. Green to the experience, he thought the polite applause for the musical version of Hellman's *The Little Foxes*, a tale of treacherous class struggle in the South, and the favorable review by the *New York Times*'s Brooks Atkinson boded well. He didn't understand Atkinson's dozen references to the show as an "opera" as the poison pill it was. Kaufman emerged from his cave to join Debuskey in a box-office vigil the next morning. There was no line. *Regina* ran for six weeks.

Another Crawford flop followed, and soon Debuskey was facing unemployment again. A call came from Gerald Goode, a press agent who had a play by Arthur Laurents called *The Bird Cage*. Debuskey was hired as an apprentice. The show starred Melvyn Douglas and was to be directed by the ebullient, erudite man of the theater Harold Clurman, another founder of the Group Theatre and a critic as well as a director.

Goode, it turned out, hadn't handled a show in several years and needed all the help he could get. Debuskey liked the men— Douglas was a consummate pro and Clurman was easygoing—but it was the foul-mouthed women of the cast he found fascinating. They included Jean Carson, Rita Duncan (wife of the boxer Tony Canzonari), Kate Harkin (Mrs. Zero Mostel), Eleanor Lynn, and Maureen Stapleton (then an unknown). They were not dainty. "Their conversation and the language transporting it could curl a steel beam," said Debuskey. "It became so colorful that Douglas went to Clurman and asked him if he could request the ladies to tone it down. Clurman's response was that their reply would probably blister the paint on the walls and suggested that Douglas accept it as a learning experience and use it as an actor."

Crawford and Clurman were cupcakes next to the employer Debuskey faced soon afterward: the flamboyant impresario Mike

Todd. In 1950 Todd was busy divorcing the film actress Joan Blondell and creating a musical revue called *Michael Todd's Peep Show*, a spectacle loaded with beautiful showgirls, extravagant costumes, and burlesque comics written and co-directed by the comic sketch performer Bobby Clark, with songs by the musically inclined twenty-two-year-old Thai royal Prince Chakrband Bhumibol. Debuskey was offered an apprentice position by Max Gendel, yet another quirky employer, who, on the first day of work, executed a version of Wolfe Kaufman's disappearing-press-agent routine. Gendel introduced Debuskey to everyone but Todd and then decamped to the Grand Street Boys Club, leaving Debuskey his phone number; after that, said Debuskey, "I never saw him again until the day after the New York opening."

Ironically, the one Broadway show Debuskey had seen before shipping out had been produced by Todd—*Star and Garter*, starring Gypsy Rose Lee. At one port of call, Chinwangtao, China, during his World War II tour of duty, Debuskey and the rest of the crew of his ship were often entertained by a Chinese "performance artist" who would set up on the dock alongside the ship and announce his presence by banging loudly on a flat drum. His pièce de résistance was inserting a small snake in one nostril until its head emerged from his mouth while the tail was still wriggling out of his nose. Debuskey described this act for Todd when he was assembling acts for his *Peep Show*. The producer growled, "Listen, kid, an act like that's a bomb unless he can work a broad into it."

Todd—born Avron Hirsch Goldenbogen, the son of an immigrant rabbi, forty-one years earlier in Minneapolis—was his era's P. T. Barnum, an "ersatz Ziegfeld," as Richard Maney put it. He is best remembered today for three things: marrying Elizabeth Taylor, producing the Academy Award–winning *Around the World in 80 Days*, and dying young when his private plane, the *Lucky Liz*, crashed in New Mexico in 1958. But, as his *New York Times* obituary reminded the world, he also found time to be "a dice hustler, carnival roustabout, trustee of a bricklaying academy, bankruptcy sale major domo, building contractor, movie studio soundproofer, plunger on horses and cards and bankrupt." The humorist S. J.

Perelman once described him as "an ulcer no larger than a man's hand."

Todd's headquarters was a maze of offices above the Broadway Theater at Broadway and Fifty-third Street. There Todd's general manager, Benny Stein, walked Debuskey into the office of his client, who grabbed his hand and said, "OK, kid. Call me Mike. Let's make a buck." "For the next couple of months he never called me anything but Kid," recalled Debuskey, who was then twenty-seven. "Me, who had recently seen combat."

Debuskey was agog at the chaotic rehearsals in New York.

> [They] were all over the place, dancers here, showgirls there, the burlesque comics in another studio struggling to learn lines and business and to perform them the same way twice, the vaude-villians—ventriloquist, jugglers, paired dance team, exotic dance act—finding any blank spot to work on their acts, wardrobe people running back and forth from the costume shop to the stage strug-gling with bundles of costumes for catch-as-catch-can fittings, music copyists furiously copying the score parts for the musicians and conductor, lead singers working with a tireless rehearsal pianist.

Debuskey quickly learned that the show's Philadelphia tryout was his responsibility alone. He worked sixteen-hour days, generating general releases, photographs, and "exclusive" stories; proposing feature ideas; writing column items; and jumping at Todd's frequent commands of "Get me the Kid!" He hit Pennsylvania Station every Tuesday morning to catch the 9:00 a.m. train to Philadelphia. Making the Tuesday train was critical to landing copy in the Sunday sections of the Philadelphia newspapers. Debuskey spent his commute picking up whatever operational tips other veteran publicists aboard the train were willing to share.

"They offered to have me tag along to learn the routine, the order of the papers to be visited, and to introduce me to the appropriate editors," recalled Debuskey.

> I had gleaned some knowledge in theory, but their practical advice saved my ass. The Philadelphia media were easy to work with, very

obliging. Aside from being decent folk, they had a vested interest in our work. It gave them material to occupy the space they were required to fill each Sunday, entertaining and informing their readers. By my fourth trip I was a veteran and proficient flack.

After an evening performance, Debuskey would sometimes chauffeur Todd back to New York from Philadelphia. Debuskey drove while Mike talked.

> Todd was normally loquacious, and with a bit of prompting would cheerfully launch into tales of his colorful gambling days in Chicago. On one trip, he suddenly became silent and began searching through his pockets and looking around the car. We were about half-way to New York when he said, "Kid, when you see one of those places with gas, food, and a telephone, pull in." When I found a restaurant, I walked in with him. He asked an attendant where he could find a pay phone, asked me for change, and placed a call. As he waited, he turned to me and said, "Kid, go to the car and get me my heater." I thought of his Chicago days and his friends in the mob and wondered. I searched the car and went back into the restaurant. He was standing by the phone. I blurted out, "Sorry, Mike, but I could not find your gun." He looked at me strangely. "Gun, you schmuck?" he said. "A heater is a cigar."

Todd did find other shady employments for the Kid, however. The producer was soon to be named a defendant in a bankruptcy proceeding, and it was not a good idea for him to keep large amounts of cash in his personal bank account, where his creditors could access it. So Debuskey became a bag man. His weekly task was to take a paper sack from his producer filled with neatly packaged bills, drive the package to Irvington, New York, north of New York City, where Todd's wife, Joan Blondell, lived, and deposit the money in a special account. "I asked no questions and never peeked into the bag," he said.

Another time, during previews in New York, the blossoming publicist was sent to a tony night spot, the Stork Club. There the owner and tastemaker Sherman Billingsley handed over a one-gallon jug of the club's exclusive perfume. Todd had dreamed up an exotic and original adornment to the first-act curtain—a bubble bath for the entire line of showgirls. As the audience ogled the beauties, the perfume would be poured into the theater's blowers, and the theater would be filled with the precious scent. The stunt was tried at a matinee. "We damn near suffocated the audience," recalled Debuskey. "The smell couldn't even be cleared during the intermission. It saturated the audience's clothing all through the second act. They took home a souvenir of the show that probably lasted for weeks. We didn't do it again."

Michael Todd's Peep Show opened at the Winter Garden Theatre on June 28, 1950. Atkinson called it "an old-fashioned girlie-girlie carnival" with "a lot of good stuff," and *Variety* labeled it a hit. But that didn't mean Debuskey had a job. When he entered the office the morning after the opening, his absentee boss, the serpentine Max Gendel, had rematerialized. "He asked what I was doing there. 'Going to work,' I replied. 'No,' he said. 'You don't work here anymore.' I was given one week's salary. I was told later that for weeks, Todd would holler, 'Where's the Kid?'" Debuskey met Todd one more time, two years later, at a press conference set up for Mike to announce his latest gambit: a plan to produce a movie version of *War and Peace* to be shot in Spain. "He did not acknowledge that we had ever met."

———

Though Todd and Debuskey were temperamentally ill-matched, they were not as different as the self-inflating Todd might have imagined. Both were from religious Jewish households, the piousness of which they had largely left behind. Both changed their names in preparation for their new lives (though all Debuskey did was shed his first name), and both found a new home in show business, where they wed actresses not of their faith. But Todd's nature had more twists than a pretzel, whereas Debuskey seemed to have been a straight arrow from inception.

Basil Merle Debuskey was born on March 24, 1923, to Freda Debuskey, born Blaustein, whose family had been in the United States since before the Civil War, and Robert Debuskey, at Mercy

Hospital in Baltimore, Maryland. He was the last of five children, following Matthew ("Buster"), Charles, Shirley, and Frank. Also in the family's Lakeview Avenue house, in the Jewish section of town, were a German immigrant housekeeper named Louise, occasional paying boarders, and a black day worker called Big Mary, who helped with the cooking, laundry, cleaning, and serving meals and who became an adopted family member. Merle's maternal grandparents lived a few houses away. Two of his mother's sisters and their families lived around the corner on Lake Drive, facing the huge Druid Hill Park. He did not want for relations.

Appearances to the contrary, the Debuskey home was not religiously united. Robert Debuskey was a quiet, dignified man who would comb the papers every day to make certain that no Jewish man had been accused of any heinous activity. He accepted his faith at face value, attended temple, performed the Shabbat rituals, and had a mystical connection with God, according to his son. His wife was less devout. Robert refused to take phone calls on Friday nights or Saturdays; Freda was devoted to her Metropolitan Opera broadcasts on Saturday afternoon. But she respected her spouse's piety and seldom questioned his beliefs.

Debuskey remembered a household of great familial camaraderie and care. The children performed myriad chores without complaint, the entire family made weekly visits to the synagogue, and they engaged in lively dinner-table discussions. Debuskey's parents never argued, to his recollection, even though his father, a wine salesman, was frequently on the road, away from his family. He often wrote to his wife during his travels using stationary from the hotels in Ohio, Pennsylvania, New York, and West Virginia where he stayed. His missives were largely professions of love for Freda and the children, and sometimes he even expressed himself in poetry. (His youngest son would echo his florid and garrulous style of writing decades later.)

The Debuskeys were not ones for confrontation or conflict. There were no grand stand-offs on points of Jewish tradition, even though three of the five children would go on to marry non-Jews. Nor were there deep examinations of the unjust climate of segregated

Baltimore, a southern city in personality, where whites, Jews, and blacks all had their separate and unequal places. "Jews were generally tolerated, but were strange, foreigners, and not accepted into the general social structure," recalled Debuskey, who, like his parents, did not question the arrangement, but merely accepted it. "Each of these groups had subdivisions based on economic, cultural, and educational levels."

Furthermore, the Debuskeys, who sprang from a mix of ethnicities, were held in lower esteem than Baltimore's German Jews, who had arrived first and, possessing higher levels of education, business experience, and culture, considered themselves superior. Among the more exalted Jewish Baltimoreans was Freda Debuskey's uncle, Louis Blaustein, whose family worshipped at a daunting German temple. The Blausteins were obscenely wealthy—they owned the American Oil Company, Amoco Gasoline, and the Crown Petroleum service stations. They acknowledged the family connection with the Debuskeys, but they didn't encourage a relationship.

As for his hometown's other large minority, Debuskey said: "During my days in Baltimore, I had no black friends, nor did any of my peers. When we were roaming in Druid Hill Park, if we encountered a similar bunch of black wanderers, our only contact was a nod and a move in another direction. We never played ball on the same park fields." That did not mean that young Debuskey was entirely insulated from the African American world. A few exceptional encounters stood out in his memory. After happening upon some Bahamians playing cricket in Druid Hill Park, Debuskey, always interested in sports, frequently sought them out and tried to learn the game. He also became friendly with a man he knew only as Hawk, a twenty-year-old African American who shined shoes at the local shoemaker and who could, for some loose change, be persuaded to sing and dance a few bars, exposing the young Jewish boy to jazz. There was also an older man who racked the balls and put up the cue sticks at the local billiard parlor, and who turned out to be a friend of Merle's brother Frank. Once Merle noticed that the sweater the man was wearing looked very much like one of his own. "He came over to me, smiling, and said it was a gift from my brother Frank."

If the Debuskey family had a black sheep, it was Frank. Frank bridled under the family's reputation for prowess on the playing field. His two older brothers had been celebrated local athletes. Frank could have followed their path—he had the wiry frame and quick skills needed to succeed—but instead he turned his back on it. "When he went out for sports they'd say, 'Oh, *Debuskey*—are you related to Charles and Matthew?' He would turn in his jock and leave. He was expected to emulate them. He didn't feel up to it, didn't want to do it, and reacted in an adverse fashion." Frank was also known to have occasionally pilfered loose change, sometimes even raiding the house's *pushke*, the charity box that is kept in many observant Jewish homes. "Once he stole from our brother Charles's pants pocket," recalled Merle. "When accused, he denied it until Buster and Charles hoisted him by his feet and shook him till it spilled from his pockets. They admonished him, gave him the change, and suggested that next time he needed some change he should ask for it. I do not think that Frank thought it much fun."

Merle and Frank shared a third-floor back bedroom. On Friday nights Frank would employ little Merle in his surreptitious Sabbath escapes, when he would climb out the window, shimmy down to the ground, and head to the local pool hall. Merle's assignment was to tie up Frank's good clothes and toss them out the third-floor window. They dropped the ruse when a police cruiser spotted Frank halfway up the house, collared him as a burglar, and woke his parents. Yet Frank continued to play hooky and spend his days at the pool hall. His parents deputized Merle to make sure Frank got to school, but more often than not, Merle would end up playing pool with Frank. He loved and admired Frank, even when his brother's boxing lessons were taught with a trifle too much enthusiasm. "He would vent his anger, because I was such a little prize to my parents," recalled Debuskey. "He would teach me to box. We go into the bathroom, close the doors. He beat the shit out of me. It hurt. I would cry in appreciation."

Eventually it became clear to the Debuskeys that they couldn't keep Frank in school. "My mother was kind of wise," Debuskey said. "She didn't rise up and strike him down. She went to educators and psychologists to investigate and decide what to do. My father deferred to my mother in these sorts of circumstances. They decided it would be foolish to push him into school, to force him into it. The best thing was to withdraw him, so he didn't leave school with a bad mark."

The wealthy Blausteins got Frank a job as a pump jockey at a gas station they owned. But he contracted pneumonia and, once well, never returned to work. "The feeling was maybe he should be away from the home environment." The boys' father asked his cousins in California, who were vintners, to take Frank in. "He thrived. He did very well. He was popular with the locals, who were largely Armenian. He married Jean Smith, raised a family, went into war, saw action. He got the Purple Heart and Bronze Star."

Merle, the apple of his parents' eyes, took a different path. He was the archetypal good boy. He learned Hebrew, took out volumes of *Tom Swift* and *Tarzan* from the library, and joined the Boy Scouts. But he retained the streetwise toughness he'd learned from Frank. On the way to scout meetings at the Haar Siani Temple, he would have to pass through the territory of non-Jewish gangs bent on stealing his dues. Sometime he would be accompanied by Warren, a blond street brawler who years before, on the school playground, used to pummel Merle and force him to cry uncle—until Frank gave Merle a tutorial in fisticuffs and Merle beat his nemesis into submission. Afterward the two boys become pals. But when Warren wasn't around to escort him through enemy territory, Debuskey would have to stand and fight. He came to look forward to fighting the toughs more than attending the scout meetings. "It advanced me as a human being more than being a Boy Scout did," he said. "You had to stand up and confront a certain unpleasant reality."

———

One unpleasant reality of the New York theater in the 1950s was the former king of Broadway, Jed Harris, an old-style producer whose bombast matched Mike Todd's. The playwright George Kaufman had one said, "Every playwright has to have Jed Harris once, like the measles."

Debuskey had a brush with Harris when he worked under Jimmy Proctor on Arthur Miller's *The Crucible*. Because Proctor, a publicist and Debuskey's boss at the time, was an intimate of Miller and handled several of his most important plays, Debuskey got to know the lanky, bespectacled, Brooklyn-born intellectual and playwright, who liked to drop by Proctor's office and chat.

Working on a Miller play was both a privilege and a problem. There was no difficulty in getting press, but at the same time, the press tended to hang on the writer's every word. "Miller accepted many opportunities to write articles on many themes, about both theater and politics," said Debuskey. "So he could and did use the much-needed ministrations of an experienced media manipulator whom he could trust. And Jim was the chosen one."

The third Miller play Proctor worked on was *The Crucible*, a play that used the Salem witch trials to illustrate the rolling dangers of mass hysteria. Widely interpreted at the time as a response to the destructive politics of the Joseph McCarthy era, it has endured as a powerful protest against unfounded accusations and the erosion of individual rights in any time of fear and suspicion. Miller felt the anti-Communist congressional hearings were very much like the witch trials—"profoundly and even avowedly ritualistic." The questioning congressmen had a prepared script, and they wanted the witnesses to name names of Communist Party members, just as Salem's seventeenth-century inquisitors had wanted the alleged witches to name their satanic colleagues.

It was an incendiary construct, and choosing a director was problematic. Elia Kazan, who had directed both *All My Sons* and *Death of a Salesman*, was the logical choice, but Kazan had since named names before the House Un-American Activities Committee, a betrayal Miller could not abide. The producer Kermit Bloomgarden had a personal and professional relationship with the writer Lillian Hellman, having wooed her away from her previous benefactor, the producer Herman Shumlin. Surprisingly, Hellman suggested and heatedly pushed for Jed Harris to be signed as director.

Harris was a storied name from the past. He was been a golden boy in the 1920s and 1930s, producing and/or directing several milestones in the Broadway theater, including *The Front Page, The Royal Family, Broadway,* and *Our Town.* But since then everything had turned to salt in his hands. Jim Proctor, who had worked with Harris, offered a two-sided appraisal. "Jim advised Miller that Harris had the capacity for genius in the theater," Debuskey recalled, "but had traded his soul to the devil in return for that talent." Harris was a spellbinder, and he effectively wove his spell in meetings with Miller and Bloomgarden and was given the reins. It was an unfortunate choice.

The play had a distinguished cast, headed by Arthur Kennedy and Beatrice Straight as John Proctor and his wife, Elizabeth; the venerable Walter Hampden as the deputy governor, Thomas Danforth; E. G. Marshall as the Reverend John Hale; and Cloris Leachman as Abigail Williams, the vengeful, sex-driven servant girl who sets the witchcraft hysteria in motion. But the director and his stars turned out to be a bad mix.

"It soon became an exercise in who was boss," said Debuskey,

instead of helping the actor develop his character or find the nexus of the scene being played out. There were days when Harris did not show up, others when he demanded the firing of an actor. It became an untenable situation, and just before leaving for the out-of-town tryout in Wilmington, Kermit and Miller told him not to come around. Jed's response was to assent, but he demanded a large percentage of the show, which was impossible. Hellman had come down for the opening, and it became apparent that she was sharing a room with Jed, who was there but not attending rehearsals.

Debuskey recounted an incident on opening night that further revealed Harris's character: "The audience responded enthusiastically, and at the curtain calls kept calling for the author. Suddenly Harris entered from the wings and took a bow with the startled and confused cast. Harris later claimed that he had been pulled onto the stage by Kennedy and Marshall, but they had never laid a hand on him."

When the play arrived in New York, however, the critical response on opening night—January 22, 1953, at the Martin Beck Theatre—

was mixed. Miller was not surprised; he felt that Harris had taken all the fire out of the play. Ticket sales weren't strong enough to keep the play running for long, even though it won the Tony Award for Best Play and Miller redirected it and removed the scenery to cut operating costs. It closed in July after only 197 performances. The play was revived in a few years' time to much acclaim, but the initial production left all disheartened. "It was the right play for the right time that went all wrong," said Debuskey. "Especially hurt was Jim Proctor, who felt he had let Miller down."

———

The antithesis of fun-loving Mike Todd was Herman Shumlin, a renowned producer and director known for a dangerously dour temperament combined with a low boiling point, and for backing and directing Lillian Hellman's work, including *The Children's Hour* and *The Little Foxes*, and also such plays as William Drake's *Grand Hotel* and Emlyn Williams's *The Corn Is Green*. He had recently mounted Jerome Lawrence and Robert E. Lee's *Inherit the Wind*, a fictionalized reenactment of the Scopes "monkey trial." It was an established hit by the time Shumlin called Debuskey. He remembered: "The theatrical community admired and respected him for the quality and success of his work, but he was not particularly liked. I had no idea of what prompted the call and was hesitant about meeting with him." Debuskey's pal Jimmy Proctor told him that he probably would not like Shumlin but added, with teasing emphasis, that meeting with him would be an interesting experience. And so it proved. Recalled Debuskey:

> Shumlin was an impressive presence. He seemed taller than he was, and he was always immaculately dressed in a suit and tie. He wore thin gold-rimmed glasses and sported a trim gray mustache. He was exceptionally well-read and, I suspect, had undergone psychotherapy. He spoke crisply, succinctly, and authoritatively. He quickly came to the subject of this interview. He was terminating the employment of Leo Friedman as the press agent for *Inherit the Wind*, which was already an established hit, and was offering me the assignment.

Debuskey was surprised. He had worked for Friedman and thought him a good press agent, and he told Shumlin so. At that, the producer's notorious dyspepsia unleashed itself. "In no uncertain terms did he lecture me on the responsibilities of the producer, adding that my opinion was of no consequence, as he had made the decision." Despite this initial meeting, Debuskey took the job.

One day months afterward Shumlin summoned Debuskey. Bowed over his desk, he let fly an attack on the press agent's character and performance. He then stretched out on a nearby couch. "When I reassembled my psyche," Debuskey remembered, "I walked over, stood over him, and informed him that he was an unmitigated and sadistic prick and could not talk to me or anyone else in that fashion. I said that he could stuff the project up his rectum and took my leave."

Shumlin's assistant later called to explain that her boss had been seized by a horrific migraine. Debuskey learned that the producer was often afflicted by these tormenting headaches, and when under their spell he lashed out uncontrollably and without cause. "He and I looked at each other differently after that incident. We worked together professionally for the life of the show—but never again."

Merle Debuskey was only thirty-two when he swung back at Shumlin. It was an impressive show of spine by any measure. But Debuskey's ability to defend himself and hold his ground had been formed many years before on the sports fields of his native Baltimore. When producers hired Merle Debuskey to campaign for their show, they were hiring a two-time collegiate lacrosse All-Star, a four-letter man.

"Sometimes he would make an observation about something going on in the theater, saying, 'If football can't knock me down, this can't,'" said Lee Silver, a Shubert Organization executive and former *Daily News* critic, who first met Debuskey in the 1950s. "'You're talking to a guy who did XYZ on the field.'"

"I enjoyed physical activity," said Debuskey, simply. He got plenty of that during his teens. Stickball, stepball, touch football, roller-skate hockey—the play along Lakeview Avenue and in nearby Druid Hill Park was constant. Debuskey was kept in equipment by hand-me-downs from his older brothers: sled, bike, tennis racquet, balls, lacrosse stick, and kites.

In the 1930s and '40s, when Debuskey was growing up, Baltimore had neither a professional nor a major college football team. Gridiron action was local and passionately followed by the citizenry. The name Debuskey was constantly found in the sports pages—first the two eldest brothers, Matthew and Charles, and then Merle. The youngest Debuskey burned to match Matthew's and Charles's achievements and, if he could, exceed them. "I think it was because it would make me significant," said Debuskey of his motivations in high school and beyond. "In college, I was aware of the anti-Semitism. To break through there was important to me. I did things that were not really reasonable. When I tore up my shoulder and couldn't play basketball, and I still had full scholarship, I let them talk me into boxing."

As soon as he started classes at his Baltimore high school, City College, the third-oldest public high school in the nation, Merle competed for places on the football, basketball, and lacrosse teams. Though only fourteen years old, about 5'8", and weighing in at 150 pounds, he made all three junior varsity squads. The coaches were tough and drilled him on fundamentals. Unlike Frank, Merle beamed like a puppy when coaches compared him to his star-athlete brothers: "The coaches of all three sports knew or knew of my elder brothers, and I believe the name Debuskey made them focus more on me than most." Schooled by Frank's tough-love training, Merle excelled, especially in football and lacrosse, and his exploits were soon covered in the local papers. In Baltimore, a big city that often functioned like a small town, he was a star.

"He was a hero of such proportions in the city," recalled Sidney Offit, a friend who attended the same synagogue as the Debuskeys and would later go on to become a novelist and develop the George Polk Awards in Journalism. "My first awareness of Merle was a picture in the *Baltimore Sun* when he was at Baltimore City High School. He wasn't just a star football player. He was legendary. This was before the television era, and local sports were given a great deal of attention."

Offit recalled his first sight of that oddest of 1940s-America specimens: the Jewish sports star. "I saw him at the Druid Hill Reservoir. I was there with a friend of mine, bike riding. Merle Debuskey was walking by with his City sweater with all its stars...for all the varsity teams he made. I remember my friend saying, 'God, that's Merle Debuskey.' I'd never met anybody at that age who was seen with that awe."

Because he had skipped grades early on, Debuskey was due to graduate in 1940, when he was just sixteen. A conniving coach named Harry Lawrence didn't like that idea. Anxious to extend City College football's five-year winning streak by any means possible, Lawrence suggested to Merle's parents that he take a year of "postgraduate study," which would, not incidentally, allow him to play an extra year of ball. As an inducement, he promised an athletic scholarship to a good college. Debuskey accepted and, in that twelve-month addendum, grew even more celebrated than before.

"I remember cheering his name: 'Give three yays for Debuskey!'" said Russell Baker. "I once clapped Merle on the back. It was like striking an oak tree."

Debuskey admits confusion as to why he agreed to an additional, unnecessary year of high school:

> Even then, I was aware that the promise of an athletic scholarship was far-fetched. An injury could easily wipe that out as a real possibility. I believe I felt that my young age had not allowed me to reach my potential.... Another significant factor was that the Jewish ghetto wherein I did dwell did not produce very many three-letter men of note.... Somewhat naively, I did hold a faint vision of breaking through the prevailing attitude the general community held about Jews.

In that final year, the papers covered him heavily, which had its rewards. Girls found him interesting. News clippings about Merle were featured in the local barber shop, and he was promoted at the soda fountain where he worked, a neighborhood hangout called the Brookfield Pharmacy. There was always a table waiting for him in the pool room, and the waitresses at Nate's and Leon's Delicatessen would take his messages.

The big games were fought on Saturday. That posed a problem for the Debuskey's parents. On the day of the momentous City College–Polytechnic Institute match—a local rivalry that stretched back to 1889 and Baltimore's annual equivalent to the Harvard-Yale game—Debuskey was mortified to see his picture in the *Baltimore Sun*. He slunk into synagogue that morning, hoping no one had read the paper. Stunned, he heard himself called up to the *bimah* by the cantor to help carry the Torah as it was covered and placed back into the ark. It was an honor, but, as far as Debuskey was concerned, an unlooked-for one just then. The cantor handed him the Torah, and Debuskey waited for a punishing lightning bolt from above. Then the rabbi walked over and whispered in his ear, "This may help this afternoon. Good luck."

After the service, a number of people offered him rides to the game. In keeping with Sabbath dicta, Debuskey declined them all and walked the several miles to the stadium, carrying his equipment. City College won 19-0, and Debuskey scored a touchdown.

———

The only person in the Broadway community that knew about Merle Debuskey's glory days in Baltimore was Ernie Martin. A tall, lethargic, cigar-smoking, Savile Row–tailored, pony-playing sports fan who would wear raccoon coats at New York Giants games, Martin was half of the powerful producer duo Feuer and Martin. Martin's mother was the sister of Debuskey's mother's sister-in-law Rebecca—Merle's Aunt Rebecca—which made Debuskey a sort of relative, though the press agent didn't know this when he received an offer to join their production team.

Debuskey, like the rest of Broadway's denizens, was in awe of Feuer and Martin's reputation. Their spectacular producing career on Broadway had so far included *Where's Charley?*, *Guys and Dolls*, *The Boy Friend*, *Can-Can*, and *Silk Stockings*—five critically acclaimed, profit-producing musical comedy hits in a row that established a benchmark for success on Broadway. It was a track record won through a hard-driving perfectionism that often punished the talent. They faced off against the legendary George S. Kaufman on the Cole Porter musical *Silk Stockings* and won, keeping him off the production and scoring a hit. When the librettist Jo Swerling refused to accept their vision of the plot for the Damon Runyon–inspired *Guys and Dolls*, they canned him. They barred Sandy Wilson from rehearsals of the 1920s musical takeoff *The Boy Friend* when the author, composer, and lyricist proved difficult, and even went so far as to hire a team of Pinkerton men to enforce the dictum.

Debuskey was friendly with Feuer and Martin's current pressman, Karl Bernstein, a gentlemanly though parsimonious Brooklynite who began his career as a vaudeville critic and whose entire life was lived within the theater trade, down to his addiction to the nutted cheese sandwiches at Times Square's Chock Full o' Nuts. Debuskey had worked with Bernstein in his swaddling days in the business and liked him, but he had also witnessed the panic attacks that would strike whenever Bernstein received a phone call from the producers of *Guys and Dolls*. With the phone to his ear, Bernstein would stick his head out the open window by his desk and continue the conversation among the pigeons.

Martin offered Debuskey a gig covering their new show, something with the ridiculous title of *How to Succeed in Business Without Really Trying*. The press agent felt some allegiance toward Bernstein. As he had Friedman, Debuskey—a fierce labor man—felt compelled to defend his colleague. "I told Martin how well I thought Karl had served, that the media certainly connected him to them, and that I honestly did not believe that I could improve on his [work]." He said he'd have to speak with Bernstein before accepting. "As you will," barked Martin, "but make it quick." He called Karl, who at the time worked in a low-rent, airless room that was part of a working dentist's office. "In a most generous manner, told me that he knew he was separated, did not know why, suggested that I take the job but that I should know that it would not be a cakewalk and that I could expect calls at all hours, that F & M had no limitations on the workday." Debuskey signed.

Before climbing aboard, Martin asked Debuskey what his salary was to be. The press agent began to rattle off the standard union terms. Martin interrupted him: "This is not a negotiation. Tell the bookkeeper how much you are to be paid." "Martin had an instinctive ability to size people up and where and how far he could go with them," said Debuskey. "He knew I would not exceed what was reasonable." Debuskey put himself down for something comfortably over minimum.

Cy Feuer and Ernie Martin were a comedy of opposites. Recalled Debuskey:

> Ernie was tall. Cy was short. Ernie was always preceded by a long cigar. Cy had an occasional cigarette. One was the good cop, the other the bad cop—roles they would switch when the occasion warranted. Ernie did not care much for the theater's citizenry; Cy was active in the League of American Theatres and Producers, eventually serving as president for a number of years. Neither was politically active, leaning toward capitalism; they despised McCarthy and his top aide, Roy Cohn, but they had reservations about the Kennedy family's political activities

Dealing with the twin act at production meetings could be a challenge. Feuer, a bundle of constrained energy, would hop up and down in a physical demonstration of his points. Martin, spread out on a couch, would change his mind with every passing argument. But Debuskey won over both on occasion, notably on the night *How to Succeed* opened to smash reviews on Broadway. They gathered in the offices of the powerhouse ad agency Blaine-Thompson with account executive Ingram Ash. The agency's spy at the *New York Times*, a typesetter who knew his way around a composing room—but not the English language—read with torturous pronunciation the rave notice over the phone. The agency began devising an advertising campaign, selecting quotes for the conventional first major Sunday ad as well as the daily ABCs (the alphabetical listing of shows) and two-column displays.

Debuskey pounced. He had long nurtured a radical idea that ran counter to all advertising theories on Broadway. *How to Succeed* was bound to sell out. What if they didn't advertise and thus reached profitability all the quicker? Debuskey argued his case. He knew Feuer and Martin hated to part with money unnecessarily; they didn't even throw opening-night parties. "Ingram, of course, did not agree," remembered Debuskey. "He advocated striking while the excitement was fresh, building the advance. Most ad people believed in their gospel: you spend advertising money to make money." Debuskey was to advance this argument several times over his career, but this was the only time he prevailed. The producer agreed. No display advertising—only ABCs. They held to it for a sold-out, standing-room-only year. The producers rewarded Debuskey for his suggestion with some of the money he'd saved them.

Blaine-Thompson didn't forget this defeat, said Debuskey.

For years after, the agency referred to this, in their esteem, as Merle's Folly, not to be encouraged. Any number of times in promoting a show the ad agency would come in with a proposed campaign and a budget which I would question. When I asked how much more this expenditure would add to the income from ticket sales, I could never get a specific response. After the fact, when the results were in and I pointed out that the return barely covered the expense, their undeniable response was, "Yes, but you do not know how much less you would have sold if you had not spent the money for the ad campaign."

—

Martin's press agent had been more than a high school star; Debuskey's athletic accomplishments continued into college. Coach Lawrence—the man who made sure Debuskey served an extra year of high school for the benefit of City College—was as good as his word, and the three-letter man entertained scholarship offers from several schools. Not Harvard, as Freda Debuskey had hoped, but august houses of learning such as William and Mary and the University of Virginia. "All this was pretty heady stuff for a young lad totally devoid of sophistication," admitted Debuskey. "My ego was so inflated that I had a difficult time relating in a civil fashion with my family and friends."

After much deliberation, Debuskey settled on the University of Virginia, attracted by the historic school's Jeffersonian aura. Debuskey was now living even deeper in the South, and he encountered more virulent anti-Semitism than he had experienced in his limited Baltimore wanderings. The university had a quota for Jews, and blacks were barred altogether. Christian fraternities courted him until he was approached by a Jewish fraternity; after that they lost all interest. There was one other Jew playing varsity football—a tackle who had been a starter the previous season—and one more with Debuskey on the freshman squad, Pinky Newmeyer. The two became close friends.

Debuskey was on a tight budget. His lodging, meals, tuition, books, and fees were covered by his scholarship. Still, he needed spending money, so he took a job at the school library as a clerk. And when he registered for classes, he also enlisted in the Naval Reserve Officers' Training Corps. On the playing field he held his own, getting off to a good start. But the camaraderie vanished after practice, when Christians and Jews went their separate ways. Said Debuskey, "We were able to depend upon each other on the gridiron each day, communicate, share the training and locker rooms, but once in the boarding house it was as if we were strangers."

Soon Debuskey and his teammates were strangers entirely. A torn rotator cuff in his right shoulder knocked him out of football in the middle of his freshman year. The basketball season was lost to him as well. He underwent physical therapy and wore a sling. For several months he had difficulty sleeping, getting out of bed, getting dressed, and eating. None of his fellow boarders did or said anything to help other than "tough shit." Debuskey also suspected that some of the football coaches thought he had not shown sufficient courage to play with pain.

Debuskey healed well enough to shine at lacrosse and prove his worth. At season's end, he was plucked to start in the annual North-South College All-Star game in Baltimore, the first player from the University of Virginia to be so honored—and a freshman at that.

But another serious decision lay ahead that fall. Early the next fall, before he returned to Charlottesville, Debuskey was asked to join a pickup team of local college lacrosse players for a scrimmage with the squad from the U.S. Naval Academy. The academy picked its team from the members of the football squad, giving the lacrosse men the advantage; Debuskey and his buddies beat them handily.

After the game Debuskey was approached in the locker room by the Naval Academy's director of athletics, who knew of his high school career. The director stunned Debuskey by asking if he would like to enter the academy.

They agreed to meet. The director told Debuskey that the necessary political favor swapping was already under way—a congressional appointment was necessary to enter the academy. "It was exceedingly difficult to gain entrance into the academy, more so than West Point," said Debuskey. "He pointed out that the academy's plebes were assured of three years of training before being called to duty." This would hand Debuskey a lifelong career and, not incidentally, three more years of football, lacrosse, and maybe—if his arm permitted—basketball. "At that moment," remembered Debuskey, "I could not say no."

But he did eventually say no. When he got a letter from John A. Meyer, a member of the House of Representatives from Maryland, saying he had been nominated for a Naval Academy appointment, he turned to his eldest brother, Matthew, for advice. "Without telling me what to do, Buster gave me a full description of what was in store for me in the regular Navy—what that life was likely to be, particularly for a Jew." Anti-Semitism, his brother said, was particularly rife in the Navy. Debuskey opted to return to Virginia.

That would not be the end of the episode, however. Debuskey would pay a dear price for having toyed with the academy. That fall, he won a starting spot as quarterback for Virginia's football team. The team won the first game of the season. The second game was against the Naval Academy in Annapolis, and the academy made clear what they thought of Debuskey's turning down an invitation to join the institution: they sent him limping off the field in the second quarter with a torn muscle in his right thigh and a split chin. He was through for the season. To add insult to injury, he saw a sneer on the face of one of his coaches. "His insinuations were very clear," said Debuskey—the boy couldn't play with pain. Debuskey didn't win over the coaching staff until the next fall, when he played through the entire schedule. For good measure, the eager-to-please Debuskey also took up boxing as a light heavyweight.

Debuskey tried boxing partly out of guilt over not fulfilling the obligations of his scholarship, and partly owing to the entreaties of Archie Hahn, the boxing coach. Hahn was an Olympic athlete who had earned the nickname of the "Milwaukee Meteor," having won three sprinting events in the 1904 games in St. Louis. He was short and light of build, always had a cigarette hanging from his lips whose ashes spilled all over his clothes, and wore a suit and tie with his trouser legs rolled up. Boxing was a major spectator sport at Virginia. The alumni would gather with their traditional mint julep–filled Mason jars in hand.

Hahn stressed conditioning, which Debuskey hated—circling the track innumerable times, jumping rope for ten rounds at a clip and repeatedly punching the light and heavy bags for three 3-minute sessions. "I couldn't wait to get in the ring with someone and learn how to avoid getting hit," he recalled. "I became quite skillful at avoiding disaster. My reflexes had been sharpened by all of my ball playing, and my legs were quick and responsive."

He won his first few fights in his 175-pound division. His enthusiasm evaporated, however, when he learned he was to meet the University of North Carolina at Chapel Hill Pre-Flight School's star, "KO" Kraus, in the ring. Kraus had won all three of his fights thus far by speedy knockouts. Said Debuskey, "I did not sleep in anticipation of my intro to Cuckoo-land." On the Wednesday preceding the scheduled Saturday scuffle, Coach Hahn took him aside and asked if he thought he could get down from 175 to 165 pounds and thus avoid being crushed by Kraus. Debuskey eagerly starved himself. At Saturday morning's weigh-in, he was at the life-saving mark of 165. "I was so relieved that once I stepped into the ring and the bell rang, I almost destroyed my surprised opponent."

"Merle was a star at Virginia," recalled the film producer Sam Goldwyn Jr., who met Debuskey at college. "But he never acted the star. He would always worry about the next game. He's always been a worrier. But he had a wonderful quality—a humble leadership, an incredible, dogged determination."

Debuskey's Navy service interrupted his education, but it did give him an unexpected chance to use his boxing skills. While his ship was docked in New Orleans, Debuskey, a commissioned officer, came upon a group of seamen who had set up a boxing ring on deck and were pairing men up to fight. Although he had stopped just to watch, the men challenged him to enter the ring. Thinking it inappropriate for an officer to fight an enlisted man, he resisted until the taunts became too much. The ship's champion was ready to take him on. "I knew they thought they had bagged an officer. Acting as if they had shamed me into it, I put on the gloves and stepped into the ring for a three-round bout. I was not polite. I proceeded to beat the guy unmercifully." Word got around to Debuskey's captain, who reprimanded him but then said with a smile that it would not go into his report.

After Debuskey returned home he found that his tolerance of Charlottesville's rigid social system had evaporated, and he transferred to Johns Hopkins for his final year of college. The dean, who had been the director of athletics there during Debuskey's time in high school, admitted him on the condition that he start on the basketball, football, and lacrosse squads. Debuskey had not held a ball in three years, but he acquiesced. Again, he shone most brightly at lacrosse, overcoming shin splits to win a starting position, achieve All-American honors, and start in his second North-South College All-Star Game, in 1947.

Though Debuskey's sports fame was largely local, it stayed with those who experienced it. Much later he met William Schaefer, the mayor of Baltimore, who surprised the press agent by bringing up his years on the field. Soon afterward a friend who had communicated with the mayor's chief assistant wrote to Debuskey saying that "all the way home on the train, the mayor kept saying over and over and over again, 'I can't get over it. I can't get over it. That famous lacrosse star, Merle Debuskey, couldn't believe that I remembered him. Who could forget him? He was so famous, so great, etc., etc.'"

Debuskey's prowess in sports had a slightly different effect on the man himself, shaping his character in the decades to come. In the 1970s Sidney Offit was playing pool with Debuskey's mentor, the press agent Jimmy Proctor, at the Manhattan Century Club, to which they both belonged. Upon learning that Offit was from Baltimore,

Proctor asked if he knew his old associate, Merle Debuskey. "Every-one in Baltimore knew Merle," replied Offit. Proctor was surprised. In all his years knowing Debuskey, he had never heard of his athletic triumphs.

"One of the reasons Merle is so fiercely honest, so straight, is because he had that confidence," said Offit. "He has that intuitive integrity of a guy who can challenge you and hit you back. He doesn't have to cheat. He just plays it straight up. When you're a hero at that age, when you've had that degree of success and idolatry at that age, it affects you. And I don't think he was aware of it."

But Debuskey does in one respect acknowledge the effect of his sporting life on his theatrical career: "Every now and then I wonder whether the uncertainty of the outcome of each play being produced and my effort to 'win' was somehow a transference from my days as a jock. From the opening whistle you pushed to win. Against whatever odds. The joy, of course, was in winning, but there was satisfaction in playing well, even if the end [was] a loss."

———

Physically, Philip Rose was the exact opposite of a sporting man. He was about "this big," Debuskey said, holding his thumb and finger about an inch apart. But Rose saw himself as a giant. "He never thought of himself as diminutive either in size or in ambition. This was evidenced by his playing tennis as if he were Pancho Gonzales or shooting pool with the confidence of a Willie Hoppe." But Debuskey admired the man's persistence in trying to advance the opportunities for African Americans in the theater, as well as his political convictions in the areas of civil rights and civil liberties.

Rose liked long shots. He gambled at cards and he gambled at theater, taking on projects with what seemed to be unlikely prospects. Steven Suskin, the general manager on several of Rose's shows, remembered calling Rose at Neil Simon's weekly card game to report the daily grosses; that was how the amateur gambler learned how his professional gambles were paying off across town. Rose remains most famous for having taken a chance on Lorraine Hansberry's 1959 play *A Raisin in the Sun*, the first play produced on Broadway written by a black female playwright, directed by a black director, and featuring an almost entirely black cast.

Rose was always a sport. In the 1960s he initiated a running pool game in a basement parlor at Broadway and Fifty-fifth Street. Regular members included Debuskey, the general manager Wally Fried, the writer Peter Udell (who wrote the books for the Rose productions *Purlie* and *Shenandoah*), and, occasionally, *Raisin*'s star, Sidney Poitier. The smoky, dimly lit hall was strictly the domain of African American men, many of them sharks. They would ignore the group of white Broadwayites as they gabbed about show business. That is, until Poitier showed up. "Then we became acceptable," recalled Debuskey.

At some point, Rose decided *Purlie Victorious*, the Ossie Davis play he had produced in 1961, would make a good musical. The story, set in southern Georgia, told of cotton pickers in the Jim Crow South and the black preacher Purlie Victorious, who wants to build a church for his people. "Phil submitted the play to a number of composers and lyricists," recalled Debuskey,

> all of whom for one reason or another turned it down. So he was surprised to get a call from the great Frank Loesser expressing interest and asking for a meeting to discuss the project. Loesser ultimately dropped out, suggesting that the play was too funny to be interrupted by songs. But soon after, Phil was approached by a lyricist, Peter Udell, who had worked in the Loesser organization and had been coached by him. Rose told me that he quickly decided that if he could not get the master, he would be happy with a star pupil.

Gary Geld, who with Udell had written the recent pop hit "Sealed with a Kiss," was hired as the composer, but he refused to leave Los Angeles. Said Debuskey, "He suggested that Phil and Peter send him the book and lyrics as they progressed, and that he would write the music, phone them, and play it for them. This seemed to me most unusual, if not a formula for disaster. But so much for my being prescient. It worked out quite well, producing a bouncing gospel [and] rhythm-and-blues score assimilated into a Broadway sound."

Debuskey had a small role in that sound. The publicist enjoyed hanging around rehearsals. Late into the last week of previews, the show was still working out the kinks. A ballet number in the second act wasn't working, and in the first attempt to fix the problem the dance was shortened. But it still remained a drag on the pacing. "I had been monitoring the audience reaction," said Debuskey, "and I thought that they were waiting for another song by Melba Moore, whom they rightly adored, and that they were disappointed when none came. When I first pointed this out to the creators, they buried my idea with assertions that the structure of the show did not call for it."

Debuskey made a pest of himself, insisting that Moore be given another song and that the ballet be dropped. Rose and Udell refused to listen—they took to ducking when Debuskey showed up at rehearsals—but Geld paid attention. "Finally," recalled Debuskey,

> they took the ballet out altogether, which eliminated one problem but left a musical hole. I kept bugging them until the fifth day before the opening, when Geld told me that they would write a song for Melba. I wondered how long it took to write a song. Geld suggested that I see the second act the next night. I did, and Melba brought down the house with her wonderful rendering of "I Got Love."

The song became a hit single and the show's signature, and Moore won the Tony as Best Featured Actress in a Musical.

Two months later Debuskey got a note from Geld, who had returned to Los Angeles: "In a frenzied and hectic time when everyone around me had a varying panacea for the real or imagined ills of *Purlie*, there was one sober, calm voice I shall always remember, of intelligence, perception, and great discretion, who said quietly, 'Drop the ballet and write Melba a solo.' That voice was yours, Merle, and we took your advice. With gratitude, Gary."

———

Not every producer Debuskey dealt with was as capable as Feuer and Martin or as brave as Rose. The publicist encountered two of these lesser beasts in a single show, Peter Shaffer's 1965 play *The Royal Hunt of the Sun*. The production was a lofty enterprise of soaring passages, mime, masks, magic, and color, all in the service of depicting the sixteenth-century journey of Spain's Francisco Pizarro, who, with 166 men, climbed the rugged Andes Mountains in Peru and conquered the Inca empire of twenty-four million. But before the huge enterprise could reach the point of performance, there were obstacles to overcome.

"My first chore was to figure out who the producers were at any given moment in the pre-production period," mused Debuskey. In May it appeared that Theodore Mann would be joined by Joseph E. Levine, David Susskind, and Daniel Melnick. Levine, nicknamed "the Boston Barnum," was regarded by the others as a security blanket. Better known as a movie mogul, he had begun—like several other film producers—in the garment industry. After switching to the film business by buying a movie house in New Haven, he made his first big splash in the 1950s importing movies such as *Godzilla*, *Hercules*, and *Hercules Unchained* and turning them into box-office hits. Levine promised to put up $200,000 of the $250,000 budget.

"Levine, I figured, was as good as his word," observed Debuskey. "It was just that his word was worthless." Levine, the press agent knew, had developed a penchant for announcing his involvement in a project that was certain to attract considerable newsprint and air time. After the hullabaloo died down, he would simply abandon it. Sure enough, Levine was soon out of the picture.

With Levine gone from *Royal Hunt* and Susskind and Melnick having dropped out, Mann soon managed to align himself with the Theatre Guild and Gerard Oestreicher. The necessary capital was soon raised, and a production schedule was finally set. Onto the scene strode Joel Shenker, representing the Theatre Guild. He became the captain of the effort. "He called a publicity and mer-chandising meeting in the conference room of the elegant Guild mansion, a couple of doors down from the Museum of Modern Art," Debuskey recalled. Debuskey attended with his associate Violet Welles. Welles, who was part of the Debuskey office throughout the late 1960s, was known on Broadway (for reasons that are lost to history) as "the Silver Bullet." She was a talkative displaced hippie who went on to write scripts for *Dark Shadows*, a daytime soap opera rooted in the supernatural.

"No sooner were we collected and seated," recalled Debuskey,

> than Shenker began pacing the room, throwing his arms around in
> emphatic gestures and speaking in operatic tones and with a melo-
> dramatic manner as he outlined his plan—and our chore—to create
> "The Year of the Inca" in New York, to turn Fifth and Madison
> Avenue store windows into dioramas of Inca life, to have fashion
> designers borrow from the motifs of Inca garb in their new lines, and
> to rename the Avenue of the Americas as Conquistador Boulevard.
> About the only stunt I thought he had omitted was having the mayor
> give the keys of the city to the Inca king.

After leaving the magnificent building, Welles turned to Debuskey
and pleaded, "Who do you have to fuck to get off this show?"

Debuskey and Mann suffered Levine's duplicity again in 1972,
when Circle in the Square, after an illustrious list of accomplishments Off-Broadway in Greenwich Village, took possession of a
new theater at Broadway and Fiftieth Street. Circle habitually lived
one step away from economic disaster, so it was particularly sus-
ceptible to Levine, who appeared at Circle's doorstep one day to
offer Mann and Paul Libin, Circle's leaders, a sum sufficient to keep
the wolf from the door. The only condition was that the theater be
renamed the Joseph E. Levine. The agreement was concluded with
a huge media event surrounding the official change of the theater's
marquee to Circle in the Square/Joseph E. Levine Theatre. Levine
and his wife, surrounded by an impressive group of stars connected
with the Circle's illustrious string of triumphs and a gaggle of press
agents, photographers, reporters, and TV cameras, watched his
name go up in lights. The only thing missing was a valid check—
which remained missing. After a couple of months, Levine's name
was taken off the marquee, an event witnessed by only the sign
makers and a few of Circle's rejoicing staff members.

———

In 1970 Sam and Cyma Rubin, near apoplectic with frustration,
were facing what seemed like the twenty-third crisis in bringing the
1925 creampuff musical *No, No, Nanette* back to Broadway when

their press agent, Merle Debuskey, summed up the show's predicaments for them and their creative partner, Harry Rigby: there was no theater, no acceptable book, no investors, a sick or senile director, and a superb choreographer who lacked expertise in tap dancing.

"Any one of the problems was sufficient reason to abandon the project," recalled Debuskey,

> and I argued forcefully for them to do so. But Cyma and Harry remained undaunted, obsessed with moving on. I often wondered how she did it, but Cyma persuaded Sam to cover the entire investment. Burt Shevelove was signed to direct as well as rewrite the script; Ted Cappy and Mary Ann Niles were hired to create the tap routines; and Berkeley's contract was rewritten so that the billing was changed to "Production Supervised by Busby Berkeley."

Berkeley, the erstwhile king of Depression-era kinetic, madcap Hollywood musicals, was the "sick or senile director" Debuskey had described. Rigby, with his passion for the past masters of American show business, had drafted the seventy-five-year-old out of retirement. Blinded by sentiment and the coup of landing Berkeley for a Broadway show, Rigby, when he looked at Berkeley, could not see the feeble old man who stared back at him.

When Debuskey first met Berkeley at the Algonquin Hotel, he thought the director was in danger of slipping down and disappearing between the couch cushions. Nevertheless, Debuskey organized a press stunt in which Berkeley would survey some hopeful chorus girls, and the media went into a frenzy over the opportunity to corner Berkeley, the tap-dancing gamine Ruby Keeler (his former star, who had come out of retirement to headline the show), and the old-time comedian Patsy Kelly in one room. Said Debuskey:

> The set-up was to line up the ladies on the front of the stage and have the fabled Berkeley examine them as he walked the line between them and the footlights edging the stage. We rehearsed it before we admitted the press, and it was a near catastrophe. Someone helped Berkeley get up the steps to the stage, and he was so unsteady that he stumbled into the footlights. When we ran it for the cameras we had

an assistant stage manager walk alongside him, between him and the footlights, shouldering him upright. The photographers had their field day, and the print seized on his comment that he did not look at their bodies but gazed into their eyes to see their souls. We all became convinced that the once-great man was physically no more. In a subsequent interview with David Frost, Berkeley was almost incoherent, nailing down the conviction that he was too infirm, physically and mentally, to direct the show.

Cyma Rubin soldiered on. She was not the sort of woman to accept defeat on any terms. A small, impeccably garbed woman with a hard, dark-haired beauty, she had won, as her second husband, the very wealthy and politically radical philanthropist Sam Rubin, who had built Fabergé into a powerful cosmetic house and then sold it for millions.

Cyma was determined to make her mark in the arts. With the famed conductor Leopold Stokowski, the Rubins had formed and financed the American Symphony Orchestra. Debuskey was brought in to raise the orchestra's profile; as a heavy contributor and board member at the New York Shakespeare Festival, Cyma was acquainted with Debuskey's work developing a profile for Joseph Papp's innovative and complex Festival.

When Cyma hooked up with the effete serial dreamer Harry Rigby—a man of ingenious ideas, a distracted sense of business, and absolutely no capital—Debuskey was again called. Given the project and the personnel, *Nanette* was a ludicrous proposition. Not surprisingly, it experienced enough out-of-town problems for four musicals. Burt Shevelove's rewrite of the book proceeded at a glacial pace. No money could be raised by either the cape-wearing Rigby or the Rubins, so Sam ended up backing the entire price tag of half a million dollars. Sensing a bomb, no theater owner would rent them a Broadway house to settle into after the pre-Broadway road tour. The show was in shambles in Boston, with a torturous run-through that ended with the star, Hiram Sherman, telling off the producers. But the Monday night opening performance in Boston improbably went like gangbusters, stunning all with the ecstatic response from the audience and the critics. The backstage joy was curtailed when Sherman, who played Keeler's husband and was sixty-two at the time, collapsed. "I rushed him to Massachusetts General Hospital, where he was diagnosed as having had a heart attack," recalled Debuskey. "The show continued to be a smash, with the understudy going on for Sherman."

Word of the success had gotten back to Broadway, so *Nanette* now had a theater. It also had a suddenly acclaimed star in Keeler. Unfortunately, Keeler now felt she was being underpaid and hired a new agent. Then Rubins hit the ceiling. "When Ruby got an agent and wanted to renegotiate," remembered Debuskey,

> Sam Rubin was incensed. "How can she do that?" he yelled. I said, "Well, if you don't renegotiate, she can get sick. I can tell you now, this show is worth a couple million dollars if you keep it intact." He said "I object to this kind of high-handed . . . ," etc., etc. I said, "Use it as an opportunity to advance yourself. You'll renegotiate but you'll want to hook her in for a couple years more. Be a gentleman, talk like a gentleman, appreciate her contribution." That's what he did.

The problem of replacing Sherman remained. The role was offered to Frank McHugh, the second-banana comic of a bushel of old motion pictures and a comrade of Patsy Kelly and Ruby Keeler. He was signed to a one-year contract without auditioning and was worked into the show in Toronto. It was another disaster. Not only could McHugh not sing, he had difficulty remembering lines and would fill in with old vaudeville shtick, and he made suggestions that would take lines from others to pad out his part. "He was dismissed and was guaranteed a year's salary for a couple of weeks' work," recalled Debuskey, "making him the highest paid septuagenarian in show biz."

With that, Cyma Rubin approved Debuskey's suggestion to get the blacklisted Jack Gilford, a close personal friend of Debuskey's who was still hurting for employment. The actor was playing stock at the time. "We went up and watched the show and said, 'Yes, Jack could do it,'" said Madeleine Gilford, the performer's widow. Debuskey, exercising flexible ethics, worked both sides of the fence by finessing

Gilford's deal behind the scenes. "I abrogated any fiduciary responsibility I had to the production by negotiating his contract," he admitted, "giving him star billing and the highest salary he had ever had for a Broadway show."

Cyma Rubin wasn't pleased about the extra money, but she acquiesced. The show opened on January 19, 1971, to extravagant reviews and was immediately established as a smash hit. It ran for 861 performances, more than two years, and made a mint.

———

Alex Cohen loved the phone even more than Merle Debuskey did. His left ear would suffer withdrawal symptoms when deprived of a receiver. He found ways to place a call even while on vacation in remote locales. He had a telephone in his limousine long before it was the norm. But he didn't want to talk to just anyone. David Merrick, with whom he constantly feuded for the title of Broadway's preeminent producer, once pulled up in his own limo beside Cohen's idling car. He had had his own phone installed and planned to one-up Cohen by calling him. But when Cohen picked up the phone and Merrick announced himself, the producer responded, "Sorry, David, I can't take your call now—I'm on the other phone."

"I may not be the smartest producer around," Cohen said, "but I have the best Rolodex in the business—it has the names, private phone numbers, contacts, favorite beverages, reading materials, restaurants and flowers of just about everyone who is anyone in entertainment. Priceless."

Debuskey and Cohen spoke every day. Only half of the time was it about business. Recalled the producer's son, Chris Cohen:

> There was a small circle of people like Merle—Gerry Schoenfeld and Bernie Jacobs, Roy Somlyo—with whom Alex communicated about the active projects they were working on, but also about the world and life in general, politics and other things. These guys were on the phone with him every single day. I remember falling asleep with two of three lines on the phone lit up conferencing together late into the evening. After dinner, after theater, for hours.

Cohen was a conspicuously high-minded producer, flamboyantly contemptuous of classless buck-chasers. "Any moron can make money, and in show business any cretin can make money," he told the *New York Times* in 1998. "My considerations have never been financial. A flop in my head is a show or an experience I didn't care for. And a hit in my head is something I enjoyed doing very much. You'd be surprised how many of my flops have been hits and hits, flops." His credits were classy, if varied. He presented Richard Burton on Broadway in *Hamlet* and *The School for Scandal* with John Gielgud and Ralph Richardson. His so-called Nine O'Clock Theatre series gave the public such cultural milestones as *An Evening with Mike Nichols and Elaine May* and Peter Cook, Dudley Moore, Jonathan Miller, and Alan Bennett's innovative comedy revue *Beyond the Fringe*. He offered one-person shows by Victor Borge, Maurice Chevalier, Marlene Dietrich, and Yves Montand.

Cohen was equally extravagant in his personal life. He ate out often, always at the best restaurants, downing two Absolut vodkas before ordering. ("He was always greeted like the Secretary of the Treasury," said Debuskey.) He threw lavish dinner parties for little or no reason, and high teas at his home in London. He swaggered about, his thick, dark hair swept back, on his face the curmudgeonly grimace of the thinking genius. He had homes in St. Croix, London, and Mougins, in the south of France, and a couple of apartments in Manhattan. The long-distance bills at each address were high, and if the conversations were contentious, so much the better. "Merle didn't hold back," said Chris Cohen. "I heard as many loud arguments between Merle and Alex as I heard soft and gentle ones. It wasn't a relationship where Merle worked for Alex. It was definitely one where opinions were heard. And, more often than not, the topics being discussed were not about the theater. He found Merle to be logical, sensitive, intelligent, well-read, well-rounded. It went way beyond the role of a press agent to the level of advisor."

His many credits notwithstanding, Cohen never wielded as much power as he did when he was the producer of the early Tony Awards broadcasts. The Tonys, from their inception in 1947 and for the next nineteen years, were a modest, genteel affair, usually presented over dinner at a hotel, and so unassuming that some winners declined invitations. The press gave the event no more than polite attention. In the mid-1960s the American Theatre Wing, which created the award, was even considering abandoning it. But the organization of Broadway producers—then called the League of New York Theatres, later the League of American Theatres and Producers, and today simply the Broadway League—eager to keep the Tonys alive, went to the Wing and persuaded it to co-produce the event with the League. The League asked Cohen to take over. Cohen got television interested and approached ABC with a deal. He assigned the writing of the show to his wife and business partner, Hildy Parks, who had no writing experience—and he continued to produce the Tonys for two decades.

In 1967 the Tonys were nationally telecast for the first time. The show began with Joel Grey performing "Wilkommen" from *Cabaret*. The broadcast was a hit. Eager to get the press on his side, Cohen hired Debuskey as his "sheep dog," in the publicist's words,

> herding a flock of able specialist press agents who titillated the media from journals all across the country. We treated them lavishly, and they returned the favor with their laudatory stories. Our first principle in dealing with the press was that we would approach each journalist as if he or she were the most important scribe in the business. We gave them freebies that would have cost a fortune—airfare, hotel rooms, limos, theater books, original cast recordings, meals, champagne— and we provided one-on-one interviews with the nominees.

Not surprisingly, the critics started calling the Tonys the cream of the awards shows. Ratings were high.

Cohen's sometimes bizarre perfectionism—in his mail room, stamps on envelopes had to be placed in a precise position, one he measured with a ruler—extended to the Tonys. Black tie on an invitation meant, for Cohen, black tie. At one awards show, a CBS news crew showed up in street clothes to cover the interviews that the media held with the winners after they left the stage. "All was going well until Alex entered the room," Debuskey recalled. "His presence was surprising because the show was still going on and you would have thought that the producer would be in the control booth, not in a hotel room across the street from the auditorium. But there he was. He saw that the CBS crew was black-tie-less, and he ordered them out of the room." Debuskey, not wanting to lose their coverage or a media friend, did some quick thinking. Dashing to a nearby restaurant, he persuaded the maitre d' to lend him a couple of waiters' black jackets and string ties until the end of the broadcast. "I got the crew in costume, brought them back in, and they continued their interviews."

The thing that brought Cohen to the pinnacle of his trade, the Tonys, would, however, eventually lay him low. "Alex's Achilles' heel was his arrogance—his belief that he could overwhelm any dissent," remembered Debuskey.

> He had essentially invented the Tonys, at least the national-television version. He was on a first-name basis with all the major figures in the theater and most of the majors in television, including William S. Paley, the head of CBS. One year, when some CBS exec wanted to drop the Tonys, Alex told him to call Paley, and Paley said to give Alex anything he wants. But Alex's arrogance made him overconfident about his ability to get what he wanted, no matter what.

In 1985, during the rehearsal for the Tony broadcast, Cohen, speaking in the Shubert Theatre to the stagehands, actors, and an invited audience of chorus members, used an obscenity in referring to the *New York Times*'s chief drama critic, Frank Rich. There was more. That evening, during an off-air commercial break, Cohen noted that although the New York State Council on the Arts was getting a special Tony, New York's Governor Mario Cuomo would not be accepting the award. "The governor of New York hasn't been to the theater in twenty-five years," Cohen quipped, "and he didn't want to break his record."

The remarks, saucy but essentially harmless, were nonetheless denounced from every corner of the theater world. Isabelle Stevenson, the president of the Wing, said she felt she should apologize for Cohen. Richard Barr, the president of the League, said they were "uncalled for." And Bernard Jacobs and Gerald Schoenfeld, of the Shubert Organization, told the *Times* that Cohen's remarks were "unfortunate." On June 4, 1985, the Monday after the Sunday night Tony Awards, Cohen quit the League of American Theatres and Producers.

Jacobs and Schoenfeld had been upset with their old friend for years by then, and to have those two men upset with you could be a chilling prospect. A pair of canny lawyers at the Shubert Organization, in the mid-1970s they had staged a coup, taking over a firm that since its beginnings had almost always been run by someone with Shubert in the name. Their takeover was so complete that they became known, collectively, as the Shuberts—and they were the most powerful men on Broadway.

In 1979 Cohen's critically trounced production of Richard Rodger's musical *I Remember Mama* was floundering at the box office. "Alex had made an arrangement to do the show with the Civic Light Opera on the West Coast in Los Angeles and San Francisco," Debuskey recalled. "They had a huge subscription sellout, and they could have made a lot of money on it. But the problem was that they had to keep the show running in New York until the California booking began, and they had run out of capital." Rodgers had put up about $50,000 to cover weekly losses, but the weekly grosses had fallen below the figure in their lease's stop clause (a standard clause stipulating that if a show doesn't take in a certain specified amount at the box office for two successive weeks, the landlord can end the lease). Cohen asked the Shuberts not to exercise the clause, and Jacobs and Schoenfeld at first assented. But then Cohen went to Europe. While he was there he got a call from Somlyo, his general manager, who told him that the Shuberts had put up the closing notice. "Alex pleaded with them. Forget the professional aspects, he told them; it was a personal request, a favor, he was asking," Debuskey recalled. "It was the last show by Richard Rodgers. Alex didn't want it to be a failure. But they ignored him and closed the show. And the West Coast trip was dead."

Cohen's pleading had annoyed the Shuberts, and he angered them further in the early 1980s in the futile battle to save two Broadway theaters, the Morosco and the Helen Hayes, from demolition to make way for the Marriott Marquis Hotel and a new theater in the hotel. Jacobs and Schoenfeld—always businessmen first, theater men second—wanted the theaters removed. They and others argued that the small theaters were no longer financially workable propositions. "Cohen knew the theaters weren't viable," observed Debuskey, "but he gave Joe Papp's committee to save the theaters working space in his offices." Cohen's aggressive contrariness to Jacobs and Schoenfeld's wishes was particularly galling because he was working out of a network of offices high above the Shubert Theatre, just one floor above the headquarters of the two lawyers themselves.

With a river of bad blood between the producer and the Shuberts, it came as no surprise that, following Cohen's Tony gaffes, with one year to go on Cohen's contract to present the awards show, the League decided to interview other possible producers. Feeding the fire were grumblings that, while the League had usually lost money on the awards, Cohen's Bentwood Productions received about $2 million a year from CBS to produce the show, though the money included payments to the stars and staff and a fee to the League. Said Debuskey,

> There were people who said, "What the fuck do we need Alex for— he's making money and the League isn't making money, and his wife gets a fee as a writer. Who is she? What do we need her when we've got people like Peter Stone and Neil Simon?" The fact was that when she wrote the show she and everyone had won awards for it. But they were pissed off that he was making the money and they felt that the League and the Wing weren't getting their fair share. Until then, there was nothing they could do about it, because he had a long-term contract. But when it was time to renew, they decided they would get a better deal if they produced it themselves. Alex was certain, because he had done it so long, that they wouldn't make a change. He was buddy-buddy with the people running the industry. Alex was relying on the Shuberts. But he never got that contract. The Shuberts claimed they couldn't convince the League. Which was a lot of baloney.

Matters grew uglier. Cohen, not about to go down without a fight, went to Stevenson and tried to persuade her to abandon the League, take back the Tonys, and present the awards herself, with him as the producer. "That started a ruckus. The League said the Wing wouldn't be able to do a show without them—they wouldn't let any of the performers appear. Alex said he expected that response but there was no way they could stop him from producing a show—he would get his own entertainment. And the Shuberts were furious at him for doing this. Really furious."

In the end, the strength of the producers' guild, and of the Shuberts, prevailed. Cohen's contract was not renewed, and the League and the Wing created Tony Awards Productions to run the ceremony together. Cohen was out. After twenty years as the king of the Tonys, he had been dethroned. The Tony ceremonies to come, many would comment, were never as successful, with the public or with critics, as the Cohen-produced shows had been. By the end of the twentieth century the program regularly dwelled near or in the ratings basement.

"No matter how badly or how well Alex was doing as a showman, he wanted to be involved in every aspect of theater he could," said Chris Cohen. "He wanted to tell Schoenfeld how to run the Shuberts. He wanted to tell Jimmy Nederlander how to run the Nederlanders. He basically wanted to rule the theater. But it came from a passion that it should be good for all."

Throughout the entire battle with the Shuberts and the League, Debuskey remained loyal to Cohen, a circumstance that engendered considerable discomfort. What's more, Debuskey was affiliated with Joe Papp, who had joined Cohen in the fight to save the doomed Broadway theaters. Displeasing the Shuberts was a risk few in the theater took willingly. Lee Silver, a friend who transitioned from reporter to Shubert executive, noticed that Debuskey, normally a regular at the Shubert offices, was staying away. "He said, 'There's a kind of an estrangement and neither one of us are comfortable about it.' He remained loyal to Alex, which imposed on his relationship to others, like Gerry and Bernie. It made a difference to Merle. He didn't like what was happening. It created a kind of a tension. Gerry and Bernie respected Merle, like everyone else in the theater, but they didn't feel as comfortable with Merle as they used to."

Debuskey stayed a friend even as Cohen's star sank further. He continued to produce shows, but there were only a few hits, one of them Peter Brooks's *Carmen* at Lincoln Center. Once Cohen had been expelled from the League and from the Shuberts' circle, his intimates in the theater disappeared. He sold his lavish homes one by one. "At the end, he was hard-pressed for cash," said Debuskey. "He was just as grand in his attitude. But his residence was such that the kitchen and the dining room were combined. Though his struggles to rise again were admirable, for me it deepened the sadness surrounding him."

Said Chris Cohen,

> When Alex's career started to ebb in the last five years of his career, which is saying the last five years of his life—he was never going to retire—the real friendships were the ones that hung in there. Schoenfeld and Jacobs were gone. Roy Somlyo was gone. My mom, unknown at that time, had begun the first stages of Alzheimer's. That, along with Alex's bitterness toward the industry and toward his own incapacity to change to fit Broadway, scared a lot of people away. It never scared Merle and Pearl away. There was clearly a relationship between Alex and Merle that was going to go on until the end. I think is had to come from an appreciation of each other as men. He's one of a handful of people who were true to the end. And Alex was not easy to deal with toward the end.

In 1990 Cohen wrote Debuskey, "Merle, some fine day I think I will find the proper way of saying thank you for what you have meant to me over the last few years. You are more than just a good friend—you are an extraordinary man."

Alexander Cohen died in 2000 at the age of seventy-nine, and with him passed the last great functioning American producer of his era.

Chapter 3

THE PRESS

Having initially wanted to become a journalist, Merle Debuskey entered his profession with a healthy measure of respect for members of the Fourth Estate. That respect disintegrated over decades of exposure to the media's inconstant mores. "I think I got a wider view and better perception that led me to believe it wasn't all that noble," he said simply, adding, "There are noble journalists, but the practice is ignoble." And in Debuskey's opinion, perhaps the noblest of them all was Brooks Atkinson, the long-serving, fair-minded chief critic of the *New York Times*, who in his time came close to deification.

Debuskey first encountered Atkinson when trying desperately to secure a review of an Off-Broadway production called *The World of Sholom Aleichem*. The cast consisted entirely of blacklisted actors. "The mainstream media responded as if they were being approached by someone inviting their attention to a befouled event," Debuskey recalled. Enter Aline Bernstein, the costume designer who had once been the much older lover of the novelist Thomas Wolfe. She was well-known in theater circles and was on familiar terms with Atkinson. She said she would call the critic and ask him to meet with Debuskey—a plan the press agent was eager to approve. The appointment was set for the very next day.

Debuskey spent a sleepless night trying to figure out how to approach the critic: "I knew that for me to touch on the political aspects of the production would be an affront to his propriety, and that to propose that the show was so good he could not responsibly ignore it would violate his journalistic and critic's integrity." He dragged his frightened self to the New York Times Building and was ushered in by Claire Rotter, a tiny, middle-aged woman who possessed no powers of intimidation except with theatrical press agents. As the drama desk secretary at the *New York Times*, she was the gatekeeper you had to get past in order to reach Atkinson. "She assumed for herself all the power of the *New York Times*," said Debuskey. "Atkinson adored her. She was fierce. You could never say no to her. You were dead if you did. You would never get a call through to anybody."

Atkinson, as ever, was neatly dressed for their meeting. He wore a bow tie, and his thin-rimmed metal spectacles sat delicately on his nose over a small moustache. A pipe was wedged between his teeth. A finer caricature of Yankee reserve had never been drawn.

> He was New England polite and proper and immediately tried to put me at ease, speaking directly, concisely and sensitively. I simply offered the modest plea that a theatrical effort was not complete without a review in the *Times*. I cited all the professionals involved in the production whose careers had earned his consideration, including Aline Bernstein. He gently and correctly pointed out that if he did attend a performance and filed a review, our schedule would have the show closed before *Times* readers could decide whether to buy a ticket. I summoned up what courage I had and suggested that it was important for the record, regardless of what his opinion might be. I told him that the show was so successful we hoped to reopen it in September for an open-ended run and would be trying to raise the capitalization during the summer.

Atkinson replied, "Mr. Debuskey, if I review it now I will not be able re-review it in the fall, when you will really need it. I understand the difficulty in raising money, but I do not wish to write a money-raising tract. Why don't you just let me figure out a way to handle this?"

That afternoon Rotter called to arrange tickets for Atkinson for the following evening. Oddly for someone with her reputation of eating publicists for breakfast, she was very friendly. Said Debuskey,

"[Atkinson] did not file a review, but in his next Sunday column he wrote a couple of paragraphs extolling the work—paragraphs that made it easy to raise the necessary money and set the show up royally for its fall reopening."

Being on good terms with Atkinson never hurt any press agent, and over time Debuskey and Atkinson developed a working relationship so cordial the critic began referring to the publicist as Professor Debuskey. Debuskey compounded his good fortune by setting up equally solid relationships with Arthur Gelb, Lewis Funke, and Sy Peck (who was at the *Star* when that publication covered the Interplayers, and who first put Debuskey's name in the paper). When prompted to memory by Debuskey's name, Joe Nederlander, a member of the powerful theater-owning family, exclaimed: "When he went into a press office, all they had to hear was that name, Merle Debuskey, and 'Oh, send him up.' He was a legend!" Don Loze, who helped run Cy Feuer and Ernie Martin's office, said he always assumed Debuskey was contracted because "Ernie felt that Merle had a straight reputation at the *Times*."

Bob Ullman, an associate of Debuskey's during the 1970s, remembered his boss being supremely, even recklessly confident of his influence with the Gray Lady. "Lewis Funke called from the *New York Times* once, so naturally I went into Merle's office," Ullman recalled.

> He was having a conversation, one of his leisurely conversations, which he was famous for. He loved to talk on the phone. He's a very loquacious man. I was trying to get his attention. So finally I slipped him a note that said, "Lewis Funke is on the phone." He signaled to me that he wasn't going to get off the phone and I should tell him to call back. Merle is the only press agent I know who would tell the *New York Times* to call back.

Herbert Mitgang, who was supervising editor of the drama section of the *Times*'s Sunday edition in the 1950s and early '60s, succinctly encapsulated Debuskey's unusual appeal: "You could trust Merle." In a sea of hacks, Debuskey knew the value of integrity, and to buttress his image, he made certain the press could also trust his staff.

"What I learned from him is you don't lie," said Judy Davidson. "I also learned that if someone turns you down on a story, you don't badger them. Merle was so different from other publicists. He'd go and talk to the press as friends. He'd go with his pipe in his mouth."

The press agent was particularly tight with Seymour Peck, the thoughtful, bearded editor of the Sunday *Times*'s Arts and Leisure section, whom Walter Kerr compared to the head of a university English department and Clive Barnes called "the dream of all culture editors." The two men navigated the same leftist circles in the entertainment community, and Peck had a political appreciation of such Debuskey projects as *The World of Sholom Aleichem* and the New York Shakespeare Festival. In 1955, during the McCarthy era, Peck, known to all as Sy, was subpoenaed by the Senate Internal Security Committee, causing the *Times* to suspend him without pay for a time. This was particularly hard on Peck since his wife had recently died and left him the sole parent of two young children. Debuskey, Jimmy Proctor, another leftist press agent, Abe Weiler, also of the *Times*, and Jack Harrison of the *Hollywood Reporter* took up a collection for the journalist, which Proctor and Debuskey hand delivered.

Debuskey was equally enamored of Gelb, whom he considered an instrumental player in the *Times*'s mindful coverage of the theater over the decades. "He was quickly favored by Atkinson," he said,

> who recognized his journalistic instincts, energy, ambition, and love of theater and provided the escalator which enabled Artie to ride to the top, variously as a critic, a news gatherer, and ultimately as editor. He was consistent in his affection for Joe Papp's endeavors and was a willing advocate. He understood and appreciated them as an elemental part of the New York theater and a social instrument that characterized New York.

The long-standing *Times* theater beat reporter Sam Zolotow was less of an intimate, but to Debuskey he was a continual source of amusement. Short and bespectacled, Zolotow was a relentless and greedy newshound. Staring at his victims with wide, surprised-looking eyes, he would demand honesty from every press agent and producer and exclusivity on every scoop. "The CIA and the FBI were but pale operators when compared with the indefatigable, devious techniques of Sam," said Debuskey,

> with his widespread network of insider implants, secretaries, waiters, chauffeurs, bartenders, printers, ad agency agents, casting agents, and even parking lot attendants. He was the first one in the office in the mornings and the last to leave. Reporters arriving at the customary morning hour found their mail had already been opened, an act he denied. But his most egregious theft was undeniable. The most widely read news column was Sunday's "News of the Rialto," assembled and written by Lewis Funke. To meet his Sunday edition printing deadline, his column of exclusives would be sent down to the composing room Wednesday evening or Thursday morning and sit there until the presses rolled the Sunday edition. Sam would sidle into the composing room, read Funke's Sunday column, and rewrite segments for his Friday column, scooping his own colleague.

Zolotow called Debuskey "boychik," and the press agent managed to keep in the reporter's good graces. When Sam retired, Debuskey headed a small group that arranged a farewell party and gift for Sam. The event was exceptionally well attended. Said Debuskey at the time, "one strain running through all the responses of people invited to this party... explains our attendance—fear."

Debuskey admitted that his close association with Peck often made it difficult for him to do his job. Peck felt a similar burden, for to be both a pressman and familiar with Merle Debuskey opened one to accusations from "upstairs" of favoritism.* It also opened you to all sorts of written and spoken "discussions" about the nature of your trade. It was not unusual for Peck and other *Times* staffers to receive from Debuskey weighty, typewritten dressings-down through the mail. Arthur Gelb once opened an envelope to find a five-page, single-spaced diatribe from Debuskey filled with dozens of five-dollar words, all in response to the *Times*'s

---

* Through Debuskey, Peck once secured for his daughter a position handling props at Joseph Papp's Delacorte Theatre.

review of the play *Does the Tiger Wear a Necktie?* Debuskey concluded the letter in typically fustian fashion: "As is obvious, this letter was not composed. It was written. Written with a halter, checkrein and a large dose of self-inflicted propriety. Arthur, I tell you, something is wrong."

These communications were usually typed on Debuskey's beaten-up old 1907 Underwood, which he loved dearly and seemed to reserve for the most serious tasks. To judge from the letters' length and unstinting deployment of an unabridged dictionary, Debuskey wrote them with relish, loading each letter with obscure cultural references and convoluted metaphors. The effect on the other end of the exchange could range from bemusement to indignation. Upon receiving a commendatory "note" on his work as a critic, Richard Eder, who covered the theater for the *Times* in the late 1970s, drolly replied, "Your note is easier to appreciate than answer."

More typical was Debuskey's war cry, addressed to Howard Taubman, chief drama critic for several years in the 1960s. It concerned a misapplied head on a *Times* article that said London critics had "lauded" the show *No Strings*, when the opposite was true. "I even lifted our thick dictionary to check out 'laud,'" he wrote. "I do not believe that the quotes in the story praised or extolled the play as indicated by the title." Taubman waited two weeks until Debuskey "simmered down a little" before responding, "Believe me, Merle, irritations of this sort will only give you high blood pressure."

Even the mild-tempered Peck's patience was sometimes tested by these impromptu lectures. In 1970, after reading a piece in the *Times* in which an "oaf" named Harris Green evaluated the Broadway musical scene, Debuskey complained about the newspaper's "irresponsible and venal whimsies." He pointedly noted that that article had failed to mention his client Philip Rose's production of *Purlie*. Peck tartly retorted, "Next time you have the impulse to write a letter like this latest one, I suggest you wait twenty-four hours, or possibly even count to ten. I work hard, I work wild hours, and I fill them as purposefully as possible, and I certainly don't intend to spend much more time defending the *New York Times* and myself against your absurd attacks." A couple of years later Peck sent a note congratulating Debuskey of the success of *No, No, Nanette*, a show he represented. Debuskey reacted by launching in longhand into yet another attack on *Times* theater coverage policy, ending with: "I labor under no misapprehension that to be liked at any cost is profitable, neither in commercial theater nor in human terms." In the final paragraph, he remembered to thank Sy for his nice note.

"If you were a member of the press," Alex Cohen once observed, "you know how often it has been pointed out to you by Merle Debuskey in an engaging and humorous manner that you are full of shit."

Marilyn Stasio recalled the sheaves of unsolicited opinion that often traveled the few blocks from Debuskey's offices to the Times Building. "He wrote very long letters," she said. "When Merle was contemptuous, he could be contemptuous or angry in a very elegant and gracious manner, always with well-chosen words."

Stasio tended to receive the brunt of these arguments in person because she and her husband at the time, the *Variety* reporter Dick Hummler, occasionally socialized with Debuskey. "He would always carry on about these dog shows that he worked on. He was incredibly loyal. Dick and I would just fume about it afterward. We kept changing our minds as to whether he was just oblivious to the fact that these shows were shit or he was just so incredibly loyal. And yet, his enthusiasm when the shows were real was just beautiful to behold. He would love the show and would be so eloquent about it."

Age did not dampen Debuskey's desire to assault the enemy in fiery-*cum*-flowery vocabulary when a published piece was not to his liking. When in 1989 Frank Rich gave the Circle in the Square production of *Ghetto* a slighting review, Debuskey told him, "Your viscera rejected it and your intelligence repudiated it," which damned the play to a bleak future. "Empirically one observes that the *Times* is virtually ceaseless in its support of a show sanctified by its Critic and obdurate in its refusal to lend a hand to a production defiled by its Critics."

Rich probably took the riposte in stride. When he joined the *Times* in 1980, Sy Peck sat him down. Said Rich at Debuskey's retirement party years later, "He gave me a lecture on press agents and how it all worked. Sy moved on to the subject of Merle. He was a good friend of Merle's and had been for a long time. He tried to be objective but he was very, very flattering... how literate Merle was, how much he loved the theater, and what a gentleman he was."

Rich later caused Debuskey some agitation. During the 1980–81 season, Rich's first as the *Times*'s chief drama critic, there was a movement on the part of producers to generate more opening-night excitement by doing away with the preview system, which had been instituted in the 1960s. In going back to the old-fashioned opening-night system, critics would simply attend the first official performance and then write their notices on a very short deadline. The devilish David Merrick had achieved this very thing by coercion: by canceling, at huge financial cost, the final previews of his musical *42nd Street*, Merrick forced the reviewers to attend opening night. Emboldened by this canny move, the Shubert's Jacobs and Schoenfeld decided they too wanted to resurrect the idea of a newsworthy opening night. But Merrick-like chicanery was not for them. Debuskey arranged a meeting with Arthur Gelb, then an assistant managing editor of the *Times*, and they implored him to have Frank Rich attend the formal opening of Peter Shaffer's *Amadeus*, return quickly to the newspaper's nearby offices, and write his review on deadline for the next day's paper. The theater owners reasoned that if the *Times* gave the nod, the rest of the press corps would go along.

"Gelb agreed," Debuskey said, "and warranted that Rich would attend the opening night of *Amadeus*, on December 17, 1980. I, as the show's press agent, was so advised and proceeded to inform all the other media and set up the opening, shoehorning everyone into the same night and guaranteeing that Rich would attend that performance." Rich arrived on opening night and took his seat for the show.

All was well until a heated Clive Barnes, at that time the critic for the *New York Post* (and perhaps keenly aware that his competitor, Rich, now held his former job), stormed into the theater in a huff, shouting at Debuskey that he had lied and that Rich had been permitted to attend a preview. "I grabbed him, pointed to the seated

Frank Rich, and suggested that he take his seat." But Barnes was right. By the time the play ended and the curtain came down, the *Times* was on the street with a rave review. Aided by Gelb, Rich had purchased a mezzanine ticket to an earlier preview and written his critique the following day.

Debuskey was suddenly faced with a hornet's nest of angry reviewers who thought they had been duped for the benefit of the *Times*. "Fortunately, the media folk believed me when I swore that I had no knowledge of this clandestine affair, and they turned their ire against both Gelb and Rich," Debuskey said.[†]

Critics and producers, of course, don't mix well, and early in his career, while under the tutelage of Jimmy Proctor, Debuskey witnessed this fact firsthand. On the opening night of Arthur Miller's *The Crucible*, the *New Yorker* critic Wolcott Gibbs was all but carried to his seat by two men, in full view of the show's producer, Kermit Bloomgarden. "The next morning," recalled Debuskey,

> Kermit comes in saying, "You better call Wolcott and tell him he was too fuckin' drunk to understand the show. He better come back again." So Jimmy called. When Jimmy was nervous he would sweat. He gets Gibbs on the phone and he doesn't know quite how to approach it. Jimmy knew Wolcott very well. He's stumbling around, and Wolcott says, "Jimmy, stop it. Tell Kermit it's a rave."

It could be argued that if Debuskey ever had any complaints about the work of the *New York Times* critics Clive Barnes and Mel Gussow, he had only himself to blame. Barnes began his career as a dance critic in London. He was married to a dancer and on one of his visits to New York in the 1960s visited the office of Debuskey

---

[†] *Amadeus* caused Debuskey another headache in the form of the playwright Peter Shaffer's agent, the legendary European expatriate Robert Lantz. They received pages and pages of publicity, but still Debuskey would routinely get notes from Lantz, with copies sent to Shaffer, about the press agent's supposed derelictions of duty. "A couple of times a week at least," said Debuskey. "I asked Alex Cohen about it. He knew Lantz well. He said Lantz was fortifying his position with the playwright. He was protecting his ass. Lantz could be the most gracious, affable, Eastern European, debonair sophisticate. But he could be scurrilous and treasonous."

and Seymour Krawitz, whose wife was also an English dancer. Barnes mentioned that he wanted to start doing work in the United States. "I first wrote to the *Times* when my son was born and I needed to get an increase of income," said Barnes. "I got a very chilly letter back. Then, both Seymour and Merle contacted Sy Peck on my behalf. Sy worked with the press agents he liked. And he took Merle very seriously." Soon afterward Peck arranged for Barnes to write pieces about London theater and dance for the newspaper. In 1967 Barnes was named chief theater critic at the *Times*.

As for Gussow, his long career at the *Times* may have been born of a bus ride. "I ran into Arthur Gelb once and we went downtown on the bus," said Debuskey. "He said they were looking for a new kind of voice to bring into the *Times*. I said, 'I know somebody who is into how the theater is developing. He writes second-string for *Newsweek*. Gelb said, 'Can you arrange for me to speak with him?'" Debuskey called Gussow and told him to call Gelb if he was interested. The editor later wrote Debuskey to say Gussow was under consideration.

———

When Merle Debuskey came to the theater scene in 1948, the principal instrument for the dispensing of news was the print media: newspapers, wire services, magazines, and, to a much lesser degree, radio. The presses turned out eleven dailies in the city: the *Times*, the *Herald-Tribune*, the *News*, the *Mirror*, the *Post*, *PM*, the *Journal-American*, the *Sun*, the *World Telegram*, the *Wall Street Journal*, and the *Brooklyn Eagle*; two papers on Long Island, *Newsday* and the *Press*; two papers in Newark; one in Westchester; two wire services, Associated Press (AP) and United Press International (UPI); and three trade papers, *Variety*, *Billboard*, and *Hollywood Reporter*. They all held an interest in theater activity, which dominated their entertainment pages.

The spread of magazines included *Time*, *Newsweek*, *Life*, *Look*, and *Cue*. There also were a couple of small weeklies important for the emerging Off-Broadway movement in Greenwich Village: the *Villager* and the *Village Voice*. "The print media was a cornucopia of outlets for the legitimate theater press agents," recalled Debuskey, "and the diligent ones worked their fingers and feet to the bone. Just servicing them was a full-time activity requiring time, energy, craft, and a thorough knowledge of their individuality, preferences, prejudices, [and] deadlines, [as well as] the idiosyncrasies of the reporters, editors, and columnists."

During his apprenticeship, Debuskey's weekly salary for all this was $25.

The duties of a lowly apprentice were not particularly glamorous. Debuskey likened the mechanics of the job back then to "the medical practices of leeching and cupping":

> The reams of material flowing out of a press agent's had to be typed or, if one was progressive, they possessed the very primitive copying machines that existed, producing flimsies that the media found barely tolerable. In my first days as an apprentice and as associate, the seniors insisted on producing original copies, and many were the evenings one spent banging them out, with carbon paper maybe two or three at a time.

Once a week press agents would pay a visit to each of the New York papers, usually on Tuesdays in order to make the deadline for the weekend edition, with its expansive entertainment sections. Each agent came equipped with story ideas, photos, or simple announcements, but the most important thing, according to Debuskey, "was to maintain eyeball-to-eyeball contact with the reporters and editors."

Columnists were another target. They were a different breed from critics. Thriving on scandal and taking a waspish perspective, they made no pretense at journalistic scruples. They were paid to a have a voice, to build up a following—and where there is a following, an ego soon grows.

When Debuskey became a press agent, the city teemed with columnists, most of them forever hungry for theatrical gossip fed to them by press agents. The publicists, he said, "had very close contacts at each paper, especially with the columnists. If you knew Walter Winchell's Girl Friday, Rosie Bigman, and she liked you, your message would get through to 'the boss.' Each columnist had a favorite restaurant hangout, and you looked for them there." Leonard Lyons could be found at Sardi's, Winchell at the Stork Club. "They also had legmen, and there were agents for press columnists, whose job it was to seek out items. If you weren't 'in' with a given columnist, these agents might get your item placed," said Debuskey.

But columnists were proud and sensitive to slights, which made them volatile. The seating arrangement for a show's opening designated a certain pecking order among the media. Making an unintentional mistake could be costly. Debuskey and Krawitz once slipped up with the opening-night press list for Jean Kerr's much-anticipated *Mary, Mary*. Noticing that the very short columnist Earl Wilson of the *New York Post* was seated on the aisle behind the very tall columnist Ed Sullivan of the *New York Daily News*, they exercised some misplaced sensitivity and exchanged their positions. "Just before the opening curtain," recalled Debuskey,

> when Sullivan was shown to his seat, he looked, spotted Wilson seated in front of him, about-faced, and angrily stormed out of the theater. We could not stop him and persuade him to return. It took me a couple of days, working through the producer of Sullivan's television show, Bob Shanks, to explain my motivation. And, gentleman that Sullivan was, he apologized. We booked him for another performance.

A few years later Debuskey tussled with Dorothy Kilgallen, the often vicious gossip columnist for the *New York Journal-American* and the nationwide Hearst syndicate. Debuskey, who can usually be trusted to find a kind word about nearly everyone he's worked with, curtly characterized Kilgallen as "a mean-spirited bitch." In 1965 the columnist suddenly began denigrating, in print, the musical *Skyscraper*. The show, which Debuskey was promoting the show for Feuer and Martin, hadn't even opened yet. "Kilgallen was generally impervious to correction or criticism," said Debuskey. "We could not figure out what had unleashed her venom." He turned to Mike Hall for answers. Well coiffed and neatly outfitted, Hall was a fabled specialist in planting column items. Movie companies paid him a healthy fee to represent their projects, a dozen at a time, and gave him inside information on the stars during the shooting of a film. That made him a gossip gold mine. Hall was therefore thick with Kilgallen, and he promised to look into her *Skyscraper* beef.

"It turned out that some fashionable organization had bought tickets for a theater party for an early preview of *Skyscraper*," Debuskey said. "They had invited Kilgallen and had had the temerity to insult her by seating her upstairs in the mezzanine. Mike was able to convince her that the show was in no way responsible for such heinous behavior." Her criticism ended as suddenly as it had begun.‡

Columnists sometimes transgressed in more unseemly ways. While handling the Alan Jay Lerner and Frederick Loewe musical *Paint Your Wagon*, Debuskey became smitten with the show's lead female dancer, a "tiny, fey, Irish, honest, quiet, otherworldly, and superb" Agnes de Mille dancer with the improbable given name of Gemze de Lappe. The two grew close after de Lappe became the target of the attentions of the *World-Telegram* and *Sun* critic and columnist Ward Morehouse. The rotund, southern-born Morehouse was a renowned dandy and bon vivant who had once had an affair with the movie actress Miriam Hopkins. "I think he was going to ask me to marry him," recalled de Lappe. "I saw what was coming."

"One day he was at an airport," said Debuskey.

In those days, airports prominently displayed machines from which you could buy very inexpensive insurance policies redeemable by a beneficiary if you were killed in a crash. At the airport and before flying off, this short and chubby Don Juan had banged out a couple of policies naming Gemze de Lappe as his beneficiary, and he had mailed the policies to her.

De Lappe panicked. She didn't know how to respond. Rebuffing a stage-door Johnny was one thing, but rejecting a critic could damage

---

‡ Kilgallen ended soon after her swipes at *Skyscraper* did. On November 8, five days before the show opened, she died in her sleep in her Upper East Side townhouse from a fatal combination of alcohol and barbiturates.

her professionally. When she appealed to Debuskey, he advised silence. "I had met and knew Ward and was sure I could jolly him off to woo and take his chances with another stage enchantress. But he never followed up."

All columnists' reigns must end one day. For the king of all columnists, Walter Winchell, the end was infinitely sad. While working for a 1967 comedy called *The Ninety-Day Mistress*, co-produced by (of all people) George Steinbrenner and directed by Phil Rose, Debuskey received a surprising request from Winchell to attend opening night. Winchell's time in the sun was long past. He no longer held the entertainment world by the throat through his syndicated column and radio program, and he lived much of the year in Miami.

Debuskey had done well by Winchell in the 1950s, when the journalist was at the top of his game, alternately making and ruining careers and dictating national policy in Washington. The fedora-sporting writer somehow knew of the press agent's background and was apparently amused at his having been one of the very few Jewish All-American lacrosse players. "Beginning with my neophyte days, press-agenting *Michael Todd's Peep Show*, I batted over .300 with Winchell, and when it was necessary and I called the office, Rose would put me through to the boss if he was in, or would take and be sure to deliver my message."

Debuskey met Winchell in the lobby of the Biltmore Theatre to hand him his tickets for *The Ninety-Day Mistress*.

> He was once a dandy dresser. I was surprised to see his shabby appearance and demeanor. At the intermission, I was standing in the back of the house listening to and looking at the audience to see if I could sense any encouraging response. Winchell, this fallen god, came up and asked if I would like a quote from him that could be used in advertising the play. I tried to summon up the response I would have given a decade or two earlier, when his words would have been like gold. I stumbled through an exaggerated gratefulness.

Encouraged, Winchell then invited Debuskey to join him at the Spindletop restaurant after the show. Recalled Debuskey, "In his heyday, just to be seen with him at his special table at the Stork

Club would have been enough to double a press agent's client list." After the final curtain and the backstage photo opportunities, as the company headed off for drinks and dinner together, Debuskey collared Rose and told him of Winchell's invitation. "Philip had grown up when Winchell was king and insisted that I could not avoid the invitation."

Sensing he was in for a depressing evening, Debuskey dragged himself over to the Spindletop. No sooner had he sat down than Winchell dug into his pocket and pulled out some tattered newspaper clips. "They were articles from minor journals, with his byline. The clips reported, in his familiar style, some retreaded gossip. I don't know who was more embarrassed, me or the young lady at his side. I managed to effect the expected awed, respectful response and downed a Scotch straight up."

Debuskey filled up time by asking about Rose Bigman and whether his Miami address was still the same. He then begged to be excused, saying that he had to look after the photographers covering the party, and fled.

> There had been a time—when he was flacking for Joe McCarthy and filling his columns with vindictive, mean-spirited, and destructive tirades about good and innocent persons—when I would have gladly pissed on the bastard. But that night, that's not what I was thinking or feeling. I was seeing the person he once was, a cornerstone in twentieth-century American history. The depth of his diminution was saddening. He had unfortunately hung around too long. He should have gone down the Ganges in flames.

———

Debuskey never did achieve his initial New York dream of seeing his byline printed in a major newspaper. But he did publish some reviews, after a fashion. Early in his press agent days he took a summer job banging the drum for a stock company called Theatre by the Sea, in Matunuck, Rhode Island, just east of Providence. The company received its primary press coverage from the *Providence Journal*. One year the paper assigned their South Shore bureau correspondent to review the plays.

"He was a competent general-news reporter, but he knew absolutely nothing about the theater and had never seen a professional production," said Debuskey. "The producers were understandably nervous. They feared the worst. Historically, a novice critic tended to make his mark with acerbic put-downs of the subject, and the *Providence Journal* was a significant make-or-break for business. The new critic visited the theater to introduce himself before it opened for the summer, and over a few drinks he confessed to me that he had no idea how to proceed." The cub critic was facing a tight deadline and feeling the pressure. Debuskey calmed him, saying he could use his office in the theater to write the notices. He told the reporter to avail himself of the desk, paper, a typewriter, the telephone—whatever he needed.

The publicist sensed an opportunity. On the first opening night of the season, when the reporter raced to Debuskey's office to confront the agony of his deadline, he discovered two sheets of paper. "On them was a review of the show he had just seen. All he had to do was phone it in. When he completed his assignment, he sauntered over to the nearby inn and slyly slipped a copy of his review to the grateful producers. After a while, he began to change a word here and there. But he didn't dare change the favorable thrust that the reviews inevitably gave the show."

The next summer, the same reporter returned, brimming with new confidence. He called Debuskey and said that he could handle things himself from now on. "I made certain he knew that he was still welcome to use my office," said the publicist. Debuskey waited until just before deadline to check on the journalist's progress.

What a sight. He was thoroughly soaked with sweat, sheets of balled-up paper were strewn around, and he was staring at a blank sheet in the typewriter. I asked if he would like a drink, and when he nodded yes, I told him to open the bottom drawer of the desk. I left. There had been a flask sitting in that drawer, but there was also a neatly typed review, ready to be phoned in to the *Journal* just in time to meet his deadline. About twenty minutes later, he came over to the inn with a copy of his review. This event was never mentioned, and for the remaining shows we went back to our established journalistic practice.

Chapter 4

THE PLAYERS

Merle Debuskey likes actors, particularly dancers, but they mystify him.

> They have persisted in pushing themselves to the outer limits of their capabilities, never satisfied with the results, always trying to get better, in an area that's not particularly welcoming or provident. They are special. I've never gotten over seeing them in the performance of a character and then sitting with them over coffee or dinner. How could this person have transformed themselves like that? I've read about all that stuff, the techniques. But I don't know how they do it. There are people who excel at finance, at real estate, but they don't transform their very being. And that's mystical to me.

As a press agent, Debuskey couldn't get away from performers even if he wanted to. But that was OK by him. His first marriage was to a dancer, and it was arranged by an actor.

Debuskey was introduced to Christine Karner by a former object of affection, Gemze de Lappe. Like de Lappe, the beautiful Karner was a dancer. Romantically, there was nothing Debuskey liked better than dancers. She had performed a series of roles in the Phil Silvers vehicle *High Button Shoes*, which was choreographed by Jerome Robbins. When Debuskey met her, she had recently returned from a tour of *Oklahoma!* and was a fixture on Sid Caesar's *Your Show of Shows*. "She was very attractive, bright, politically aware, and active in the performers' unions," remembered Debuskey, "and she fit my vision of the ideal woman—she was a consummate dancer." In 1958, after living together for a few months, they decided to marry.

The couple wanted to hold the ceremony in Baltimore so Debuskey's family could attend. That complicated matters, since Maryland recognized only marriages performed by a licensed clergyman, and in the 1950s it was simply not possible to find a rabbi in the Baltimore area willing to perform a ceremony between a Jew and a Christian. The nuptial plans stalled.

That summer Jimmy Proctor invited Debuskey and Karner for a weekend visit at his Montauk estate. Proctor was pals with the playwright Arthur Miller, whose plays he had often promoted. That Saturday night Proctor decided to cook up one of his exotic (for the time) spaghetti dinners and invited Miller and his wife, Marilyn Monroe, who were living on Long Island's East End.

Monroe wore a light peasant blouse, a long full skirt, and no makeup. The film actress had converted to Judaism in order to marry Miller, and, somehow, said Debuskey, "in the conversation's mix of fishing, the correct al dente level for spaghetti, beachcombing, theater, and politics, Chris mentioned the dilemma that was holding back our wedding." Monroe jumped up off the couch and insisted that she could and would settle the problem. Debuskey and Karner had previously nixed the idea of conversion, thinking it too significant an act to use as a technical device for getting hitched. But Monroe ignored their protests. "She insisted that it had been one of most educational and gratifying learning experiences of her life."

Monroe pushed the rabbi who had instructed her, Robert Goldberg, as the man for the job. The head of a congregation near New Haven, Connecticut, he was politically progressive and very active in the civil rights movement. Recalled Debuskey, "By the middle of the week, [Monroe] had spoken with Rabbi Goldberg and convinced him that we were friends and good people." Karner made an appointment and was soon undergoing a reading course in the essentials of Judaism. A month later the conversion ceremony was held in Debuskey and Karner's apartment. They were married soon afterward in the groom's hometown.

—

Growing up, Debuskey had good reason to despise all actors. His only family connection to the profession was his older brother, Charles, who had married his high school sweetheart, Florette, and moved to Pottsville, Pennsylvania. Pottsville did not contain sufficient excitement for the ambitious Florette, who fancied herself an actress. When their daughter, Nan, was three, Florette abandoned her husband and daughter, moved to Hollywood, and changed her name to Maggie Hayes. Though she never achieved stardom, she did manage to put together a long career, taking roles in the films *Blackboard Jungle*, *The Glass Key*, and *Sullivan's Travels*, as well as many television shows. Her most significant achievements were her marriages. After Charles, she next wed the actor Leif Erickson, and then, after him, the director Herbert Bayard Swope Jr. The forsaken Nan was sent by her father to Baltimore and raised by Debuskey's parents. In interviews, Hayes never mentioned her daughter by her first marriage. For Debuskey, his sister-in-law's betrayal was unforgivable, and from then on he referred to Hayes as "the vixen."

Debuskey was more tolerant of other vixens of the stage. During his salad days as a summer stock flack, he was assigned the care and feeding of Eva Gabor, who had been engaged to perform at Theatre-by-the-Sea. The producers had found her a house with a swimming pond about half a mile from the theater, and one night after a performance Debuskey and his assistant were told to drive her home.

> It was a balmy country night, and Miss Gabor, a lively soul, suggested a swim. But we demurred, as we did not have bathing suits. She smiled. "Don't be silly," she said. And in a matter of seconds we had all shed our summer clothes and dived in. She behaved good-naturedly, simply, joyfully, and without affectation. And she was a proficient swimmer. "Momma made all of us learn to swim almost as soon as we could walk," Eva said. "She wanted us to be prepared for any occasion."

Another time the erstwhile film siren Veronica Lake was brought in to perform. The week went smoothly until just before the final performance, when the alcoholic Lake ran off with—appropriately enough—the bartender at a nearby inn. "The alert went to police precincts from coast to coast, and the tabloids were full of rumored sightings," Debuskey remembered. "She was nice enough when sober, but unfortunately that wasn't often enough." Neither Lake nor the bartender ever returned.

Blonde bombshells of every description and all eras haunted the stock company. The most memorable of Debuskey's term there was undoubtedly Mae West, who was in her late fifties by then but still a huge attraction on the circuit. She traveled with her companion, a hulking piano player, and her brother, who acted as her chauffeur, bodyguard, and general factotum. West's contract called for special housing, very private and isolated. The producers agreed that for her one-week engagement they would rent her a stone mansion just off the highway skirting Narragansett Bay.

Debuskey waited at the house to meet West on the evening of her arrival with a writer and a photographer from the *Providence Journal*. "As dusk was giving way to darkness, an imposing black automobile turned into the driveway, turned off its lights, and came to an abrupt halt. It looked as if it belonged in an old James Cagney movie. It had spare tires in metal casings embedded in the front fenders, a running board, and a tiny oblong rear window." The reporter began to grow impatient. Finally Debuskey screwed up the courage to approach the car. A tinted side window opened, and a man's deep voice informed Debuskey he would not budge until the photographer was gone.

Returning to the porch, Debuskey asked the writer and the photographer to wait in the billiard room. "They did, and the car came to the steps. The chauffeur emerged and opened a rear door, and out came this big guy who turned to assist someone whose head was wrapped in a scarf and whose body was enveloped in a voluminous, shapeless dark wrap. The companion told me to wait until he called down, and then to bring the reporter and photographer to the suite. In the meantime, the drinks were on Miss West."

An hour passed. Finally the three were invited to come up to the suite. "Apparently it had taken that long to manufacture Mae West," remarked Debuskey.

> We walked through an ornate sitting room, gilded from wall to wall, into the bedroom. There, our eyes marveled at the sight of this bewigged, bejeweled, gowned figure carefully displayed on a huge bed, her wide, smiling mouth filled with sparkling ivories, inviting us to "come on in." The room was heavily mirrored, the walls painted as a garden of flowers. There was a chair, but as the writer prepared to sit, Miss West patted a space beside her on the bed and suggested that the scribe make herself comfortable beside her on the bed. He did. West then beckoned the photographer, asked to look at the camera, smiled, returned it, and said, "Sonny, you just click away until you get tired."

After a bit she looked at Debuskey and said, 'Why are you so shy, young man? Climb in and join the party.'"

The play she was starring in was a ribald romp called *Come On Up*. Remembered Debuskey, "After each performance, West, in costume and makeup, would stand on the stage and invite the members of the audience to come up and say hello. She stayed until she had shaken every hand. Then she sashayed back to her dressing room, removed all her appurtenances, and came over to spend some time at the inn and its bar—just plain folks." Before she departed, West left Debuskey an envelope stuffed with a crisp $50 bill.

Later on another purring feline crossed Debuskey's path. While working under the press agent Bill Doll on a show called *Mrs. Patterson*, he met the singer Eartha Kitt, who was young, ambitious, and red hot. "Kitt had earned a deserved reputation for being difficult, demanding, arrogant, nasty, and racially sensitive," remembered Debuskey. "Her career was rocketing, with recordings, nightclub gigs, and TV appearances. She was sensual and used her sensuality teasingly. She was also suspicious of everyone and was determined not to be exploited. No one wanted to handle her."

Doll was a tall, country boy with a laid-back, aw-shucks attitude and a million stories. Journalists liked him, but he was an alcoholic.

He was more than willing to let someone else run his office while he held up the east end of Sardi's bar, a position he assumed at lunchtime and relinquished only in time to return to the office before it closed. Kitt, as inviting as she was, wasn't nearly as attractive to Doll as a stiff drink. So Debuskey, the youngest man in the Doll office, was designated the sacrifice and sent into the cat's lair.

Debuskey saw that Kitt was intelligent and, moreover, that she could smell fear. So he came up with a strategy for dealing with the actress: he would make transparent his fascination with her—which Kitt liked—and he would do nothing without first getting her approval—which she liked even more. It worked. "We got along quite well," deadpanned Debuskey.

Debuskey was equally bewitched by Irene Pappas, the fiery Greek star who teamed with the director Michael Cacoyannis on a series of productions of Greek classics. In 1967 Circle in the Square hosted their rendition of *Iphigenia in Aulis*. The press agent and star hit it off famously. "She and Merle were very friendly," remembered Leo Stern, who was working in the Debuskey offices at the time. "She was often up at the office to talk to Merle, chatting for a long time. She was quite unusual. She certainly was a passionate-looking woman. She once said she wanted to buy one of these water towers they have on top of buildings in New York and make a house out of it."

Debuskey thought the *Zorba the Greek* star earthy, sensual, and smart. Whenever he joined her at the expensive Greek restaurant she favored on Fifty-seventh Street, every head would twist on its axis. Debuskey thought of making a move on Pappas, but, like many others before him, he was too intimidated. And so Pappas herself made the proposition. One evening after Debuskey had driven her to a late-night radio interview and then back to her hotel, "she turned to me and asked, 'Why did you not ask me to go to your apartment?'" The press agent was too stunned to think. He remained silent and affected "what I hoped would be a sophisticated, enigmatic expression." Pappas kissed him and said goodnight.

"I knew I had blown what could have been a glorious night, never again to be an option. That was one of the worst mistakes I ever made," Debuskey said.*

———

Two of Debuskey's longest-lived and closest friendships with actors began with Tennessee Williams's 1951 play *The Rose Tattoo*. It starred Maureen Stapleton as a once-lusty Sicilian American widow, Serafina Delle Rose, a dressmaker who has been in mourning for three years since the death of her young husband, and Eli Wallach as her new love interest. Williams's original plan had been to cast the Italian film actress Anna Magnani as Serafina, but after months of negotiations, she eventually turned it down. The show made stars of Wallach and the twenty-five-year-old Stapleton, cast as a forty-year-old woman.

Stapleton was unpretentious and casual—too much so, thought some women in the show. They conspired to elevate Stapleton's schlubby wardrobe so it would be fitting for a prominent Broadway actress who was constantly being photographed and interviewed, receiving awards, and making personal appearances. They led her on a shopping tour, dressing her suitably but not ostentatiously, and convinced her to toss out her everyday clothes.

"Maureen and Eli were unaffected by their eminence and continued to be members of the show's extended family," Debuskey recalled. "This was particularly true of Maureen, who was as open as a Montana sky and actually needed to be surrounded by people." Debuskey became a member of the social circle that began to congregate at the Fifty-seventh Street apartment of Stapleton and her husband, Max Allentuck, both of them evidently addicted to the game of charades.

---

* A few years later Debuskey's second wife, Pearl Somner, flew into a rage when she found out he had arranged a dinner with the visiting Pappas. Recalled Debuskey, "She went into a remarkable tirade of insult, denigration, and threats——How could I have a dinner with that woman and exclude her?! I'd better call it off or else." Somner had, in fact, planned a surprise party for her husband's fiftieth birthday that same night. After Debuskey cancelled his appointment with Pappas, Pearl called her, explained her husband's behavior, and invited her to the party. Pearl judged that tirade "the best performance of my acting career."

A few years after *The Rose Tattoo*, Debuskey was called in to handle the press for *Inherit the Wind*, Jerome Lawrence and Robert E. Lee's dramatization of the court face-off over the teaching of evolution in schools between Williams Jennings Bryan, arguing for the state, and Clarence Darrow, defending the teacher, Henry Scopes. The play starred Paul Muni as Henry Drummond (the Darrow character), and Ed Begley as Matthew Harrison Brady (the Bryan role). The show's irritable producer, Herman Shumlin, had warned the young publicist to handle the show's principals with kid gloves. But Debuskey found Begley and his co-star Tony Randall not only easy to deal with, but vastly entertaining.

> While they applied their makeup and prepared to go on, their room was a veritable verbal boxing ring. They hurled imaginative, raunchy, and occasionally witty insults at each other. One evening I was visiting them and found Randall up close to and peering intently into his makeup mirror, which was ringed by small light bulbs. Begley was wondering out loud how Randall could possibly tolerate his reflected image. Tony proclaimed that he would become a Hollywood star and offered this bit of supporting evidence: "I have fuck in my face."

Begley jumped on the phrase, unleashing a hilariously apoplectic three-minute riff on a camera's response when challenged by Randall's face and other elements of his physique.

Muni was an unusual case. He began his career as Muni Weisenfreund in the Yiddish theater on the Lower East Side. He was one of only a few from that self-enclosed world to find fame in mainstream films. Muni became associated with serious "quality" biopics such as *Scarface, Juarez*, and *The Life of Emile Zola*, his Academy Award–winning performance. In an era of stars and personalities, he was most famous for his acting process. By the mid-1950s he was a living legend. Shumlin claimed that the actor was generally averse to personal publicity and that Debuskey should not attempt to speak to him once had he arrived at the theater, usually sometime after 4 P.M., to prepare for the night's performance.

Debuskey first met Muni and his wife, Bella, in their apartment. The actor, elegantly dressed in smoking jacket, shirt, and tie, was engrossed in a live television broadcast of the United Nations. When they broke for lunch, the highly political Debuskey endeared himself to the actor by calling him "Mr. Muni" and asking him what was up at the U.N. They hit it off, and after that Muni had no objection to seeing the publicist after 4 P.M.

The show had already opened, so Debuskey's job amounted to press maintenance. But that pacific period ended suddenly on the evening of Monday, August 29, 1955, five months into the run, when the producers learned their star might soon be dead.

Earlier that afternoon Muni, who had been having problems with his left eye, had gone to a doctor. He was told the eye had a tumor that was probably cancerous. The actor did not want to wait: he decided to have the necessary surgery as soon as possible. Shumlin and the authors were not optimistic about the possible outcome. Said Debuskey, "Mrs. Muni proclaimed that her husband would be back in the show before the end of the year—by Christmas. But the rest of us did not agree."

Debuskey now had to execute the flip side of a PR man's job— he had to keep the press *away* from the Muni story. No stories, no coverage, no attention. "The intent at first," said Debuskey, "was to make the situation seem modest so as not to cripple the show—to say as little as we could and to not make it seem catastrophic. Any news that did get out should at first make it appear to be a minor ailment requiring a brief absence, until it was clear what was going to happen." Another goal was to protect what would be, in time, the "major story": Melvyn Douglas would be taking over the role. "We wanted to make Douglas's appearance as dramatic as possible. There were many opportunities for the story to leak, and all the holes had to be plugged."

The first story about Muni's absence appeared on September 1. The *New York Times* reported that Muni was out of the play because of an eye infection and that his understudy, Simon Oakland, would fill in. Shumlin told the paper he was waiting for a specialist's diagnosis of the problem before deciding what to do. The next day the *Times* revealed that in fact Muni had a tumor on his eye and that further examinations would reveal whether surgery was necessary.

Shumlin and Debuskey continued their tap dance. The showman said he was searching for a prominent replacement and refused to confirm reports that Douglas had agreed to take the part. The next day the official announcement came that Douglas would indeed assume the role and that performances would be suspended until September 17 to give him time to rehearse.

Muni's surgery was scheduled for September 6. His eye was removed. He went to his Los Angeles home to recover and be fitted with a prosthetic eye. Meanwhile, Douglas opened in *Inherit the Wind* on September 17.

In the end, Bella Muni's improbable prophecy proved right, and by December 1 the actor was back on stage as Drummond. Muni was adamant that his return to the stage not be publicized. "He had no idea of how his condition would affect his performing on the stage and, ultimately, how he would be seen by the uncompromising eye of a camera," remembered Debuskey. "We talked about it, and he agreed to a television interview, so long as the interviewer agreed not to mention his eye operation. This was delicate, as I would have to tell all to the interviewer and trust that he would oblige the preconditions." Debuskey met with Mike Wallace, who at the time had a hard-hitting interview show with a large viewing audience. The newsman, who had begun his career as an actor, greatly admired and respected Muni and agreed to the stipulation. "Mike was like a puppy in Muni's presence," said Debuskey.

The evening of Muni's return performance, as Jerome Lawrence recounts in his book *Actor: The Life and Times of Paul Muni*, the house lights dimmed to half.

> The audience settled back. Douglas walked out front of the curtain. The audience moaned, sighing with disappointment—he wasn't in costume or makeup. Some unknown understudy was probably going to play the part. Then Douglas spoke with eloquent understatement. "According to the rules of Actors' Equity, a public announcement must be made from the stage whenever there is a cast substitution. Tonight the role of Henry Drummond will be played by Paul Muni."

The next day a large feature article appeared in the *New York Times* under the headline "Actor Returns to 'Inherit the Wind' in Atmosphere Fraught with Emotion."

Debuskey is undoubtedly right when he says that this scenario could not possibly be replicated in the Broadway of today. "It turned on the relationship of one producer and one actor—their closeness, trust, respect, and affection. And I must add Douglas to the mix. The events of that year are a reflection of the theater in the days when a producer was and could be a producer. In the forty years and hundreds of shows I later represented, I never encountered anything approaching this experience."

———

While he was with *Inherit the Wind* Debuskey entertained Muni with tales of working with his comrade in the arts, Joseph Schildkraut, who was the son of a famous Yiddish theater actor and had co-starred with Muni in *Zola*. At that time Schildkraut was starring in another Broadway hit, *The Diary of Anne Frank*, the dramatization of the famous journal kept by a teenage Holocaust victim who had gone into hiding in Amsterdam. Schildkraut played Otto Frank, Anne's father, and if the actor could have had his way, the play would have been called *The Diary of Otto Frank's Daughter*.

"He had a reputation of squeezing every advantage out of his status," said Debuskey.

> He had grown up in the shadow of his father, Rudolph, who was a star and a beloved figure of the Yiddish theater. Joseph's instinct as an actor led him to emote excessively and to maneuver in a scene to keep himself the dominant character onstage, much to the despair of the other actors. Schildkraut really wanted this part, both as an actor and as a Jew. He sensed that this could be the climactic performance of his career, and he was incessant in his attempts to get the role.

Schildkraut's attempts to remain in the spotlight were frustrated, however, because Susan Strasberg, the young woman cast as Anne, had inconveniently become an overnight star. The selection of Strasberg had been surprising and risky. The fifteen-year-old daughter of the daunting acting guru and director Lee Strasberg, founder of the Actors Studio, and the actress Paula Miller, Susan had no perceptible acting experience, and her parents denied having tutored her. "Susan built her character slowly but steadily, showing a remarkable instinct for embodying Anne," Debuskey remembered. "Her mother attended all the rehearsals and was surreptitiously coaching her, which occasionally led the director Garson Kanin to take Susan aside and remove some of the 'improvements' her mother had made overnight."

Debuskey and his boss, Jimmy Proctor, had no trouble interesting the media in the production. Their problem was keeping the coverage balanced enough so as not to bruise Schildkraut's ego. Most outlets were eager to cover the pretty, talented Strasberg, but she and Schildkraut had developed a tender affection for one another during rehearsals, and the publicists did not want to smash that relationship. This became more tricky after the reviews. Brooks Atkinson's last paragraph read: "It is Miss Strasberg who put the clearest print of truth on the whole enterprise. Her Anne is the Anne that won so many hearts when the book was published. Out of the truth of a human being has come a delicate, rueful, moving drama."

Good notices like that were manna for the producers but a huge headache for Proctor and Debuskey. They racked their brains trying to figure out how to make the needy Schildkraut feel cared for and appreciated while capitalizing on Strasberg's sensational reception. It was also vital not to make the show's future too dependent on Strasberg's remaining in it, because at some point, of course, she would leave. Furthermore, they had to figure out how to keep the domineering and newly empowered Mama Strasberg at bay.

"Paula Miller intended to dip into her store of alchemy and transform Susan into family gold," said Debuskey. "There was nothing wrong with that decision, except that it emerged from Miller, whom I came to dislike and distrust. She had set herself up as the doyenne of the theater community, at least among those notables devoted to her husband." Miller ran a salon in the Strasberg apartment, and an invitation to an evening there was almost a coronation. "I attended a couple," he recalled, "but I found the sycophantic environment, and the accepting of their absolute wisdom, the pontificating opinions of Lee and Paula . . . , as well as their enormous egos, insufferable."

The prickly Schildkraut was just as difficult, but he was easier to manipulate. He made certain his contract dictated that his name alone appeared above the title on every venue—in the Playbill, in advertisements, and on posters and theater houseboards. Most significant, his name was spelled out in light bulbs on the theater's marquee. To make hay out of Strasberg's rising star, the producers wanted to put her name in lights as well. Proctor and Debuskey concocted a publicity scheme that would temper Schildkraut's jealousy. Said Debuskey:

> We would have Strasberg's name go up on the marquee alongside Schildkraut's, at first unlit. We tried to get Schildkraut to agree to stand at the top of a ladder, pointing to her name with one hand and holding Susan's hand with the other—the grand old man of the theater leading the shining new actor up the ladder to star billing as the bulbs lighted. Papa Frank and daughter Anne. Simpleminded? Yes! A sure-fire publicity event? You could wager a year's rent on it.

Schildkraut's first reaction was both predictable and apoplectic: he threatened to call his agent, his lawyer, and Sam Zolotow, the *New York Times* theater reporter. It was a violation of his contact, he fumed, and he would not give one more performance. "But after an hour," said Debuskey,

> during which I pointed out what accolades would accompany his generous behavior—an ennobling, landmark act in the history of the theater—he actually turned completely around and began suggesting a trove of further events. The staged event went off famously, capturing an incredible amount of ink and a photograph that actually was wired around the world. He was celebrated as never before, a magnanimous actor of rare proportions.

Not every actor was as receptive to Debuskey's counsel as Schildkraut. One such was Mort Sahl, whom Debuskey treated to some tough love. Sahl was an innovative stand-up comedian who in the late 1950s and early '60s culled his material from the morning paper. He was the unusual choice for the lead in Lorraine Hansberry's second and final Broadway play, *The Sign in Sidney Brustein's Window*.

Debuskey described Sahl as

> a cup of bitter vetch. He was an original entertainer, having invented a new form of stand-up comedy—sardonically, savagely, and amusingly ripping prominent political figures and current headline news. His television and nightclub appearances had established a visual image—he wore an open shirt and a sweater, with a rolled-up newspaper under his arm and a sneer on his lips. Unhappily, as it was to turn out, his performance character was not so different from his personal demeanor.

Rehearsals, Debuskey said,

> did not progress smoothly; rather, they regressed into an almost catatonic state, and the director, Carmen Capalbo, was wise enough to recognize his inability to move the cast along. A destructive nastiness had crept into the environment, and he formally took his leave. He was replaced by a personable, confident, and intimate one-on-one-style director, Peter Kass. Peter gained the trust of the actors, and they responded productively, with one exception. Sahl, inexperienced as an actor, grew more and more surly as he became more confused.

One day Debuskey had business backstage at the Longacre Theatre, which he conducted during a rehearsal break. Suddenly he was interrupted by a vicious and vituperative verbal attack from Sahl. "I responded by grabbing him by his sweater, lifting him against the back wall and daring him to say another word." Sahl clammed up, and the production stage manager, Steve Gardner, pulled Debuskey off the comedian. Sahl left the theater, never to return.

"I was taken aback by my actions and I did not know to react," remembered Debuskey. "My unease was relieved when co-star Rita Moreno gave me a hug and a kiss and Kass announced to the cast that I had made a significant creative contribution to the play." The producers, far from wanting to fire Debuskey, were relieved to be rid of Sahl. They quickly recast the part with Gabriel Dell.

Decades later Sahl and Debuskey would work again on another show. Sahl had since mellowed. No one mentioned the earlier incident, and the two became friendly.

———

Laying hands on a V-neck-sweater-wearing comic was one thing. Doing the same to the bullish, hot-tempered, and often intoxicated George C. Scott was another. But Debuskey, confident in his athletic frame, did just that one night in 1960.

Scott's performances at the New York Shakespeare Festival and Circle in the Square gave Debuskey many opportunities to interact with him. The publicist found the Scott among "the most interesting, complex, confusing, ingratiating, antagonizing, intelligent, scholarly, and bedeviled" performers he had ever encountered, and the finest actor, period. But Debuskey also described him as "infused with a subcutaneous anger that was eager and ready to flare, an anger that one sensed while watching him." Debuskey once looked on in dread as, during a 1957 outdoor New York Shakespeare Festival performance of *Richard III*, a glass Coca-Cola bottle rolled down the concrete steps of the auditorium just as Scott was beginning his "Now is the winter of our discontent" soliloquy. "Fortunately he did not hurl the bottle back into the audience, but used his annoyance in his portrayal."

In 1960 Scott was starring in one of his first Broadway roles, *The Wall*, a play about the Warsaw ghetto. One fateful Wednesday between the matinee and evening performances, Scott and Debuskey, separately, were having dinner at Patsy's, a theatrical hangout. "I noted that Scott was obviously drinking his dinner, and as the clock moved closer to the show's half-hour, he gave no indication of leaving. I paid up, walked over to him, and suggested he go to the theater." Scott answered him with sarcasm and anger. Debuskey walked away to call the stage manager at the theater and alerted him to the necessity of getting the understudy ready. He then returned to Scott.

I grabbed him by the arm and pulled him through the crowds down to the Billy Rose Theatre on Forty-first Street. He was in no condition to resist. He was also in no condition to go on, but at least he was at the theater. I do not remember whether it was that same day or another when he drove his fist against the brick wall at the back of the stage, breaking it—his hand, that is—and was forced to miss a couple of performances.

Twenty years later, Debuskey witnessed an even more explosive eruption. It was the opening night of Sidney Michaels's mystery play *Tricks of the Trade*, starring Scott and his wife at the time, Trish Van Devere, and directed by Gilbert Cates. "I knew that George was well aware of the show's deficiencies and the likelihood of its being raked over the coals by the New York critics," Debuskey remembered, "and had his co-star been anyone other than his wife, he would have withdrawn it before New York. My educated guess was that he felt obliged to allow Trish a shot at a major role on Broadway."

The night of the opening, as was traditional, Debuskey, the show's general manager, Paul Libin, and the advertising executives Jeffrey Ash and Jon Wilner gathered up the reviews and convened in the ad agency's offices. There were careful not to tell Scott of their whereabouts.

> As we ... received one bit of bad news after another, gloom permeated the rooms. The quiet was interrupted by the sound of the elevator doors opening, followed by the growling, gravely voice of George directing Trish to walk straight into the gathering. He was jovial, like a manic-depressive on a high, requesting refreshments for Trish and himself. He was already in an advanced state of inebriation, and the tall drinks he tossed down converted him into a fiercely angry avenging devil.

The television reviews came on, and they were universally horrible. Then Scott charged Ash to read the *New York Times* review aloud. Another death knell. Recalled Wilner:

> "Scott turned to me and said, "Didn't *Deathtrap* get the same review in the *New York Times*?" I said, "Yes, Mr. Scott, it was just as bad.

However, the TV reviews were wonderful for *Deathtrap.*" Scott stood up and said, "Who the fuck are you?" I said, "I'm the advertising agency." He said, "Well, I'm going to get you." Trish said, "Go get them. We're just a bank account to these people!" And Merle Debuskey said, "Jon, get out of the room."

Scott then threw Ash to the floor, and with that Wilner took off down the hall, the actor in furious pursuit. Libin and Debuskey reached him in time, pulling Scott to the ground and sitting on him. "Trish said, 'Get off my husband. Let him up!'" said Wilner. Debuskey continued the story:

> When Scott quieted down, Libin literally dragged him into the elevator, accompanied by Trish. During the descent, George was vilifying Paul, and just before the elevator reached the ground floor he stepped over the line by accusing Paul of being an incompetent leech who had attached himself and fed off of George's pal, Ted Mann. Fed up, Paul laid one up alongside of George's ear—a punch that knocked him to the floor of the cab. When the door opened, Scott's chauffeur, bodyguard, and loyal caretaker pulled him up and tried to get him into the waiting limo. George resisted and in a swift and startling reversal averred that Libin was his kind of guy, insisting that Libin join him in a comradely visit and drinks in the nearest saloon. But Scott was finally stuffed into the limo and driven to his country home.

There was no need to worry about getting Scott back on his feet for the next night's show. *Tricks of the Trade* closed after that performance.

Debuskey was on equally close terms with Scott's on-again, off-again wife Colleen Dewhurst. As with Scott, the roots of their relationship went back to the beginning of the New York Shakespeare Festival and continued through the years Debuskey worked for Circle in the Square. "Colleen respected him because she knew him from the days of Joe Papp," said Paul Libin. "They got along well. He wasn't fearful of actors. He was able to communicate with them, talk straight. And at Circle you were dealing with the best of the best."

Debuskey had first met Dewhurst in the early 1950s when she came to his office for a lengthy interview. He was hoping to elicit from her a thorough background that he could stockpile for publicity purposes. "She had insisted that as a youngster she was a tomboy, more interested in playing ball with the boys than indulging in 'sissy' activities generally pursued by young girls. To exhibit her toughness, she challenged me to punch her in the stomach. I gently poked her, but she refused to accept that as a proper test and insisted that I punch her properly. Reluctantly, I obliged—and my fist met a brick wall."

Debuskey worked with Dewhurst not only on several shows, but outside the theater; their union presidencies overlapped—his of the Association of Theatrical Press Agents and Managers (ATPAM) and hers of Actors' Equity. "Colleen was easy to like, to love. So open, quirky. So loving of life, adoring of her friends in the business, so committed to action in behalf of those less fortunate than herself." Occasionally he would visit the actress at her farm in South Salem, New York, a ragged estate and house overrun with animals and people, invited and uninvited. Said Debuskey, "She often came to breakfast to discover friends who had not been present when she had gone to bed the night before. Her home became a welcoming haven for the lonely, the troubled, or those there simply because it was a pleasing ambiance to share with the garrulous host."

In 1989 Dewhurst was diagnosed with cervical cancer. She chose not to seek treatment. Recalled Debuskey,

> Surprise—rather, shock and confusion—permeated my thinking of Colleen when I learned that she had refused to consider medical care, preferring to place her faith in . . . Christian Science. At no time during the forty years I had known her was I made aware of that inclination. But it became known among friends that her mother was a Christian Science practitioner and that Colleen had turned to an old school friend, now a practitioner, for guidance. Very close friends, including the producer Robert Whitehead and Zoe Caldwell, had tried to steer her to doctors, but she was resolute, and they gave up and devoted themselves to supporting her in her endeavor.

Dewhurst died on August 22, 1991. Debuskey's last service for her was to supervise events involving the commemoration of her death. He arranged for obituaries and handled the press for her memorial at the Martin Beck Theater. "I resolved then," he said, "to never again be the publicist for the death of a friend."

Debuskey was reluctant to work with another stage diva, Lauren Bacall. She was reputed to be, in the publicist's words, "the most difficult bitch of all time." When the producers of the musical *Woman of the Year* came to him soliciting his services, he said, "I know her. I like her. But I don't want anything to do with her." They pleaded, "You're wrong. She really is terrific. You'll have no trouble with her."

A lunch was arranged for them at the Russian Tea Room. "She swept in with her cape," recalled Debuskey.

> She couldn't have been more loving and sweet and friendly. She said, "You'll have no problems with me, as long as we understand each other." I said, "I'm not going to do anything without your assent. And if something comes up, you'll be the first to know." She said, "There's only one thing. I don't want to do interviews pre-Broadway. It's too tense." I said, "You have to do it. I'll tell you what I'll do. I'll have one mass press interview."

Bacall agreed, with one provision: they could not ask her anything about Frank Sinatra, whom she had been dating. Debuskey dutifully corralled the members of the press, who, knowing the press agent, agreed to the rules of play. The day of the press conference came. The press corps played fair, but Bacall called an audible. "*She* brought up Frank Sinatra," remarked Debuskey, dryly. (This apparently was a recurring *faux* demand of Bacall's. A reporter assigned to interview her in 2000 was admonished not to bring up Humphrey Bogart by any means. Within five minutes, Bacall was discussing Bogey in depth.)

Bacall did not keep her word: she gave the publicist trouble, and plenty of it. Debuskey assigned his pretty associate, Diane Judge, to the show, but she could get nowhere with the star. Imperiously, Bacall instructed Judge, "If you want to meet with me, you meet with me after the show." Judge would go over at 11 P.M.—and Bacall would make her wait. "At one point, she got nasty with Diane and chastised her in no uncertain terms," recalled Debuskey. "I said to her, 'You can't talk to me that way, and I won't let you talk to anyone who works for me in that fashion.' She told the producers." Thereafter, the producers hired a personal press agent for Bacall, a solution that suited all parties.

———

Debuskey stood in stalwart opposition to Joe McCarthy and the blacklist, and he was friends with several of its victims. One of his closest relationships was with the actor Jack Gilford. They worked together of several shows, including *The World of Sholom Aleichem*, *The Diary of Anne Frank*, *No, No, Nanette*, and *Sly Fox*.

"Jack absolutely adored Merle," recalled Gilford's widow, Madeline Lee Gilford, "and Jack had no male friends." Gilford, born Jacob Gellman on Manhattan's Lower East Side, had been an uncooperative witness before the House Un-American Activities Committee and consequently was blacklisted from the early 1950s to the early 1960s. Debuskey, who liked Gilford and despised the hysteria that had jeopardized his career, frequently welcomed the actor into his offices to talk over his affairs. The press agent's devotion went so far that not only did he lend Gilford money from time to time, but Debuskey's mother and his niece, Nan Rosenthal, would arrange for the performer to visit Baltimore to entertain an organization to which they belonged. The honorarium they got him served to cover a couple of months' rent.

Debuskey and Gilford would exchange visits at each other's homes, Merle's on Westhampton Beach, Jack's on Fire Island. They would talk of politics, family, the theater. Debuskey would take the Gilford kids to the beach to give their parents a break.

"[Jack] was a big worrier," Debuskey remembered. "He was a worrier even when things were good." Gilford once arrived in Debuskey's office to fret over a coming audition. He hadn't worked a lot and needed to win a part in the new Stephen Sondheim musical *A Funny Thing Happened on the Way to the Forum*. But he was going to audition opposite the production's upstaging star, Zero Mostel, and worried, "Who's going to look at me?" Gilford returned to the office after the audition and announced that he had the part. Mostel had insisted on doing the reading with his back to the audience while Gilford read, ensuring that the casting agent and director would focus on him.

After Gilford's death in 1990, Debuskey spoke at his memorial, followed by Milton Berle, whom Gilford had often spoken of as a mentor. On the way up to the podium as the publicist was leaving it, Berle whispered to Debuskey, "Schmuck. You stole my material."

Debuskey's ferried Mostel through near-death and, finally, death. Mostel was an uncontrollable stage presence, a ham's ham who considered his stage career secondary to his true identity as a painter. While teaching painting he was encouraged to audition for Café Society Downtown, New York's preeminent jazz nightclub. He was hired after an initial rejection and began performing in clubs across the country. Then, just as his career was gathering steam, he was subpoenaed by HUAC. He testified that he was not a Communist but refused to name any names. With that, his television and film work evaporated.

Debuskey and Mostel first worked together on an obscure comedy called *The Good Soup*, by a prolific Belgian French writer named Félicien Marceau. If they hadn't, Mostel's stage career might have ended in 1960. David Merrick was behind the show, which was adapted and directed by Garson Kanin. The play's cast was loaded with fine actors, including Ruth Gordon, Sam Levene, Mildred Natwick, and Ernest Truex. Debuskey had no desire to work for Merrick, whom he considered "sadistic, a cheat, [and] a liar," but he took the job because Kanin and Gordon had insisted upon the Debuskey-Proctor team.

Late in the evening of January 13, 1960, Debuskey arrived home to find a message to call the city desk of the *New York Times*. "When I returned the call, I was asked if I knew which hospital Mostel had been taken to." After rehearsals, Mostel had ventured into the freezing night and hopped a bus. Upon disembarking he had slipped on the ice, and the bus ran over his leg.

"The on-duty doctors told us that the damage to his leg did not seem too bad and that he would probably be able to get back into rehearsals in a couple of weeks," Debuskey recalled. The next day Mostel's doctor had him moved to the Hospital for Joint Diseases for further examination and care. Debuskey relayed the news to Kanin and Gordon, who promised to hold off any changes and rehearse with an understudy until Mostel could return.

Merrick was being fed optimistic reports, but the news from the hospital grew grimmer with each passing day. Debuskey decided to consult one of his closest friends, Joe Wilder, the hospital's chief of surgery. Wilder and Debuskey had known each other since their Baltimore lacrosse and football days in high school. Back then, Wilder—who was, like Debuskey, an All-American—had been a showboat who wore white shoes. He attended Dartmouth and thereafter established himself as a talented surgeon.

Debuskey laid out Mostel's situation to Wilder, and Wilder said that he would look into it if Zero's doctor asked him to. "Joe took over and discovered that the damage was so severe that there was a strong possibility of losing the leg. Over a five-month sojourn in the hospital and four operations, the leg was, remarkably, saved from being amputated."

Mostel's part in *The Good Soup* was assumed by Jules Munshin for all of its twenty-one performances. But Mostel and Wilder became unlikely pals. "Zero, ever the teacher, persuaded Joe to take up painting, and Wilder did, often working alongside Mostel in his studio." The doctor turned out to be a gifted artist. After retiring from medicine, he embarked on a second career as a full-time painter, earning a living with commissions, gallery exhibitions, and book illustrations.

Mostel died in 1977 while performing out of town in *The Merchant*, a modern adaptation of Shakespeare's *The Merchant of Venice* by the English playwright Arnold Wesker. Debuskey was hired to represent the show, which was to star Mostel as Shylock. With Mostel's involvement, as well as the reteaming of Wesker and the director John Dexter, who had made each other's reputations in the 1960s with a series of plays, the project had potential. And yet the experience was a nightmare from first to last.

Those who knew and worked with Dexter tended to agree on two things: he was brilliant, and he was hateful. Debuskey knew of the director's malevolent ways from having worked with him on *Royal Hunt of the Sun*. He had a tendency to target the weakest member of the cast, slowly undermining his or her confidence. In the case of *Merchant*, the victim was Julie Garfield (daughter of John Garfield), who played Shylock's daughter. Dexter thrived on creating adversarial relationships; he divided the cast by referring to them as either Jews or Christians, depending on the religion of their characters.

Dexter was a close friend and associate of Wesker. When the director was released from jail in England after his conviction on charges of homosexuality, it was Wesker who took him in.

Recalled Debuskey:

> I was in tight with the producers, so I knew what he was telling the producers, and I knew Wesker, and what he was saying was diametrically opposed [to Dexter's view of the facts]. Dexter was saying to the producers, "I cannot get Wesker to change a fucking word. He's crippling the show." And Wesker would say, "I can't get him to talk to me. I have pages of suggested changes." I told Wesker this. He found it hard to believe.

Mostel felt *The Merchant* to be an important assignment for him, and he took it very seriously. "It was a huge departure from how he was regarded," said Debuskey. "Z loved the part. Shylock was indeed a Jew, but his relationship with the character was quite apart from Shakespeare's vision, and Z's Shylock was a gentle lover of books and learning—as was Zero. To physically prepare for the role and to compensate for his damaged leg, he had lost considerable weight."

The show, aimed at Broadway, tried out in Philadelphia. Debuskey attended the first preview, thus becoming one of the few people to see Mostel perform the part. "The result was more than promising; it was a revelation. He was simply brilliant and was set up for a clamorous reception when the show, reworked, opened on Broadway."

After the performance, Debuskey drove back to New York with Gerald Schoenfeld. From there, he and his companion Pearl Somner (whom he would later marry) drove to their home in Westhampton.

"Sometime the next day I received a call from someone in Philadelphia, informing me that Zero had collapsed and had been hospitalized." Performances of *The Merchant* were canceled while Dexter rehearsed Mostel's understudy. Debuskey issued notices to the press downplaying Mostel's physical state and indicating he would soon return to work. "He improved to the degree that a stage manager met with him in the hospital and ran lines with him. On the day he was to be released, his pal, Sam Levene, who was in the show, went to the hospital to help him dress, pack, and go back to his hotel room. While dressing he collapsed and died in Levene's arms." The diagnosis was a brain embolism.

Debuskey now had to supply his friend's obituary. He had perhaps saved Mostel's leg during *The Good Soup* by steering him toward the right surgeon, but his grief at being unable to help the actor this time around was profound. "I was clinically depressed [over] having been involved in shows involving Zero's accident and his death."

Dexter insisted on persisting with the understudy and forcing the play onto Broadway. Predictably, it closed after six performances.

———

Debuskey was also successful in his efforts to help another blacklisted American actor, Sam Wanamaker. Sam and Debuskey's second wife, Pearl Somner, had a long history. Wanamaker's brother and Somner's brother had been the closest of friends back in California, so Somner had known the whole Wanamaker family since the 1940s. In later years, when business brought Somner to London, she reunited with Wanamaker, who had moved there to escape the effects of the blacklist. For a time she lived with Sam and his family, including his daughter, the future leading actress Zoe Wanamaker.

By the time the Debuskeys came to visit the Wanamakers in the late 1970s, the actor was suffused with the quixotic mission that was to consume the latter half of his life. "Sam took us on a tour of the South Bank," recalled Debuskey,

> and showed us where he thought Shakespeare's Globe had been. He
> was saddened that there was only a plaque on a disintegrating wall

to note it and was castigating of the lack of activity to make it prominent, like a reproduction. A couple of years later when we visited, he
showed me the plans he'd drawn up for a reconstruction of the Globe
Theatre and his ambition to get it built. He knew of my relationship
with the New York Shakespeare Festival and had a lot of questions
about its origins, growth, and sustenance.

After that, Debuskey and Wanamaker would meet whenever the
actor came to the United States. When he had pushed the project
far enough along to form an American committee for the building
of the Globe, he installed Debuskey as a charter member of the
board. "At some point," said Debuskey, "he asked me to intercede
with Joe Papp and bring him aboard as a supporter. Joe declined."
Debuskey placed major pieces in the *Wall Street Journal* and the
New York Times on the progress of the project. "They got on well,"
recalled Zoe Wanamaker. "Daddy was very forceful, very strong,
and Merle is used to that kind of personality."

Wanamaker's dream reached fruition in 1997—twenty-seven
years after he began the project. Recalled Debuskey, "We were there
when the theater was able to offer its first performance in the
incomplete building and later when it was officially opened by the
royals. His was an astounding accomplishment, especially so as he
was an American, Jewish, and a political refugee."

———

In the end, Marilyn Monroe's matchmaking skills did not prove any
more durable than her marriage to Arthur Miller. Shortly after
marrying Christine Karner, the newlyweds embarked on a tour of
Europe. One stop took them to an afternoon cocktail party at the
London flat of Pearl Somner, an American costume designer who
had come to England to work on a new musical. Somner took one
look at Karner and remarked, "How did Merle ever choose that one?"

Debuskey had, indeed, not chosen wisely. Karner was an alcoholic.
Everyday social drinking was commonplace at the time, but Karner
imbibed excessively. Debuskey did not recognize the problem for a
while. "I just thought she was a heavy social drinker," he recalled.

"When we went to the theater, we always had to go across the street at intermission to get a drink. The only time I saw her drunk was at the party for *Little Me*. She fell when she was dancing."

After two years of marriage, Debuskey perceived the pairing for what it was: a mistake. He and Karner separated—amicably, though Debuskey was burdened with remorse for years, leading him to pay the rent on their two-bedroom apartment on East Forty-sixth Street, which Karner retained, and all the attendant bills, in addition to her monthly stipend. The press agent moved into a one-room Murphy-bed apartment on Abingdon Square in Greenwich Village. When asked why he supported his ex-wife so comfortably, he said simply, "I had my Jewish guilt."

———

In retrospect, it seems natural that Debuskey and the actress and costume designer Pearl Somner should end up together. They had spent their professional lives in the theater, and both were to the left of the political mainstream. Pearl was a genuine Red Diaper baby, born on May 5—Karl Marx's birthday.

After working for the Office of Strategic Services (OSS) as an executive secretary in Washington during the war, Somner made her way to New York where she worked with noted set designer and Theatre Guild official Lee Simonson, before eventually turning to acting full time. Somner won her first Broadway job, as a dancer, in a 1946 Ben Hecht play about the birth of Israel called *A Flag Is Born*.

Somner and Debuskey first met in 1951 during the run of *The Rose Tattoo*—he was doing the press and she had a small role in the play that featured her husband at the time, Martin Balsam— but for a long time their orbits seldom coincided. After a part in *The World of Sholom Aleichim* in 1958, Pearl left acting to work as a photo stylist and to pursue costume design, which led her to work on shows in New York, California, London, Berlin, and Bejing. (Somner's career as a costume designer included the Broadway shows *Shenandoah*, *Who's Life is it Anyway?*, *84 Charing Cross Road*, and *Ulysses in Nightgown*, the Bejing production of *The Music Man*,

and the film *Love Story*.) When they met up again in 1966 at a
political event at Town Hall, Somner had just returned to New York
after working with the Berliner Ensemble, and Debuskey had only
recently separated from his wife Christine Karner.

Drawn to the beautiful recent divorcée, he suggested dinner. "I
was forty-five at the time," recalled Somner, "and I'd had a very
'lived' life. The thought of dating was not thrilling." She calmed
Debuskey's skittish nerves by saying, "Don't get antsy. Nothing can
happen between two people called Merle and Pearl." Nonetheless,
they began to see each other, and Debuskey frequently invited her
out to his house in Westhampton. "We were like old friends,"
remembered Somner. "It was very comfortable." They even knew
many of the same people. Somner was already friendly with the
producer Alexander H. Cohen and his wife, Hildy Parks, with whom
Debuskey would become very tight. Debuskey also became friends
with the Sam Wanamakers. And it didn't hurt that she was a good
tennis player; the duo often hit the court.

They moved in together in 1969 and eventually married twenty
years later. Debuskey continued to immerse himself in pro bono
political work, but Somner, who had been raised by her activist
mother, steered clear of it. "I've had my bellyful of political life," she
said. "This is something new for him. It's not new for me." Yet she
admired his devotion to noble causes. "It endeared him to me. I
don't know of many people I approve of, but I approve of him."

There were some difficult times during the early years of their
union. Debuskey always got up at 9 A.M. and never went to office
until 10:30. Once there, he stayed until at least 7 P.M. Somner
adjusted her schedule to make sure she was around in the morning
and abandoned her desire to eat dinner at 6 P.M. She also sometimes resented the time he gave to people in the business—time that
could have been spent at home. The two never had children—"I was
not a mother type," Somner said simply. She has characterized the
union as "better than ever" since her husband's retirement.

The world often sees their relationship as idyllic. Pearl attributes
this in part to their names-those two singsongy rhyming handles that,
she had said years earlier, would prevent their becoming serious

about one another. "There's a lunacy about those names," she theorized. "People meet us and they smile. They think it's kind of cute—'Merle' and 'Pearl.' Young people I meet say, 'Oh, I'd like to be just like you when I grow up.'"

Chapter 5

THE AUTHORS

For a time in the 1950s Debuskey lived on the top floor of a four-story building at 104 Washington Place in Greenwich Village. The ground-floor space was taken up by a Russian restaurant, and the owners, the Nemiroffs, lived on the second floor. Spotting Debuskey as an unattached male alone in the city, the Nemiroffs adopted him and regularly foisted food on the young man. "They thought Debuskey was a Russian name," he recalled.

Many evenings, after Debuskey had come home late, the Nemiroffs and their son Robert, a songwriter, insisted that he join them for leftovers and lively disputes about the topics of the day. Later he joined in the making of their storied Russian pastries, the recipes for which were closely guarded.

Often joining them would be Robert's young wife, a petite black woman with strong opinions named Lorraine Hansberry. He remembered her as "attractive, elfin, tousle-headed, personable, loyal, humorous, and authoritative on black American writers and the early black social and political movements. However, nothing about her would have made anyone suspect that she was interested in or capable of writing a play, certainly not one as well-crafted and as substantial as *A Raisin in the Sun*."

When in 1959 the producer Philip Rose approached Debuskey and Proctor about doing the press for *Raisin*, the first thing Debuskey did was read his friend's play. Debuskey remembered his reaction well: "I was literally stunned." Hansberry had been born on Chicago's South Side to middle-class parents. Her father was a successful real estate broker who in 1938 agreed to battle segregation by moving his family into an all-white neighborhood near the University of Chicago, where they encountered much worse than unpleasant resistance—experiences she would later incorporate into *Raisin*. Hansberry wrote that she remembered being "spat at, cursed and pummeled in the daily trek to and from school" when she was eight years old. Her mother kept a loaded pistol to protect the family against "howling mobs" that threw bricks and broke windows. After attending the University of Wisconsin, Hansberry moved to New York, where she took classes in writing at the New School and worked as an associate editor of Paul Robeson's *Freedom* magazine. She met and became friendly with black writers—among them James Baldwin, Langston Hughes, and her hero, Robeson.

Raisin is one of the great long-shot stories in theater history, a Broadway success in which practically no one involved had any previous Broadway experience. Rose, a music publisher with no theatrical bona fides, had found *Raisin* at Nemiroff and Hansberry's Greenwich Village apartment. After the three friends had dinner, Nemiroff read aloud from the play. Rose was thunderstruck, and the next morning he called and told her he intended to produce the play on Broadway—with a cast made up almost entirely of black actors.

Rose had one ace in the hole: he was friends with Sidney Poitier. If the film star could be signed, the play had a chance. Poitier read the play and agreed to take the lead role. But even so, it took Rose eighteen months to raise the money. Hansberry has been quoted as having remarked, "Potential backers read my play and cried: 'It's beautiful! Too bad it isn't a musical. White audiences aren't interested in a Negro play.'" To direct the play, Poitier suggested an old acting school friend named Lloyd Richards whose only prior Broadway credits had been small acting parts in a couple of flops. The cast was filled out by unknown black actors who would go on to become stars: Louis Gossett, Claudia McNeil, Diana Sands, Douglas Turner, Ruby Dee, and Dee's husband, Ossie Davis, who understudied Poitier and later took over the role. Rose and Richards were able to pick from the cream of the crop. "Word of its original and true-to-black-life characters had gotten out into the black community," Debuskey said, "and literally hundreds of black actors showed up at auditions for the nine black parts."

Yet with every element in place, including the money, the play could still not find a place on Broadway. "The Street exhibited its opinion of this breakthrough production by refusing to rent it a theater," recalled Debuskey. And so Rose, bucking tradition, booked a four-day pre-Broadway run in New Haven and a two-week tryout in Philadelphia while keeping his fingers crossed that a theater would open up in New York.

Reviews in New Haven were good, though audiences were middling. Weekends, however, sold out. "There were more blacks in the audience than the theater's employees remembered ever seeing," said Debuskey. The show moved on to Philadelphia. Again, there was little advance, despite a lot of media attention. This time, however, the rave reviews had an effect. "The box office became besieged." So, Debuskey remembered, "here we were, a happy extended theater family, sitting in Philadelphia with a smash groundbreaking hit that had emerged from an improbable set of circumstances, and with the end in sight just two weeks away. A very strange, frustrating, and perplexing state. But once in a while, the deserving do get served, and this time the fairy godmother was a man, Jack Small, an executive of the all-powerful theater-owning Shubert Organization."

The reviews had reached the previously deaf ears of the Shuberts, and Small jogged down to Philadelphia to catch the show. Afterward "he came backstage and met with Rose, the general manager, Wally Fried, and me," recollected Debuskey. "He asked if we would hang around for a couple of minutes while he made a phone call." Small returned with a proposition. The Shuberts would rent them the Barrymore Theatre, but they needed a couple of weeks to clear it of the long-running hit *Look Homeward, Angel.* To give the show a home and playing time after Philadelphia, they would book *Raisin* into the Shubert Theatre in Chicago, guarantee the show against losses, and share in the cost of transportation. Rose, stunned by the offer, grabbed it.

The show again triumphed in Chicago, and Proctor and Debuskey soon found themselves fielding calls from the emerging black media, a source of publicity they had never before explored. "They had previously had little interest in Broadway," explained Debuskey, "for good reasons, as there had been nothing there of interest to their readers and listeners. *Raisin* would break down that neglect and open the doors for all that would follow."

The show had a smash New York opening, and it became the first play truly depicting black life to become a financial bonanza. It went on to win the New York Drama Critics Award as Best Play and earn Tony nominations for Hansberry, Poitier, McNeil, and Richards. Recalled Debuskey:

> That opening night offered me a moment the equal of which I never again was to witness. At the curtain calls, Lorraine, seated in the third row, rose to acknowledge the tumultuous ovation. Poitier, tall, lean, handsome, and very excited, leaped from the stage, ran to Lorraine, lifted her up, and hoisted her over the footlights onto the stage. The audience went berserk in adulation at this most rare moment—the first play on Broadway to have been written by a black woman.

Debuskey would later handle Hansberry's next play, 1964's *The Sign in Sidney Brustein's Window*, but the cast of characters surrounding the playwright had changed, and ultimately the production gave little cause for celebration. Hansberry was now divorced from Nemiroff, though he was still producing the play. Rose was out of the picture. The play was about Brustein, a disenchanted white intellectual who is persuaded by a black activist in love with Sidney's sister-in-law to support a reform politician, who Sidney discovers is corrupt. Rehearsals did not go smoothly. The director was replaced and the star, Mort Sahl, bolted after an altercation with Debuskey (see page 98). Moreover, the script was in need of work.

"My perception of it was that she had drawn too many threads to weave into a completed fabric," recalled Debuskey. "I also thought that she was too perceptive an editor not to perceive and correct the problems she had built into the script as it then was. Unfortunately, there was an explanation. Lorraine was ill." Hansberry had cancer and was confined to the hospital during rehearsals.

> My after-the-fact observation is that she was aware of the odds against her defeating the cancer and wanted to see the play produced, believing that it could be tightened during rehearsals, with her contributing to the extent she was able. Also, Nemiroff was anxious to get the play on out of regard for Lorraine and presumptuously believed that he would be competent enough as a writer to make the necessary rewrites as rehearsals progressed and highlighted the script problems.

For weeks Debuskey had walked around with Hansberry's obituary in his pocket, a copy of which he had given in confidence to the *New York Times*'s obituary editor. Hansberry revived sufficiently to leave the hospital and attend the opening night, all dressed up and carefully attended in a wheelchair. Debuskey embraced and kissed her. The reviews were mixed, and the black community was not in evidence; the resultant business was insufficient to keep the show open. Nemiroff appeared onstage at the curtain calls and made impassioned pleas for contributions to keep the show open, playing on the audience's sympathy—a circumstance Debuskey found embarrassing and demeaning to Hansberry. This situation continued for a couple of months until the Shubert Organization, which owned the theater, decided that soliciting non-charitable contributions from the stage was probably illegal and exercised the stop clause in the rental contract. The play closed on January 10, 1965. Two days later Lorraine Hansberry died at the age of thirty-four.

———

Another playwright whose Broadway debut Debuskey handled was Neil Simon. Simon had made his name as one of the fabled bullpen of writers who each week created Sid Caesar's television vehicle *Your Show of Shows*. Simon's first play was called *Come Blow Your Horn*, and in 1961 it became the first show Debuskey handled from its inception as a senior press agent. The producers, William Hammerstein and Michael Ellis, were seasoned theater people, but it was the first time they had worked together as Broadway producers. "The only well-known name in the cast was Hal March," recalled Debuskey, "but his fame was part notoriety. He had been the emcee of the popular TV quiz show *21* and had been cleared of wrong-doing in the scandal that broke out in the mid-'50s over providing answers in advance to successful contestants, chief among them Charles Van Doren."

The play, about a playboy and his impressionable younger brother, was a modest family comedy steeped in saleable New York Jewish humor. Schooled in prime-time television, Simon was even then a joke machine. But when it came to the theater, he was an unknown. When the play opened, the *New York Times*'s Howard Taubman damned it with faint praise, calling it "an old-fashioned Broadway product that seemed to have gone out of fashion—a slick, lively, funny comedy."

"The reviews did not launch a hit," said Debuskey. "But the show was able to limp along, losing a bit one week and making a similar bit the next." The novice producers were weighing the words of the theater owner, Michael Meyerberg, who offered well-meaning advice to close the show and not take a chance on suffering any more losses. Debuskey, however, had been carefully studying the audiences. "I learned over a period of time how to read an audience. And I knew that that audience was having one good time." He recommended another road. "I argued that this was one of those rare occasions when advertising and publicity could support the show long enough for positive word of mouth to take over and carry it. Hal March was terrific in interviews, and I thought I could take him from one TV or radio interview show to another, all over the broadcast bands."

Moreover, Debuskey floated an unorthodox advertising notion. He contacted Sydney Hoff, a well-known cartoonist for the *New Yorker*, and asked him to create a series of small cartoons that showed the characters from the play in comic situations, captioned with the appropriate joke line. "He was amused by the concept and was so successful that readers would actually look for his recognizable drawings, enjoy the ad in the *Times*, and talk about it," Debuskey said. *Come Blow Your Horn* ran for 622 performances and began Simon's Midas touch at the box office. "I would never mention it to anyone," said Debuskey, "but I became convinced of my genius."

The following year Debuskey's new bosses, Cy Feuer and Ernie Martin, were looking for a show to follow up their hit musical *How to Succeed in Business Without Really Trying*. They settled on *Little Me*. The musical, based on a book by Patrick Dennis, was the first-person account of Belle Poitrine, born Mayble Schlumpfert, who rises from a poverty-stricken childhood on the wrong side of the tracks to surprising stardom on the silver screen, stranding husbands or boyfriends in her wake amid multiple mishaps.

Martin mined Debuskey for a possible librettist. "What about Abe Burrows?" the press agent asked, naming the bookwriter for *Guys and Dolls* and *How to Succeed*. Martin shook his head; Burrows wasn't right for this show. So Debuskey suggested Simon. "Do you think he would be interested?" Martin asked. Remembered Debuskey, "I called Neil, and he said he was very interested in the material." Simon signed on and suggested the central change that made the show what it was. Instead of making the story about Belle, they'd make it about all the men in her life, who could be played by a single actor. As far as Simon was concerned, that star could be only one person—his old employer, Sid Caesar.

The Philadelphia tryout was at the Erlanger Theater in the fall of 1962. The composers were Cy Coleman and Carolyn Leigh, who had previously collaborated on *Wildcat*. The choreographer and co-director, Bob Fosse, was having trouble fixing a song-and-dance number about the women sent to entertain the troops in World War I. After a few performances Fosse threw up his hands, and Feuer decided to cut the number. The easygoing Coleman took it in stride, but Leigh went berserk. She didn't want anyone to cut her song and started blaming Fosse for not choreographing it right. Feuer stood his ground. That night, as the show was starting, Debuskey was standing in the lobby with Feuer, Martin, Fosse, Simon, and Coleman when a furious Leigh came in with a policeman. She ordered the officer to arrest the lot; they were "violating her rights under the Dramatists Guild agreement."

"We were dumbfounded," recalled Debuskey, "and nobody was more confused than the cop. 'They cut my lyric!' she screamed." The policeman, having never confronted this particular crime, asked if he could watch the show. Afterward, he came over to the creators, said, "Looks pretty good to me," and left.

—

The composer Jule Styne was a restless man, a child prodigy who grew up to live fast, write fast, and talk fast. "He had this endless energy," remembered Debuskey. "His body was pulsating. He talked so fast the sentences would jump. His syntax was not beyond criticism, because his mind was working so fast that his mind was way ahead of the last expression from his tongue, teeth, and lips."

Endlessly productive, Styne had written a dozen shows and a thousand songs before working with Debuskey on 1967's *Hallelujah, Baby!* The show survived its Boston tryout, and Styne survived a surprise visit by a couple of friends. "One day, I was in the box office maneuvering some press seats with the treasurer," Debuskey recalled,

> when two gentlemen, led by their rearranged noses, approached and inquired as to the whereabouts of that little guy named Julie who wrote songs. Their speech pattern identified them instantly as having originated in Brooklyn. The treasurer turned to me for a judicious answer, and I suggested that he inform them that Mr. Styne had returned to New York the day before yesterday and was not expected to return. "T'anks," they responded, and they left, not to be seen again.

Debuskey never discovered the reason for their visit, but he surmised that it was related to Styne's penchant for placing bets. When he found Styne and described the incident, the composer unloosed a typically incomprehensible verbal avalanche directed at cruel fate.

Melvin Van Peebles was another composer who had reason to worry about being assaulted. By the time he crashed Broadway with his show *Ain't Supposed to Die a Natural Death*, he was already a unique eminence in the African American community. A year before, he had brought to the screen *Sweet Sweetback's Baadasssss*

Song, a film he wrote, directed, produced, and starred in. Credited with beginning the genre of blaxploitation films, *Sweetback* had grossed a startling $10 million on an investment of $500,000, so at the time he was mounting *Ain't Supposed to Die a Natural Death*, Van Peebles was a rich man.

His wealth made Van Peebles a target. Once Debuskey booked him for an interview on a black radio station housed in Harlem's famed Hotel Theresa, where all famous black personages used to gather. Melvin agreed to do the show, but only if Debuskey would bring along another male associate to drive him back and forth. Said Debuskey, "He did not want to try and get a taxi on the Harlem street, as there were too many youngsters in that neighborhood who would like to make their mark in a challenge to the iconic Sweet Sweetback."

Van Peebles was born on Chicago's tough South Side in 1932 and claimed to have had a happy, bourgeois childhood. He joined the Air Force and became skilled as a bombardier and navigator. He also claimed to have lived in the Netherlands, studied astronomy in graduate school, and gone on tour with a Dutch theater troupe. There he added the Van to a name that had originally been Melvin Peebles. He directed several short films that were seen by the Cinemathèque Française's Henri Langlois. He showed them in Paris, where Van Peebles lived for the next nine years, having become a celebrity. He sang and danced on street corners and in cafés, performing songs he wrote and providing his own guitar accompaniment, and he wrote five novels in self-taught French. He turned one of them, *The Story of a Three-Day Pass*, into a movie script, persuaded the French Ministry of Culture to give him an advance, accepted a substantial stipend from a very wealthy French woman friend, and then made the movie, which was released in 1968. The film, the story of a black G.I.'s weekend with a white French girl, became a hit in France. It had a more modest reception in the United States, but it did attract the attention of Hollywood moguls. With *Watermelon Man*, in which a white man wakes up one morning and discovers that he's become black, he became the first black to direct a Hollywood film.

"I do not believe they make them like Melvin Van Peebles any-more," observed Debuskey with considerable understatement. "Probably never made anyone like him before." Despite his recent wealth, Van Peebles's wardrobe was of the casual, thrift-store variety. A droopy mustache hung around his mouth, from which protruded a mangled, chewed, unlit cheroot. He had a tattoo around his neck, a slim necklace with the words "Cut on the dotted line—if you can."

Debuskey enjoyed talking with Van Peebles but quickly sized up his client as at least part con artist.

> Despite his remarkable assortment of talents and significant accom-plishments, I thought he also was full of shit. He knew I thought it and I knew he knew I thought it. I never did learn to differentiate which of his tales were fact and which were verbal manifestations of his creative imagination. And in truth, I did not care. I was just careful to put quotation marks around some of his remarks to me—and around those lines of his I extracted from printed news stories.

Natural Death was based on an album of songs Van Peebles had written and recorded for A & M. A lawyer named Robert Malina encountered the album and took it to the Broadway producer Emanuel Azenberg, who thought there might be a show there if a linking concept could be found. Van Peebles took time off from hustling *Sweet Sweetback* and went to work on the project with the director Gilbert Moses. They were given a back office in Azenberg's suite that Van Peebles immediately named the Black Room.

The show that emerged consisted of a series of vignettes of life in the ghetto, accompanied by music. The reviews ranged from fiercely angry denunciations to ecstatic praise for a show that delved into a kind of real life never before presented as a Broadway musical. Mixed reviews meant an uphill battle, but Van Peebles was game for a fight. At the customary post-opening meeting of producers, general managers, press agents, and advertising agents, Azenberg laid out the facts to the author. There was no money left to carry the week's expected losses and additional advertising. The prudent business decision was to post the notice and close on Saturday. Fine—but what if the immediate obstacle could be shoved aside?

"With no great show of bravura," said Debuskey, "Van Peebles offered to put up $65,000, and he purchased the screen rights for $50,000. 'What's the difference to me if I've got $2 million or $1.9 million?' was his only comment." The producers put into effect all possible financial cuts—on royalties, office expenses, producers' salaries, and rent alleviation. Advertising was diverted from the normal Broadway venues to black radio stations and newspapers. Debuskey concentrated on assaulting the black media. A specialist was enrolled to push parties from black church and social groups. But perhaps most important, Van Peebles was unleashed on the public.

The entrepreneur persuaded his black friends and black film stars to make special appearances, each in one performance of the show, and he wrote special material for each individual. Said Debuskey, "He began with his pal Bill Cosby, and there was a parade of actors led by Ossie Davis, Diana Sands, and Nipsey Russell, and followed by a politician, Shirley Chisholm, the first black woman elected to the House of Representatives. Word got around about this extra fillip. The box office was instructed that if a kid came up and only had $2, it should sell him a newly created $2 ticket in the balcony." And prior to every performance, the charismatic composer would show up on the sidewalk outside the Ambassador Theatre, slapping the palms of customers, listening to their stories, telling them where to buy cigarettes. After the show he'd ride up to Harlem and go after customers in bars.

Debuskey, entertained by Van Peebles's antics, took to hanging around the Ambassador to catch the street theater taking place before the real show.

I made it a routine to join with him on Saturday matinees. At one of those matinees, a woman accompanied by an infant was complaining to him outside the theater before the show that the box office had apologetically refused to sell her a ticket, as there was a policy not to admit an infant. Melvin offered to nanny the baby during the show, and she gave him a blanket, a pacifier, and a supply of bottled milk and purchased her ticket. He, I, and several others went across the street to the Hotel Edison's bar and took turns occupying the infant, feeding it as we downed a few libations from the bar. Melvin kept us all entertained until the show ended and the mother returned, reclaimed her baby, and said that she would tell all her friends about the show and how well her baby had been cared for.

———

Ain't Supposed to Die a Natural Death was nominated for seven Tony Awards. It won none. A couple of years later, though, the black South African actor-playwrights John Kani and Winston Ntshona did win Tonys for their performances in *Sizwe Banzi Is Dead,* a play about life under apartheid written in collaboration with Athol Fugard.

In 1976 Kani and Ntshona performed the play in the Transkei, a part of South Africa that was shortly to become a separate homeland, and were arrested. The report of their arrest quickly got to Broadway, and the producer Alex Cohen, incensed, immediately set to work, though he had had nothing to do with the Broadway show.

Cohen called Debuskey and a group of others into his office and gave them orders. Remembered Debuskey, "Committees and a formal organization were set up to receive cash donations, and I was to function as the principal press agent. A demonstration was planned, and notables were sought to bolster the importance of the event. Press releases were issued almost hourly, and interviews with the media were set up. We reached throughout the United States and abroad. Somehow, we hit a nerve." Contacts were made with theater people in London and Paris who agreed to conduct simultaneous marches. In Atlanta Jimmy Carter, then a candidate for president, announced that he would make a statement about artistic freedom and the plight of Kani and Ntshona. Eighteen affiliated unions of the AFL-CIO, with more than three million professional workers, issued a proclamation denouncing the actors' imprisonment.

At the United Nations there was diplomatic confusion because the South African representative transferred the complaint to personnel from Transkei since it would be an independent homeland in a matter of days. But it wasn't just yet, and that meant there was no one to formally receive the complaint. Fugard, in Port Elizabeth, South Africa, was able to do nothing except confirm the arrests, reporting that the actors had been separated and denied any contact with family, friends, or lawyers.

Cohen decided that he would not wait for money to be raised and personally guaranteed payment for a full-page ad in the *New York Times*, to run as soon as possible. He, the principals of Blaine Thompson (at the time Broadway's leading ad agency), the producer Norman Kean, the press agent and former writer for *Variety* Dick Hummler, and Debuskey worked through the night and came up with the text for the ad. It was bordered in black and had a headline in big, bold black type: "two tony award winners are in jail!" The subhead read, "In Transkei, 'Independence' Means Arrest." Readers were implored to march in front of the United Nations. The ad was signed by a slew of theatrical organizations, collected together under the title "Committee to Free John and Winston!"

The ad never ran. It was replaced by another, headed by the bold headline "john kani and winston ntshona are free!" On Saturday, October 23, at 11:30 a.m. Eastern Standard Time, a phone call from Kani and Ntshona went through. The Transkei had dropped all charges and released them. "We were later thanked by Kani and Ntshona," recalled Debuskey, "who informed us that the incoming Transkei independence government had let them go, as the government did not want its installation to be tarnished by all the noise we were making."

———

One playwright that Debuskey ultimately could not help was Leonard Melfi. He had come up with the group of writers who in the 1960s orbited around Ellen Stewart and her Off-Off-Broadway theater La MaMa. The son of a Binghamton, New York, tavern keeper, his name was routinely mentioned in press accounts with those of Terrence McNally, Sam Shepard, and Lanford Wilson. He had a critical hit with a one-act called *Birdbath* but never managed to capitalize on it, though he did pen a sketch for the successful revue *Oh! Calcutta!* Debuskey did the press for *Six from La Mama*, the evening of plays that included *Birdbath*, as well as a 1968 Broadway triptych of one-acts, *Morning, Noon and Night*, to which Melfi contributed a play.

Around this time Melfi began to drop by Debuskey's office to talk. "He used to come up all the time. We were very friendly. He was always broke. He was a poet as well. He couldn't earn a living. He was a heavy drinker." At one point Melfi was forced to hock his typewriter for money. Debuskey was appalled when he heard about this and gave the writer the money to get it back.

As the years went by, drinking began to dominate Melfi's life. He moved about and would disappear for months at a time. In the 1990s Melfi was in and out of alcohol rehabilitation until, in 1999, a friend helped him find a room at the Narragansett, a single-room-occupancy hotel at Broadway and Ninety-third Street, where he lived without a telephone.

In late October of 2001 paramedics, who had been called by Melfi's niece, arrived to find the playwright pale and unable to move. He was strapped into a stretcher and rushed to Mount Sinai Hospital. Four hours later, at the age of sixty-nine, he died of congestive heart failure. Because of an administrative mix-up, Melfi's body was sent to the hospital morgue. It lay there for a month before city workers transferred it to the morgue at Bellevue Hospital Center. No family members were contacted.

On Thursday, December 20, according to the *New York Times*, a morgue truck carried Melfi's body to a dock on City Island in the Bronx. It then took a five-minute ferry ride to Hart Island, where the city has buried the indigent and unclaimed since 1869. It wasn't until February that employees at the Narragansett noticed that Melfi had never come back from the hospital. After finding out that he had died at Mount Sinai, they called Melfi's niece. The playwright's brother drove down from Binghamton to have Leonard removed from potter's field.

Melfi was buried in the family plot just outside Binghamton on April 18, 2002. At his funeral Melfi's old Smith-Corona typewriter—the one that had been saved from the pawnshop—was given a place of honor.

Chapter 6

CRISES

Two stories.

Merle Debuskey graduated from Baltimore City College in January of 1941. Since he was not to enter the university until fall, he killed some time by joining a neighborhood softball team as catcher and clean-up hitter. The group played in a league made up of teams with players of the same age from all over the city. The squad was good, with a dominant pitching staff that kept the scores of the opposing teams low. Once, they traveled to a southwestern part of Baltimore to play a team in a low-income, white Christian area. "For all they knew, a Jew could have horns," remembered Debuskey.

The Christian softball team was the pride of its community, and everyone who wasn't at work had turned out for the game. The pitcher on Debuskey's team was hot, averaging two strikeouts an inning. No one was scoring, but, Debuskey said, "sooner or later we would, and the crowd sensed it, taunting us with every pitch, every swing. We became frightened, with reason. We'd better not win. And we played to make sure."

Just before they came to bat in the last inning of the regular game, the coach gathered the players together out of earshot of the crowd. He suggested the pitcher throw the game, toss up a couple of floaters that they could smack, and make an error or two, allowing them to score.

Debuskey flinched. He hated the idea. Brazenly, he countered the coach and suggested an alternate way out: "that we be careful not to score, and that we hold them scoreless, until it got too dark to continue." The game dragged on through fourteen innings. Debuskey prayed that the pitcher's arm would not fall off. Finally the umpire called the game on account of darkness. "Many in the crowd came over to tell us it was the greatest game they had ever seen. In truth, it was the greatest acting job they had ever seen."

Four years later, in February 1945, while serving on a landing ship tank (LST) in the South Pacific, Gunnery Officer Merle Debuskey was officer of the deck, looking out for 341 troops and 400 tons of cargo. Captain Leon Manees, a dead ringer for Ichabod Crane, was in ultimate authority, but he was in his quarters when the ship's radio man told Debuskey that a destroyer escort had heard the sounds of a submarine's engines a short distance ahead of the convoy. Debuskey sounded general quarters and had a messenger rouse Manees. Mitchell Resha, who manned the intercom, shouted that the bow lookouts had called in: a destroyer escort was making a run that would carry it across the ship's bow as it tossed depth charges. A moment later Manees was standing there in a terrycloth robe. "I was focused on the destroyer running from our starboard to port and I was deciding what maneuver to make, as it appeared we were on a collision course," Debuskey recalled. "Manees grabbed the voice tube that went down into the wheelhouse and to the man on the helm—the steering wheel. He shouted, 'Left full rudder.'"

Without a moment's hesitation, Debuskey grabbed Manees, pulled him away from the voice tube, and shouted down: 'Belay that order. Right full rudder. Starboard engine back full speed.'" Debuskey had remembered something from training: when on a collision course, if you turn in the direction taken by the other ship, you extend the potential of a collision; to reduce that chance, you turn in the opposite direction so you pass the point of possible collision sooner. The two vessels barely avoided a calamity.

———

It could be argued that the art of creating theater is nothing more (and nothing less) than repeated bouts of crisis management. Debuskey has seen his share of crises and seems preternaturally disposed to facing them without losing his cool. "When you were troublestruck, you were glad to have Merle in your corner," observed Bernard Gersten, a stage manager, producer, and all-around theater person who met Debuskey in the early 1950s when Gersten was working as a stage manager on a Philadelphia show that Debuskey was flacking. The two worked side by side for years at a time, first at the New York Shakespeare Festival and later at Lincoln Center Theater. "He would bring his own steadiness. Merle had broad, dependable shoulders; you could lean on Merle."

Steven Suskin worked on many of the Philip Rose productions Debuskey handled. He recalled:

> Whenever business was bad, whenever there was a problem, when-ever the producer needed hand holding, Debuskey would always be there. He knew to be around in a crisis. You didn't have to track him down. With *Shenandoah* we got lousy reviews, and we struggled the entire time. He was always very matter of fact about it, very stoic about it. . . . In those days when you had a sole producer, when the grosses were bad, these guys bled. It was almost like Greek tragedy watching these producers. Merle was a great listener. He made them feel like his arm was being cut off, too, when in fact it wasn't.

Debuskey always endeavored to keep his wits about at all costs, regardless of the circumstances. It almost seemed a point of honor. At the surprise party Pearl threw for his fiftieth birthday, attended by many of his closest friends and associates, Debuskey opened the door to his apartment, the lights flicked on, and the crowd roared "Surprise!" Instead of breaking into a smile or stumbling back in shock, he turned around and walked slowly to the end of the outer corridor. Once he had thoroughly composed himself, he returned to the door and began to happily greet his guests.

Though they were as proficient a couple of showmen as ever crossed Forty-second Street, Cy Feuer and Ernie Martin were fre-quently in need of a crisis manager, even when the impasse at hand didn't seem especially critical at the time. During the Philadelphia tryout of *How to Succeed in Business Without Really Trying*, Abe Burrows, Feuer, Martin, and Debuskey were sitting on the steps to the mezzanine in the theater lobby, moping. Despite good reviews, despite the reputation of the composer, Frank Loesser, despite the presence of the name star, Rudy Vallee, business was tepid. The lines of customers at the box office were buying tickets to the next show booked into the theater, *Kean*—general-managed by a man the producers had just fired. Loesser walked in. He had just seen the box-office agents and was apoplectic. The treasurer had told him that an elderly lady had arrived at the box-office window and asked, "When does the Rudy Vallee lecture begin?"

Said Debuskey, "That opened an angry window to the accumulated frustration, and everyone tried to come up with a remedy for the lack of business. The final solution was to change the title." The normally composed press agent threw a fit. "I said, 'Guys, that title's going to be worth a fucking fortune! Do you know how many playoffs you can get with that title? In every area that title is going to be used. That's a Pulitzer Prize title.' At the mention of the Pulitzer, Abe's ear pricked up. Loesser's ears pricked up. Feuer said, 'Listen to the guy. Let's not change the title. Let's go back and change the show.' I was trying to be forceful. It had gotten out of hand. They were crazed."

Debuskey also wanted to ensure that Vallee wouldn't be scapegoated. Vallee's star had dimmed since his heyday as a crooner in the 1920s and '30s, but he still comported himself like a headliner, infuriating all around him. During rehearsals he repeatedly insisted that he be allowed to make "improvements" in Loesser's score. "When he exasperated Loesser with his musical demands, Loesser implored Feuer to physically punch him out," said Debuskey. "Feuer ignored the request, and Loesser quit the show for three days, returning only when Feuer agreed to punch Vallee out at the end of the run—something that of course never happened."

The star also irritated his colleagues with his notorious parsimoniousness. The success of *How to Succeed* proved uniquely profitable for Vallee, who had a regular order with the box office for ten standing-room tickets. He could not resell them for a penny more than the actual price, but he sold them only if the buyer would also rent a seat cane that he provided. "I thought, at this juncture Rudy

Debuskey, *far right*, at a City College lacrosse practice.

The boxer Debuskey at the University of Virginia.

The City College three-letter man.

Left: Debuskey, *right*, in the South Pacific during World War II.

Bottom: Debuskey and his gunnery mates, somewhere in the South Pacific, prior to a full-dress inspection in the fall of 1944.

The fledgling press agent Debuskey with Mae West.

Left to right: Zero Mostel, the composer Gary Geld, Debuskey, and the producer Philip Rose at Mostel's house. Debuskey's friendship with the right surgeon saved Mostel's career and possibly his life.

Left: "King of the Press Agents."

Bottom: The syndicated columnist Liz Smith, who called Debuskey "downright couth."

Debuskey with his lifelong pal, the actor Jack Gilford. Debuskey secured Gilford the highest salary he had ever gotten in the Broadway show *No, No, Nanette,* even though he had been hired by the show's producers to represent the musical.

Left to right: Pearl Somner, Jack Gilford, Debuskey, and Madeleine Gilford.

Debuskey and Pearl Somner with their friend, the producer Alexander H. Cohen. "He's one of a handful of people who were true to the end," said Cohen's son Chris of Merle.

The director Mike Nichols with Debuskey.

Debuskey talking with the playwright, librettist, and legendary wit Larry Gelbart. The two men worked together on *Sly Fox* and *Mastergate*.

Top: Debuskey would spar from time to time with Frank Rich during the latter's thirteen-year tenure as the chief drama critic of the *New York Times*, but they retained a mutual respect. Rich spoke at Debuskey's retirement dinner.

Left: Debuskey handling a photo shoot for *How to Succeed in Business Without Really Trying*.

Merle on the set of *How to Succeed in Business Without Really Trying*.

Vallee is a handicap," recalled Debuskey. "But after this show opens, I can use him forever. What a subject!"

Once *How to Succeed* was ensconced on Broadway, its Pulitzer Prize earned and received, Debuskey found ample opportunities to publicize the show. None were so ripe as the night the recently inaugurated president of the United States, John F. Kennedy, attended a performance. "All presidents drew media coverage, but the romantic aura surrounding Kennedy early in his term exceeded [that around] any of his predecessors. Also, by now television had become a consuming journalistic player. Combining the newly elected Kennedy with the title of the show and its cynical, satirical nature added up to a blockbuster event."

On the appointed night it was arranged for Kennedy, his companions, the Secret Service agents, and the White House press corps to be seated up front. The agents had scoured the theater beforehand, searching under the seats, backstage, in the lighting and sound booths, and in the overworked men's and women's toilets. They also met with the heads of all the theater's departments, who could identify and warrant the rightful attendance of every worker.

The huge crowd that gathered to catch a glimpse of Kennedy began arriving before 6 p.m. The New York City police had taken over the neighborhood. Debuskey had arranged areas along the sides of the theater's marquee and entrance for the still photographers and television cameras, positioning them so all would have a clear view. One of his arrangements, however, was skewered when the police spotted the Associated Press photographer on top of the Hotel Edison marquee across the street. Debuskey had placed him there so that he would have an unobstructed view of the president as he passed under the marquee and would catch the bright lights spelling out *How to Succeed in Business Without Really Trying*. The cops ordered him down: anything could happen, they said, if one of the police officers or Secret Service agents saw someone on the hotel's canopy holding what looked like a gun pointed at the president. "There went a photo that would have been inked in journals all around the world," sighed Debuskey.

After order had been established in and about the theater, Debuskey gave the stage manager the word. No sooner had the orchestra struck the first notes of the overture when the head usher grabbed him: there was a problem. Lined up in the outer lobby was a nest of angry reporters from the New York dailies. "The Secret Service would not let anyone in and did not give a hoot about what paper they represented," said Debuskey. "My pleas to the officers did not even get a sign of recognition." Debuskey told the house manager to get Kennedy's press secretary, Pierre Salinger, out of his seat and down to the lobby.

"I acquainted him with the problem, but he said that he had arranged with the Secret Service to admit only the White House press corps. I told him I feared that if these guys could not get in they would return to their papers, tell their editors that they had been locked out—and the next day's newspapers would report on the lockout instead of providing the large, positive displays that had been planned." Salinger got the drift. He walkie-talkied the head of the Secret Service unit, who passed on the word to the officers posted at the doors. "They swiftly ushered the reporters to the standing-room area at the back of the orchestra. The reporters long remembered my help."

Finally, thought Debuskey, he could relax and enjoy the show. He ran up the mezzanine steps and sat down. A few songs in, the "Coffee Break" number began, and Debuskey suddenly thought, "Uh-oh." The song was a satire of the daily coffee fix the office workers needed to get through the workday. Debuskey's mind went spinning back in time; he could hear in his head Feuer's insistent voice in rehearsal: "It ain't got no button!" That is, the number didn't end with a bang, on an audience-gratifying high note. So Bob Fosse restaged the song the next day, and now "Coffee Break" had a button. Oh boy, did it have a button. In the new staging, as the words and music become more agitated, one of the men, squeezing his paper cup with both hands, separates himself from the crowd and slowly moves to the front edge of the stage. On the last note, he leaps into the orchestra pit.

"What flashed through my head was a vision of Abraham Lincoln in Ford's Theatre with John Wilkes Booth leaping onto the stage.

How would the president's security team react to an actor jumping into the orchestra pit?" Debuskey leaped out of his seat and grabbed a patrolling Secret Service agent. The agent gave the publicist his earpiece and speaker, and Debuskey described to the chief agent the finale of "Coffee Break." All he heard on the other end was, "Oh, shit."

"He rang off. Immediately I could see the agents press their earpieces close to their heads, stop moving, and stare at the stage with their mouths hanging open." But now that they knew, all went fine.

The actor jumped. Nobody shot him.

Harry S. Truman was another president who visited a Broadway show on Debuskey's watch. Truman was out of office, and the show he attended was the forgotten 1963 satirical comedy *Nobody Loves an Albatross*. The event wouldn't have been terribly newsworthy in itself if it hadn't been for a man who was a member of the same audience.

On April 21, 1964, just before curtain time, Debuskey's home phone rang. It was the house manager at the Lyceum Theatre, where *Albatross* was playing. Did Merle know who was in the crowd? Yeah, yeah, said the press agent: Truman. Big deal. Debuskey had arranged house seats for him and his son-in-law, Clifton Daniel, then the slim and dashing managing editor of the *Times*. "Right," the manager said. "But guess who else?"

"The publicist's hairs in my nose began to twitch as I grabbed my coat and hailed a cab to the Lyceum," Debuskey recalled. He entered the auditorium. Sure enough, there was Thomas E. Dewey, of "Dewey Defeats Truman"—that had been the infamous headline on the front page of the *Chicago Tribune* sixteen years earlier, when Truman had won an upset election victory over his Republican opponent. The polls before voting day had clearly showed that Dewey was going to trounce Truman, the unpopular Democratic incumbent. After the votes were counted Dewey called Truman to concede, and the two men had not met or spoken since. Said Debuskey:

> These two former antagonists [were] now occupying the same space
> for the first time in the sixteen years since their historic, bitter contest

for the world's most powerful elected office. At intermission I went down the aisle, got Daniel's attention, pointed out Truman's former rival, seated across the orchestra, and politely, very delicately, asked if he would ascertain from Truman whether the ex-president would meet with Dewey. Daniel whispered in Truman's ear, and the old pro immediately nodded his assent.

Next Debuskey trotted around to Dewey's seat, introduced himself, informed him of the situation, and asked if he would agree to meet with Truman. Dewey quickly said yes. "Before the curtain went up for the second act, I was able to advise both to remain in their seats until the audience exited. I said I would gather them up and escort them to the stage to meet with the cast, who were aware of their presence." Debuskey went into the manager's office, seized the phone, and alerted a select group of media—the *Times's* city desk, the *Daily News's* photo assignment editor, and the AP and UP wire services.

> After the audience left, I led the men to the stage, where Robert Preston assumed the role of referee—he later described himself as being "the third man in the ring of a heavyweight championship bout." The two former politicians greeted each other graciously. Dewey remarked that the occasion was a pleasant surprise. Truman, asked when he had seen Dewey last, smiled and said, "When I licked him."

It was, said Debuskey, "a case of sheer luck being more productive than anything provided by the wisdom, craft, and effort of a working publicist."

———

Every few years during Debuskey's tenure on Broadway, the *New York Times* would get the bright idea to look into "ice." "Ice" is slang for the illegal surcharge on tickets otherwise impossible to get for an immediate performance—tickets sold by scalpers. "The question under investigation was to discover how those precious tickets got into the hands of the scalpers," explained Debuskey, "and there were indictments from time to time, usually of box-office treasurers."

When *How to Succeed* was established as the hottest ticket in town, Debuskey received a call from Louis Calta, a drama reporter for the *Times*. "In an embarrassed fashion, he told me that he had been assigned by the *Times* to investigate the house seat sales of the show's tickets." House seats were the fixed allocation of tickets for every performance that were assigned to the producers, the theater owner, the press agent (who could give them free to journalists assigned to writing about the show), and the creators and stars, who were given house seats as part of their contracts. "I told him to come up to the office and said that I would be pleased to help him. All knowledgeable press agents knew enough to help a reporter on a story."

When Lou arrived, Debuskey told him that he would cooperate if he reported truthfully. Calta was taken aback. Was Debuskey questioning his integrity? Said Debuskey:

> I handed him three long sheets of lined foolscap, each line containing the name, date, and seat locations of a pair of my house seats that I had assigned to someone from the *Times*. The list included the publisher, the circulation manager, the managing editor, editors of sections, and a myriad of reporters in all departments. It totaled somewhere around a hundred. He was shocked and was uneasy about being the messenger of this news, which he had to take back to his editor.

The blackmailing press agent, pulling the noose tight, then told Calta that if the *Times* ran a story and did not include this juicy piece of information, he, naturally, would have to tell the other papers of their omission.

Later that afternoon Debuskey got a call from Sy Peck, the editor of the daily Arts section and the Sunday Arts and Leisure section. "He thanked me; the story had been killed, and he assumed that I would bury back in my file the records I had shown Calta."

——

Debuskey's dousing of fires didn't end after he retired in 1995. In 1996 Jeffrey Horowitz, artistic director of Theatre for a New Audience, called him in a panic. TFANA, working with London's Globe Theatre, was preparing to present *Two Gentleman of Verona* at the New Victory Theater, a newly refurbished jewel box on the city's reclaimed Forty-second Street. Horowitz then got a call from someone at the stage union, ATPAM.

"They said we're going on strike against the New Victory Theater," recalled Horowitz. "They said, we're handing out information and we're telling you that you're not going to be able to do your show there because Actors' Equity is going to rescind its approval and not let the company play." ATPAM insisted that Horowitz go to Cora Cahan, the head of The New 42nd Street, which ran the New Victory, and convince her to hire the union. This wouldn't be easy. Since New Victory's rebirth, Cahan had insisted that it was a children's theater with a top ticket price of $25, and consequently there would be no unionization save the limited participation of the International Alliance of Theatrical Stage Employees, the stagehands' mother union.

Cahan refused to cut a deal. The production was endangered. Horowitz phoned Debuskey, whom he had convinced to take on TFANA a year before he retired from the business. Debuskey had been ATPAM's president for twenty-five years and was an agile thinker when it came to labor negotiations. Said Horowitz:

> Merle came up with this idea. He said, "I want to call a meeting of all the involved unions at ATPAM. You should go in front of them and say you will be happy to hire anyone they want on a union contract on a one-time basis, but that you're the producer, and Cahan is the landlord. If they want TFANA to recognize them, we will recognize them, except the union can't be on the premises of the New Victory. Debuskey advised the union representatives to take up offices in the rooms at TFANA. They can represent us and come down to our offices. We'll pay your people, but they can't go into the New Victory. And he said to ATPAM, if you turn this down, you're going to bankrupt us.

ATPAM agreed, and for three weeks TFANA had union members nesting in its offices. Cahan agreed to the arrangement, but "she was very angry with me," said Horowitz. "To this day—we now work in the Duke Theater—we have a clause in our contract that says if we ever make an agreement with another union that threatens them, they have the right to immediately cancel our engagement."

——

Feuer and Martin knew how to put on a Broadway show. The music-and-lyrics team John of Kander and Fred Ebb knew how to write one. Liza Minnelli knew how to perform one.

Martin Scorsese knew how to direct films.

Nevertheless, Scorsese was the one Minnelli insisted upon as her helmsman when Feuer asked whom the young star wanted to direct *The Act*. "She shocked Cy," Debuskey said. "Scorsese was a brilliant film director, historian, and teacher, but he was also a theater virgin." Scorsese had directed Minnelli in the 1977 film musical *New York, New York*, and the actress had become infatuated with the diminutive, bearded Italian American New Yorker. Now either she got Scorsese or she walked. Feuer, uncharacteristically, gave in. Minnelli was at the top of her career at the time, and the prospect of luring her back to the stage was too hard to resist.

The show was based on a libretto by George Furth about the rise, fall, and rise again of a fictional onetime movie-musical star named Michelle Craig, a woman in her forties. He had started off with Marvin Hamlisch (*A Chorus Line*) as composer, and among those considered for the role had been Doris Day, Shirley MacLaine, Mary Tyler Moore, and Debbie Reynolds. But Minnelli wanted the part—and the character became thirty-two, closer to the star's age. Plans were for a fifteen-week tour through Chicago, San Francisco, and Los Angeles before arriving in New York, where the top ticket price would be $25, a record for a Broadway show.

That is, if they ever got there. "The first warning signal went up on the first day of rehearsal," Debuskey remembered, "when Scorsese asked to be shown his dressing room. When shooting a movie, there always were intervals between shots when the director could retire to his trailer. Scorsese insisted on having a dressing room, despite being informed that in the theater, the director was always out front watching and directing."

During rehearsals Feuer and the production stage manager took turns babysitting Scorsese, advising him what to do next. This cordial co-dependency broke down during technical rehearsals in Chicago, when the director was overwhelmed by the hundreds of lighting, music, dance, and scenic cues that had to be set. Tech was exhausting at best, and if the director did not understand it all, chaos would be certain to reign. Recalled Debuskey: "Scorsese was lost, patience was strained, and completing the tech in the time allowed was obviously going to be impossible. Aware of the delicacy of the moment, Cy spoke to Minnelli. Feuer took over tech. Liza, a seasoned pro, recognized the situation and led the company in a workmanlike, positive attitude."

The musical opened in Chicago to mixed reviews. Furth's backstage story—which involved abortion, infidelity, death, bankruptcy, and onstage violence—was considered too dark and confusing. The costumes and costume designer were abandoned, to the tune of $92,000. Changes in the sets eventually were to mean the loss of an additional $80,000. When they moved on to San Francisco and Los Angeles, the creators tried to fix it, but the show refused to respond. In San Francisco the directors Michael Bennett and Ron Field came to a performance and were asked for advice. Rumors of a romance between Minnelli and Scorsese were constantly surfacing in the press.

When the musical opened in Los Angeles, the reviews were brutal. Then Scorsese's wife filed for divorce. It was clear to the producers that the director had to be replaced. But Minnelli reportedly said—though she later denied it—that if Scorsese was fired, she would quit. Then Scorsese took ill. He was troubled by asthma and symptoms of a cold. "He would retire to his dressing room for lengthy absences and was missing performances," Debuskey said. "It was clear that he was baffled. He approached genius with a camera, but he had no idea how to stage a show. Replacing the director was ordinarily the producer's option. But in this situation only Liza could make the decision." Feuer prevailed upon Minnelli, and she persuaded Scorsese to check into a hospital and cure his cold, allowing their friend Gower Champion to step in. Said Debuskey, "He restaged the show and molded it into a possible hit."

Opening night was a press agent's nightmare. The audience members delayed taking their seats so they could see Minnelli's glamorous friends, among them Sammy Davis Jr., Ethel Merman, and Elizabeth Taylor, glide into the lobby. Inside the auditorium, before the curtain went up, theatergoers tried to get autographs and snap photographs of the stars. Because of all the publicity, real and potential, Feuer and Martin, who'd earned their notoriety as penny-pinchers, were forced to depart from their frugal policy of no opening-night party: Minnelli's return to Broadway had to be celebrated. They planned an opulent outing at Tavern on the Green in Central Park, with six hundred guests. "I convinced them that we could turn the evening into a media feeding frenzy that could overwhelm any unpleasant reviews," said Debuskey, "and that we could cut down on the advertising budget to compensate for the cost. The reviews were mostly good, Minnelli earned extravagant praise, and we had the good news available to spread around by the time the mob assembled."

Party logistics were handled gingerly. Scorsese would be there, of course, but so would Minnelli's husband, Jack Haley Jr.—a romantic triangle just made for tabloid headlines. "In an attempt to forestall any embarrassments," said Debuskey, "I set up separate rooms for the Minnelli and Scorsese groups—he was there with his parents and his twelve-year-old daughter—to prevent him and Liza from being photographed together." To ensure the arrangements, Debuskey hired security personnel. He set up holding pens for the photographers along the path where the limos and taxis were to unload their notables near the entrance. Paparazzi were welcomed but placed so they wouldn't interfere with the accredited press. Minnelli's personal press agents were ordered to keep her and Haley together as they entered and to have them stop long enough to satisfy the cameras. Only a select group of photographers were permitted to enter the party—"those I knew and could trust to respect the agreed-on limitations to their roaming, and the hour they would be asked to leave." The columnists were seated according to their prior reporting on Liza and the show. "The ones who were kindest were put closest."

Everything went smoothly for about half an hour. Then Scorsese became aware that the media were concentrating on the Minnelli room. So, as clueless in social politics as he had been in the rehearsal hall, he decided to join the celebrants swarming around Liza. Debuskey sent out new forces.

> I had the show's creators and cast members gather around him and greet him, so they could keep him away from Liza and Haley until the photographers were politely reminded of their agreement and were asked to exit. Then I got a stiff Scotch, straight up, and sat with Ernie Martin to talk about what a dreamy circumstance this was for a press agent. And I comfortably watched the love triangle's maneuvers as the alcohol took over and caution was abandoned.

Debuskey's headache did not end with the opening. Rumors whirlpooled about Minnelli. She was thought to be bedding a black musician from the pit. She kept friends in her dressing room until 1 a.m. and then headed over to Studio 54. She missed so many performances that Debuskey found himself in the ridiculous position of holding a press conference to announce the return of *The Act*'s star of record. And those were just a few of the absurdities surrounding the whole venture.

The Minnelli-Scorsese affair was the most nagging problem. Speculation wouldn't cease. "Her entanglements, real or rumored, were a veritable cornucopia for the columnists, keeping my office inordinately busy deflecting their inquiries for affirmation," said Debuskey.

> Some of their questions were quite bizarre, if not too far off the mark. The babble achieved such a crescendo that Liza's personal press agents asked me to arrange an after-show dinner with Liza, her husband [who would go on to divorce her in 1979], and the syndicated columnist Earl Wilson, so he could observe and report on the solidity of the marriage. Haley flew in from L.A. to participate in

this charade. I had them seated at a table where they could be seen but not approached, and I headed for Sardi's for a respite of alcohol and a communion with acquaintances of a less complex domestic existence.

For all the trouble she gave him, Debuskey still likes Minnelli.

Liza was a phenomenon. A bleacher-bum psychologist's analysis of her behavior was a postulation that this inherently sweet woman was consumed with a desire to be liked/loved, professionally and personally, and committed every fiber of her body and soul to that end. She gave and gave and gave until she emptied out. It was too heavy a load for anyone to carry, and the devices she sought to carry her along led to her undoing. She is a great performer, emerging from and surviving the umbra of an icon from a mother whom she loved dearly and whom she witnessed in inescapable turmoil. Despite stumbling on so many pitfalls, she has survived.

———

In all these frays, Debuskey pretty much dug in his heels and faced adversity head-on. Sometimes, however, the only logical response to sudden catastrophe is to get the hell out of town. This is just what happened during Debuskey's first, quite unexpected visit to New York, his future home.

Her name was Marie. She worked at the Oasis, a noted "night club" on Baltimore's bawdy, tawdry, neon-lit waterfront. The city sex district, on a stretch of East Baltimore Street, was known as The Block, and it had a bit of everything, from the venerable and comparatively upscale burlesque house the Gayety—which presented the nobility of its art form, such as Ann Corio, Gypsy Rose Lee, Georgia Sothern, and those classic comics Hi "Wilberforce" Connolly, Joey Faye, Jack "Peanuts" Mann, "Reds" Marshall, Mike Sacks, and Phil Silvers—to the Globe, a "scratch house" across the street that appealed strictly to the raincoat-in-the-lap crowd. Scattered along The Block were a covey of saloons inhabited by ladies of the evening, available for "conversation" while being treated to glasses of "champagne." The Versailles among these houses was the

408 Club, ruled over by Big Mike, a mountain of a man and the unofficial mayor of The Block. According to Debuskey, Mike had a library of home movies he had shot to document the accounts of his citizenry and their occupational behaviors. The 408 Club became the meeting-house for Debuskey and a few intimate chums, all pumped up with self-assumed sophistication, higher education, and World War II combat medals.

The Oasis built its reputation by promoting itself as having the world's worst floor show, featuring a Battleship Chorus, a line of dancers weighing no less than two hundred pounds each, some admittedly lousy stand-up comics, and a bevy of shapely, barely clothed showgirls from seaports around the globe. It was run by a family friend of the Debuskeys, and Merle would visit it in the company of his cousin Jerome Robinson, a lawyer for the joint. Marie was an illegal immigrant from Cuba who had seen Debuskey's photos in the town's sports pages. Attracted, she encouraged an affair. Debuskey obliged. On visits to her apartment, Debuskey was sometimes introduced to Marie's "brother," who regularly cited a pressing business meeting as an excuse to leave.

One Saturday morning, following a Thursday-evening, between-shows tryst with Marie, Debuskey was breakfasting over the *Baltimore Sun* when he read on the front page the bold-type news of a "showgirl" at the Oasis having been stabbed to death by a person unknown, who had immediately fled the club. The description of the victim left no question that it was Marie. The police had already taken in her "brother" in for questioning and were looking for anyone else associated with her.

Tossing a toothbrush and a change of underwear into a suitcase, Debuskey dashed off to the train station and leaped aboard the first train to New York, where he moved into the Thirty-fourth Street YMCA. Like a fugitive in a film noir, he wandered around midtown New York for days, grabbing first editions of the *Baltimore Sun* and *News-Post* from the out-of-town newspaper stand at Forty-second Street and Broadway.

On Tuesday, exiled to the back pages, came the finale. The killer had been captured. A merchant sailor had struck up an acquaintanceship with Marie and accompanied her home after the club closed. There he was accosted and robbed of his wallet by Marie's "brother." The next evening he returned to the Oasis and exacted his revenge.

And that was Debuskey's introduction to New York City.

Chapter 7

CAUSES

For many years Merle Debuskey did not need to make plans for New Year's Eve. He knew he would be at one of a few large apartments on the Upper West Side, the home of either the screenwriter Ian Hunter, the screenwriter Ring Lardner Jr., or the Zero Mostels. The other attendees would all be from the entertainment world, all members of the Left. Writers, actors, lawyers, composers, journalists, agents, and assorted others would gather to talk, debate, argue, drink, and amuse one another.

"While few needed being compelled to imbibe because of the holiday, the evenings were long and increasingly less reserved," recalled Debuskey.

> Musical talents took to the piano, among them Burton Lane, Yip Harburg, Saul Chaplin, Elmer Bernstein; singers, celebrated and non; and the comics would take over, including Zero Mostel, Jack Gilford, and lesser names who dared to follow. The night usually ended with Lardner and Hunter describing the rambunctious Hollywood poker-and-drinking evenings with Dalton Trumbo and other big-time scripters.*

---

* It was after leaving one of these parties that the *New York Times* editor Sy Peck was killed. On New Year's Eve 1985 Park left the party at a late hour. He was driving home, traveling north on the North Henry Hudson Parkway, when a car came out of the exit from the Cloisters, turned south, and smashed into Sy's car. Debuskey and his wife, Pearl, were not at the party that year. They were vacationing in a village on the Spanish coast when they learned of Peck's death from a day-old copy of the *Herald Tribune*.

Many of this same "shtetl of political victims" would take part in weekly poker games, which were characterized by heavy drinking and high-flown literary venom as the players entertained the table with recountings of their pre-blacklist evenings. The games were dealer's choice and some that were unfamiliar to the New York players, such as "three-card hi-lo," introduced by the Hollywood contingent, with which they could sandbag an innocent into relinquishing his next month's rent. If Mostel or Gilford found he was losing, he would fight the tide by breaking into his Cafe Society Downtown routines. The games would last late into the night, and the room would become infused with the aroma of pastrami and corned beef sent up from a deli, either the Stage or the Carnegie.

From the time he reached adulthood, Merle Debuskey was never anything but a political progressive. He was president of the press agents' union for twenty-five years and even after leaving could rarely if ever be made to admit that labor was capable of any wrongdoing. He never joined the Communist Party, but he bent over backward to help any Party member or past member he knew whose life or career had been damaged by the McCarthy-led Communist witch hunts. He lent his assistance to the civil rights, women's, farm workers', and anti-Vietnam movements when called upon. He was attracted to any theatrical project that embraced integration and color-blind casting. In fact, it is difficult to find a liberal cause of the past fifty years that he didn't embrace without reservation.

These political leanings later won him enemies. The press agent, general manager, and producer Arthur Cantor—whom Debuskey regarded as an "insatiable, upwardly mobile operator" who would "elbow aside anyone between him and advancement"—once confronted Debuskey in Shubert Alley, asserting that he and fellow Communists were trying to throttle his professional career. "I was so startled that I could only retort ridiculously with, 'No, Arthur, we had more important people to throttle.'" Bill Fields, who wore high-top shoes and handled the Playwrights' Company, would hit the ceiling whenever Debuskey, as head of ATPAM, sent out one of his political missives. "I would get these nasty letters from Bill Fields," recalled Debuskey. "He was a reactionary. He was somebody who hated me. He said it."

Unlike his colleagues at the Public Theater Bernard Gersten and Joseph Papp, his fellow press agent Jimmy Proctor, and his actor friends Jack Gilford and Zero Mostel, Debuskey was never brought before the House Un-American Activities Committee. Some associates secretly joked that Debuskey was so liberal-minded that he was actually envious of his friends' persecution and regretted not being "in the club." But the government wasn't wholly uninterested in Debuskey's actions. In 1972, to help his press office function better, Debuskey had a complicated telephone system installed. One day the system went haywire. The telephone company denied responsibility, so Debuskey sought help from the company that had sold him the equipment. "A couple of technicians responded and spent hours investigating and ultimately restoring the complicated system. When they were finished, they came up from the basement, which housed the control boxes, and said they were curious about the line of work we were in. They had discovered that someone, obviously very experienced, had rewired the system to include participants outside our office." He had been wiretapped.

So Debuskey arranged to get his government file from the Federal Bureau of Investigation and the Department of Justice under the Freedom of Information Act. When it arrived, every line had been blacked out except for those with his name and address and one on the final page that read "New York State Subversive." He appealed the blackouts to the Department of Justice, which denied his appeal and supported its decision with a notice that he had been declared a threat to national security.

A threat to national security. That was news to Debuskey, who had served proudly during World War II.

Debuskey cannot track his conversion to liberal causes to any particular epiphany in his past. Rather, he said that "incidence and coincidence played a major role." But it is not difficult to put together how he came to his way of looking at the world. He was born into a middle-class Jewish family, to parents shaped by the Great Depression and the presidency of Franklin D. Roosevelt. His parents gave clothes to charitable agencies, and his mother was a lifetime volunteer at the pediatric ward of a hospital.

His experiences with the cruelty of segregated Baltimore were followed by those of religious and racial discrimination at the University of Virginia. That was where Debuskey's political education likely began. But his sense of human fairness and equality was cemented during World War II.

He received his commission as ensign in the United States Naval Reserve on February 27, 1944, while at the University of Virginia. He had to make his own way to Camp Bradford, Virginia, just south of Norfolk, by March 10. His assignment was a distinctly unglamorous one: he was to be part of the crew on an LST. "Like many others, my romantic notion of warring at sea was to be aboard 'the greyhound of the deep,' a destroyer," recalled Debuskey. "My ambition was to fight in the Atlantic theater so I could grab Hitler by the throat. We had studied the destroyer in class and had some idea of what it would actually be."

An LST was hardly a greyhound—more of a big sitting duck. The vessel was a huge, lumbering, amphibious ship designed to run aground. Its missions involved hitting a designated beach, discharging the troops and equipment (tanks, trucks, jeeps, ammunition, gasoline, and whatever else was needed in an assault) it held onboard, and then getting the hell away from shore before the tide went out. They were big—328 feet long, 50 feet wide, and flat-bottomed, with a blunt bow fashioned by two doors that opened just before beaching—and clumsy to maneuver. Debuskey and his shipmates came to refer to their LST as a "large, slow-moving target."

Debuskey soon learned why the LSTs existed. The Axis powers occupied most of Europe and the islands of the Pacific. Before the Allies could engage the enemy, they had to invade the beaches and quickly get troops, equipment, and supplies ashore in great numbers. The conventional mode had been to load troop ships and cargo vessels, lie off the land, load up barges with men and equipment, and tow them to the beach. This was slow work and left the soldiers exposed to fire from the beaches and the air. The enemy had time to dig in and load up. The projected losses were enormous, even calamitous.

There had to be some other way. The Navy came up with the LSTs, which were being designed and built in huge numbers in unlikely places all over the country—Debuskey's came from Evansville, Indiana.

Debuskey had one advantage over his fellow trainees: he had actually seen the ocean. Most of the others were farm boys and such who knew the nomenclature of the Navy—"all engines ahead standard speed," "rudder amidships," "drop the anchor," "let go the bow line," and the like—but didn't have the foggiest idea of what would result when those orders where given. Said Debuskey, "We were tadpoles expected to jump as frogs. In no time at all, we would be given the responsibility of operating a huge floating machine costing millions of dollars, with hundred of lives and considerable equipment on board, theoretically, in combat."

Debuskey was made a gunnery officer. An LST was equipped with six 40mm automatic cannons, eight 20mm automatic cannons, six .50-caliber machine guns, and an assortment of sidearms, rifles, and signal guns. After two weeks of specialist training, he and his mates went to sea, where the groups began to actually function in their specialties. "We fired the guns using live ammunition at targets towed in the air and on the sea's surface. Firing was easy, hitting was difficult, but by the end of the two weeks at sea our batting average had improved—though not sufficiently to have us anxious to meet up with an attacking Zero bomber or torpedo boat." After two more weeks of land-based training, the men again went to sea. During all of these weeks every officer also learned the duties of the officer of the deck, who was responsible for operating the ship for a four-hour watch.

After just eight weeks of training, the crew was sent off to Evansville, Indiana, to pick up the ship, putting in some additional training in Chicago while they waited for the craft to be finished. They were not impressed. "Our commonly held opinion," Debuskey remembered, "was that the damn thing would hit the water and go directly to the bottom. What was worse was that if it did not, we would have to live and fight on it." The LST was slipped off the quays into the water on June 5, 1944. It floated.

The LST sailed down the Ohio and then the Mississippi River to New Orleans. During this time the crew became aware that theirs was in fact a command ship and would house a staff that would be on board but not involved in its operation. Debuskey also discovered that only one officer had been to sea before: Captain Francis Canny, a cultured, kindly man who had been a personnel officer for Macy's.

LST 574's orders were to proceed to Espiritu Santo in the New Hebrides. The voyage lasted thirty days, during which the crew never saw land. This was when the novice crew truly learned how to operate the ship, every day simulating breakdowns, lowering and retrieving the small boats while at sea, perfecting navigation, communicating with signal flags, firing the cannons at targets, sounding, and getting to general quarters as speedily as possible, over and over again. And they learned other tricks that aided their new life on the water. The LST's unique motion made sleep difficult. Debuskey began sleeping with a pillow between his knees, bracing his legs against the sides of the bunk to counter the tossing of the ship. He also got in the habit of never filling his coffee cup more than two-thirds from the top.

They hit Espiritu Santo exactly on schedule. After loading provisions they headed for Manus in the Admiralty Islands, a significant forward naval base. Debuskey ran into a man who had been in his unit at Virginia. "He had gone into the underwater demolition groups and had seen action, swimming in to the beaches of islands occupied by the Japanese in order to map the beach for the amphibious forces that were to come. He had aged visibly."

The LST was then directed to Hollandia, New Guinea, where General Douglas MacArthur had set his command.

We spent several weeks there, preparing for the invasion of the Philippines. We loaded 306 troops and 720 tons of trucks, tanks, and ammunition, anchoring them to the tank deck and the main deck. On November 5 we departed for Leyte, P.I [Philippine Islands]. The convoy consisted of fifteen Liberty ships (AKAs), thirty-six LSTs, and twenty-five LCIs—seventy-six ships. We had destroyer escorts and air coverage. Now we were in it for real.

On November 12, just after MacArthur posed for his famous "I have returned" photo op, the convoy arrived at White Beach, near Tacloban, Leyte. The total number of troops under MacArthur's command was reported to exceed the number under Eisenhower in Europe.

An LST operation went something like this. First came wave after wave of high-altitude heavy bombers, dropping masses of large bombs. Next, medium bombers blanketed the attack area with high explosives, followed by volleys of heavy cannon fire from the battleships and cruisers beyond the convoy. This went on for hours, the sound deafening, the exploding shells sending up a heavy cloud of black smoke. A cessation of fire cued a phalanx of landing craft infantry ships (LCIs, smaller than the LST) that had been converted into rocket ships. They headed in a line toward the beach, firing off rack after rack of rockets, then reversing direction firing the rockets in their stern. After several waves of these frightening maneuvers the firing ceased again, and the LCIs, carrying troops but no equipment, dumped the doughboys, who immediately dug foxholes and waited.

Debuskey found these horrendous assaults comforting, since, he concluded, no living thing could withstand them. Yet when the LSTs were called in and hit the beach, the nearby hills suddenly erupted with mortar shells the Japanese tossed at the beach and the ships. "How could they have survived those damnable assaults?" Debuskey wondered.

On the way back to Hollandia, Debuskey's ship was subject to six kamikaze attacks. On the way to their next combat delivery, in the Linguyan Gulf, Luzon, Philippines, the ship met more kamikazes. Recalled Debuskey: "The suicide pilots would circle above the convoy, out of range of our anti-aircraft guns, until the pilot chose his target, nosed over, and came straight down at full speed. Tough to hit it on its rapid descent. I for one, and I'd wager that many others felt the same, was certain that it was headed for me. Nothing to do but wait." The ships had to cease fire as the plane descended so as to avoid shooting each other, and as long as the ships were firing at the Japanese planes, U.S. fighter planes could not enter that airspace for fear of getting hit. Before air cover could drive them off, the bombers and kamikazes had hit and damaged two Liberty ships, killing twenty-five.

Having taken the island of Leyte and a couple more adjacent islands, MacArthur planned to go north to Linguyan Gulf, skipping all the Japanese-held areas between, secure the gulf, and land an army big enough to sweep south and retake Manila. The first week of February 1945, the LST took on a third combat load, consisting of 341 army personnel and 400 tons of cargo. It departed on February 6 for Linguyan Gulf. The next initial assault, in March, was Zamboanga, on the southern tip of Mindanao, Philippines. This time, instead of carrying troops and equipment, they were loaded to the scuppers with fifty-five-gallon drums of high-octane gasoline for airplanes. Said Debuskey:

> We all were aware of what we were carrying. Any kind of a hit, a spark, would fashion this ship into a Macy's Fourth of July fireworks display, and we would not be around to write home about it. The mood was tense. Anyone caught lighting a cigarette would have been heaved overboard. Captain Manees was well aware of what was sitting on the tank deck and, concluding that he was too valuable to the war effort to be shredded off of Zamboanga, made an instant decision to revise our beaching spot in the battle plan and ordered our captain to belay his written orders and to take the ship down the line and beach it beyond the designated area. Away from the other ships and away from the shelling of the Japanese.

It also was well away from the overall plan of having equipment and materials organized and in place within easy reach. The crew offloaded the gasoline at record speed, while the Army beach control sent bulldozers to scrape a path from where they were to where they should have been.

Manees's instincts, it turned out, were right. "Just minutes after we had retracted from the beach," said Debuskey, "a grenade or mortar shell detonated that gang of gasoline drums, sending sky-high hundreds of hours of future flying time."

Debuskey and company were then sent to the island of Morotai, in the Dutch East Indies, which became the staging area for two invasions of Brunei Bay in British North Borneo. On the beach they set up a huge outdoor movie theater and screened Humphrey Bogart pictures, dousing the projector whenever an alert came through. The LST carried Australian troops. When they hit the beach the first time in Brunei Bay, bodies floated around the ship.

These visits turned out to be the last amphibious operations of World War II. "While heading back to Morotai, we were startled by news of an atomic bomb having been dropped on Hiroshima," said Debuskey. "We did not know details of the horrendous result, but at that time, if we had been polled, there would not be a single vote against that momentous act."

Research shows that if the Pacific war had not ended, LST 574, as part of the Seventh Amphibious Fleet, would have taken part in Operation Olympic, the Allied plan to invade the Japanese island of Kyushu on November 1, 1945. Debuskey experienced a war largely free from danger, one he admitted sometimes resembled the war comedy *Mr. Roberts*. "You got sucked in and got so bored, you couldn't wait for action." But had LST 574 taken part in Operation Olympic, his Life of Roberts would surely have ended.

"Nothing in the future would be as awesomely frightening as the death and destruction we had witnessed," said Debuskey, reflecting on the effect his service had had on him. "No threat by an individual, institution, or event could be as intimidating. I—we—could look the perpetrator in the eye, remember what we had lived through, and stand straight. I came away with the belief that with purpose, sacrifice, willingness to work diligently, and respecting the efforts and choices of others, almost anything was within one's grasp."

As in Baltimore, life in the Navy had been segregated. Debuskey had done what he could to shift the order of things. The black men on the LST could serve only as stewards to the officers. As gunnery officer, Debuskey selected and trained the gun crews. He took the black stewards and made them part of the crews. "One, I liked them," he explained. "Two, I thought, this is a way to get them up a little bit."

Beyond that, Debuskey could not explain why he had gone to the bother of integrating the gunnery crew. It just seemed right to the liberal conscience he only dimly realized was his.

"There was no epiphany. My political education just slowly evolved, and somehow by the end of World War II I was ready."

———

After returning from World War II and moving to New York, Debuskey's theatrical companions kept him attuned to political liberalism. "They all leaned to the left of the political spectrum," he observed, "and most had to endure the vicissitudes of appearing before congressional committees. They all were very decent persons, and all were willing and did put themselves on the line in supporting causes, events, and movements that were then labeled suspect by the hysterical anti-Communists."

His political attitudes did not lose him much work in the New York theater of the 1950s and '60s. Then as now, the stage arts were populated by more liberals than conservatives. "Part of the attraction was he was a good left-winger," said the producer Emanuel Azenberg. "It sounds dirty now, but it wasn't then. It was correct. Merle was lovable *because* of his politics, *because* he was committed to something. That was absolutely respectable." (Notwithstanding, few other press agents trod the political Left with as heavy a foot as Debuskey.)

Most of the producers who employed Debuskey again and again were progressives themselves, and none more so than Phil Rose, whose list of credits—the landmark black drama *A Raisin in the Sun*, the interracially cast *The Owl and the Pussycat*, the antiwar *Shenandoah*—read like a résumé of American social movements from Eisenhower to Nixon. "They saw eye to eye on the things that needed to be done," said Doris Belack, Rose's wife. "They had a social conscience that was agreeable to one another."

"Philip was a member of this left circle that Merle was in," recalled Steven Suskin, Rose's general manager during the 1970s. "To the left-wing guys he was the man. Merle always supported them. What he said when he got off the phone with them, I can't tell you. But he always gave the impression of 'Sure, let's do it.' That's why he got that loyalty."

Added Larry Belling: "His charitable work and his political commitment made him more real and lasting friends than anyone else in the press agent fraternity."

Debuskey's usefulness derived not only from his sympathetic, on-his-sleeve political beliefs, but also from his special status as a functioning professional. A lefty who had never been jailed or subpoenaed and a sympathizer who had never joined, the careful tightrope he walked allowed him to move easily between the powerful mainstream media outlets and the counterculture underground. It was true, as Bob Kamlot said, that Debuskey was "politically left of left wing," and that he ran ATPAM with "a kind of socialistic attitude," according to Mickey Alpert. But it was also true that, as Bernie Gersten put it, "I was a member of the Party and he wasn't. His characteristic was that he *wasn't* a member. It gave him a good position. It was useful. He wasn't subject to so-called Party discipline." (Debuskey stated, rather evasively, that he never joined the Party because "no one had ever invited me.")

If one had to point to a specific turning point in Debuskey's political consciousness, it would likely be his meeting up with Jimmy Proctor. Proctor, a big bulldog of a man who had been a wrestler at Cornell, was, despite great success in the field of press agentry, a nervous man who could be thrown into a panic by an angry phone call from a producer. He was always fearful he was about to be fired. When anxious, he would sweat, and his elbows and knees poked holes in the air. His worrying would cause him to hover over every press release, checking and rechecking the copy, Larry Belling recalled.

Once, when trapped by Jed Harris on a yacht that the irascible and unpredictable director-producer had temporarily procured from its owner (with the spurious excuse that he needed to live with it before actually purchasing it), Proctor put his wallet in a plastic bag, put it in his pants, took off his jacket, tied his shoes around his neck, left a "thank you" note, dived into the water, and swam ashore. Another misadventure involved a gathering, upon the announcement that *The Diary of Anne Frank* had won the Pulitzer Prize for Drama, at the offices of Kermit Bloomgarden. In attendance were the general manager Max Allentuck, the writers Albert Hackett and Francis Goodrich, Proctor, and Debuskey. The clan waited for the arrival of the director Garson Kanin and his wife, Ruth Gordon, and, when they entered Jim leaped from his chair, ran across the room, wrapped his arms around Kanin, and gave him a hug—cracking one of Kanin's ribs. "A bit later we repeated the arrangement with the news of the Drama Critics award," said Debuskey. "Again, we waited for Gar and Ruth. The phone rang. It was Kanin announcing that he and Ruth were on the corner but would not come up until they were assured that two people were sitting on Jim."

A heavy drinker, Proctor was pointedly conscious of the low status to which he felt his profession regulated him. "He assiduously and nervously aspired to become a member of an elite private Manhattan club, the Century Club, and he worried that because he had been an unfriendly witness before HUAC, someone would blackball him," said Debuskey. "Eventually, through the efforts of a friend, the painter Joseph Hirsch, he succeeded in becoming a member, securing him the imagined stature that he sought."

Despite his insecurities, however, Proctor had principles and assiduously stood by them. He was instrumental in the formation of ATPAM and was a dedicated publicist for Kermit Bloomgarden and Philip Rose, who backed such progressive, liberal-minded plays as Arthur Miller's *All My Sons* and *Death of a Salesman* and Lorraine Hansberry's *A Raisin in the Sun*. Moreover, he had taken the Fifth before the House Un-American Activities Committee. Said Debuskey:

> I admired, respected, and liked Jim, and quite naturally I assimilated his political views and those of his friends—who generously accepted me into their intimacy. It was during the early years with Proctor that I became acutely aware of blacklisting, its motivations, maliciousness,

practitioners, and, most intimately, its victims. For me, it became a vicious fracturing of America's democratic principles by a few amoral, power-seeking demagogues. On a personal level I viewed and felt the anguish of an ever-increasing group of friends who were wounded by this infectious disease, and I joined and became active with those who stepped up to oppose it.

Proctor also secured for Debuskey the show that, perhaps more than any other, changed his life, both politically and professionally, and dictated many of the directions he would follow in the future. The 1953 Off-Broadway production of *The World of Sholom Aleichem* was perhaps as unlikely a prospect for a hit play as was possible at the time. It was conceived, produced, directed, and performed almost entirely by blacklist victims, among them Howard Da Silva (who would direct and act), Phoebe Brand, Morris Carnovsky, Jack Gilford, Arnold Perl, and a young, unknown black actress named Ruby Dee. Dee's husband, Ossie Davis, was the stage manager. (Dee had given an impassioned speech at a Carnegie Hall rally against the execution of the Rosenbergs; Da Silva had heard her and offered her a role.) The evening consisted of three one-act plays, only one of which, *High School*, was based on a story by Sholom Aleichem, who is now considered the greatest of the Yiddish writers but at that time—way past his Yiddish Broadway heyday and before riding the coattails of *Fiddler on the Roof* to immortality—was largely forgotten. The other two plays were based on an anonymous Jewish folk story, "A Tale of Chelm," and a short story by the Yiddish writer I. L. Peretz, "Bontche Schweig." ("Bontche" was Debuskey's nickname for Bernie Gersten—which Gersten hated—after the silent Jewish peasant played by Jack Gilford.) Da Silva would play the narrator, Mendele the bookseller.

Da Silva and Perl were in charge of the enterprise. Both had been robbed of employment by the blacklist, and they were desperate to see the show succeed and resurrect their careers. For publicity they turned to Proctor, knowing his political past and sympathies. "They had raised enough money to put it on for a limited number of per-formances, seventeen, on an irregular schedule in the auditorium of a hotel," recalled Debuskey. "The title page of the program would read like a page out of Red Channels. While the play would be special in its mining of Yiddish culture, its main thrust could not be more obvious: Theater artists could be blacklisted and obliterated from the more mainstream entertainment venues, but they lived, their talent remained, and they could still find a home in the world of New York theater."

For a number of reasons, principally financial, Proctor turned them down. "I believe that he also worried about adding another subversive credit to his already burdensome list," observed Debuskey. "And he was also unfamiliar with the Off-Broadway scene. After he turned them down, they went to several well-known press agents with whom they felt comfortable, all of whom also said no—which was not surprising, given the national political psychosis that prevailed."

This opened the door for Debuskey. Proctor asked his young associate if he could give his name to Da Silva and Perl. "I was well aware of the problems inherent in connecting with and trying to promote their effort—but in fact, I lusted for the opportunity and encouraged him to let me give it a shot." The desperate Da Silva and Perl assented, and Debuskey signed an ATPAM Off-Broadway contract. Proctor generously permitted him to work out of his office, and the show went into rehearsal. Bernie Gersten—an avowed leftist whom Debuskey had met the previous year—was to be the lighting designer.

Soon afterward it became apparent that Perl and Da Silva—whom Debuskey grew to dislike—had no management skills. According to Debuskey, he and Gersten assumed many of the duties of producer and general manager, though they never bore those titles: "We set up the box office, hired the stagehands, arranged for the signing of contracts for actors and the creative elements, worked with the hotel manager to get house personnel, and worked out the performance schedule around the prior bookings in the space."

Performances began in the late spring of 1953, and the artistic elements came together in a way that exceeded everyone's expectations.

With an enthusiasm not dampened by the intervening decades, Debuskey remembered the show as "very special, supremely entertaining, expertly acted, and beautifully presented using a minimum of scenic and costume elements and musical instruments, all carefully husbanded and artistically fashioned. It was a consummate realization of simplicity and skill seldom seen on the stage."

The play attracted the expected audience of the politically sympathetic, as well as a smattering of individuals who were instrumental in the constructing and dissemination of the blacklist; according to Debuskey, they were "checking us out to see if they could do damage." But the press stayed well clear of the show. And since Debuskey had been hired to drum up interest, all eyes fell on him to break the publicity logjam. "The media knew of the creator and the actors," he said, "but it was, to varying degrees, suspicious of the political motivations and unsure how to regard the brief and interrupted performance schedule of a presentation far from Broadway." It was also somewhat confused by the title. Some journalists assumed it was being performed in Yiddish.

"All this created a sweaty, conflicted press agent. While no fingers were pointed and nothing said, I felt everyone's eyes on my back." He succeeded in provoking the interest of the Yiddish journals, "which were probably flattered by my unusual persistence," but little else. Nonetheless, thanks to word of mouth, the show became a sold-out hit. Brooks Atkinson of the *New York Times* was enticed to attend (see p. 69) and praised it in his Sunday column: "Everyone involved in the production was ecstatic. Its future was assured. Everyone was guaranteed being reemployed."

Well, perhaps not everyone. Sometime in the middle of that summer Debuskey read a mention of the show in the *New York Post*. Since he had not placed the item, a warning bell went off in his head. He called Frances Herridge, who had signed the piece, and asked her where it had come from. She said it had been sent in by Barry Hyams, an ATPAM press agent who said he had been engaged to handle the show. Here was early proof for Debuskey that in the theater loyalty could not be assumed as a given, even among a group of artists who knew betrayal well.

Debuskey was surprised and hurt. After taking on a hot-potato show that no one wanted and getting no lesser personage than the *Times*'s Atkinson to see it, he had been knifed in the back. Proctor found out that Victor Samrock, one of Broadway's top general managers, had seen the show, spoken with Da Silva and Perl, and advised them to replace Debuskey with Hyams, who was familiar with Yiddish culture and had represented the attractions of Sol Hurok, a leading impresario (who also happened to be Hyams's father-in-law).

Debuskey confronted Da Silva and Perl and told them what he thought of them. "They were apologetic, expressed remorse, and said that they would immediately correct their lousy action. I think that the word had gotten about in the theater community, the media, and the potential investors from leftist circles. This may have been more forceful than their consciences in repairing their damaging deed."

The producers had opened an office, and Gersten and Debuskey gave up all their other work to manage the play. The show reopened to ecstatic reviews. Atkinson wrote two pieces, declaring that the reopening was "a time for rejoicing." *Sholom Aleichem* immediately became the hottest ticket in New York.

The show's success drove Vincent Hartnett, the author of the anti-Communist tract *Red Channels: The Report of Communist Influence in Radio and Television*, to sputtering distraction. "We heard from union meetings and from conversations that Eliot Sullivan, a blacklisted actor, had met with Hartnett," recalled Debuskey. "The two lived near each other in Peter Cooper Village in Manhattan, and Hartnett tried to befriend Sullivan and convert him to the cause—for a small fee. They would converse when they bumped into each other strolling the housing development's paths. Hartnett was obsessed with the existence of *Sholom Aleichem* but did not know how to destroy it, as almost everyone was already blacklisted."

Much of Debuskey's future would be strongly influenced by the associations that grew out of *Sholom Aleichem*. Davis and Dee became his guides into the civil rights movement; Gilford became an intimate; and his apparent willingness to accept the realistic danger inherent in publicizing what were then politically unpopular causes led to his being invited to participate in many battles yet to come.

The experience also formed an activist mindset that ordered his political attitudes, not only toward himself and his work, but toward others. "One thing I've noticed about Merle," said his old college chum Samuel Goldwyn Jr., "is that he's very contemptuous about people who live without an ethic of any kind. He's very strong in his convictions, and he can't work with people he can't respect. He likes to feel he's a part something that's moving forward in some way, that's bigger than just him, whether it's in politics or theater."

———

None of Debuskey blacklisted friends made more headlines than John Henry Faulk.

The Texas-born Faulk was a CBS radio personality and humorist. He and Debuskey had been members of the publicity, journalism, and entertainment unit of the American Veterans Committee. Debuskey was impressed that when some members attacked the songwriter Earl Robinson for his leftist views, Faulk strongly defended him, ending the assault. Debuskey introduced himself after that, and the two became friends.

On his radio program *Johnny's Front Porch*, Faulk told stories about people he had met on trips through the South. By the mid-1950s he had become a popular regular in New York social and entertainment circles. But in 1955 he and others won election to the board of the American Federation of Television and Radio Artists by opposing the blacklist. Reprisals were swift. The next year he was named in a blacklisting pamphlet distributed by AWARE, one of the major anti-Communist organizations, in part because he had once been a guest, along with Eleanor Roosevelt, at a United Nations dinner honoring a Soviet official. He soon lost his sponsor, and before long his show was canceled.

"John was unemployable," said Debuskey, "and unable to maintain a life in New York for his wife and children. So they moved to Austin, where he was promised a radio program by Lyndon Johnson.

Johnson reneged, and Johnny and his wife set up an advertising and public relations business."

Faulk bravely confronted his accusers and sued AWARE with the help of the prominent attorney Louis Nizer. Nizer, who took the case pro bono, was a noted trial lawyer given to aphorisms such as, "When a man points his finger at someone, he'd better remember he has four fingers pointing at himself." In 1955 he won a landmark libel decision in which the journalist Quentin Reynolds successfully sued the ultraconservative columnist Westbrook Pegler.

The trial took place in 1962 and lasted eleven weeks. For much of those eleven weeks—and for the weeks needed to prepare for the trial—Faulk roomed with Debuskey, who had an extra bedroom and bath. Debuskey helped raised money to sustain Faulk and cover the huge expenses of the trial. Some contributions were fantastic and comic. A prominent Broadway producer once arrived at their door with a big brown bag stuffed with cash.

Debuskey and his wife at the time, Christine Karner, sat in court every day of the trial to support their friend. They also helped research relevant material for his lawyers. Every day Helen Sofer, a close friend of Abraham Geller, the presiding judge, picked them up in a car. Debuskey recalled one major moment in the proceedings when Nizer was cross-examining Vincent Hartnett, editor of the "naming" weekly sheet *Counterattack* and a hub of the blacklisting apparatus.

> Hartnett's lawyers had led him through a long examination to prove him an experienced, careful, knowledgeable, and precise investigator whose deductions and accusations were unquestionably accurate. Hartnett had seen John Henry, Mrs. Sofer, Chris, and me arrive at court every morning and saw where we sat together during the day. Lynn Faulk, Johnny's wife, had returned to Austin, Texas, to take care of the children and the tiny public relations business.

"Do you know Mr. Faulk's wife?" asked Nizer. Hartnett said he did. "Can you identify her?" "Yes," said Hartnett—and pointed directly at Helen Sofer. "Helen went apoplectic. She asked to rise and give her name. When she had, the whole room—press, officers, visitors, and jurors—went ape. Hartnett was now a dead duck."

Faulk won the case and was awarded $3.5 million. An appeals court later lowered the amount to $500,000, and legal fees and debts erased even that.

Debuskey's political forays influenced Christine, and when she left the stage she became involved in a number of causes. One was Women Strike for Peace, founded by Bella Abzug and Dagmar Wilson in 1961 in the wake of an international protest in November 1961 by thousands of women around the world against nuclear testing in the atmosphere. During the height of the Vietnam War, the group organized many antiwar demonstrations in Washington, New York, and elsewhere.

Christine, a bit out of her depth and having difficulty finding her niche, was funneled into the role of publicist. But she lacked practical experience in this too, and so for a time her husband became the closeted press agent for the women's group—the only man in Women Strike for Peace. "Chris would come to my office with the information to be released, and I would write it and instruct her on where and how it should be disseminated," he recalled. "She was the front."

In December of 1962 Debuskey called on his old Baltimore acquaintance Russell Baker, who was by then working for the *New York Times*, for help. The result was an early column that Baker wrote under the heading "Observer," a title he would go on to use for the next thirty-six years. The House Un-American Activities Committee had subpoenaed some of the group's members, claiming that they had been associated with the Communist Party or its front groups. Baker assailed the hearings:

[They] covered [the committee] with foolishness. The lesson is as old as Aristophanes, who lived four hundred years before Christ: Men confronted by women peace strikers should either make peace or leave the ladies alone. In *Lysistrata*, Aristophanes' Athenian women, disgusted with the endless Peloponnesian War, shut themselves off from their husbands until peace was concluded. The men at first retaliated with the same guile that animated the Un-American Activities Committee this week. But when the ladies refused to be persuaded that peace-striking was an un-Athenian activity, the hapless males surrendered. The three congressmen who challenged the American Lysistratas this week did not end up begging for mercy but they spent most of the week looking badgered and miserable.

In 1964 Debuskey got a phone call from Murray Levy, who knew the publicist through *The World of Sholom Aleichem*. Levy was a young white member of the Free Southern Theater, a group intent on bringing integrated theater performances to southern towns in the teeth of the civil rights movement.

"The Free Southern Theater was a courageous anomaly," Debuskey said. "It was the first integrated theater to be established in the Deep South, bringing to the people of rural Mississippi their first exposure to live drama, and it added a new and vital dimension to the struggle for civil rights." But every movement, however virtuous, needs the oxygen of publicity to survive. Levy provided Debuskey with materials and asked what he could do. The press agent used his *Times* connections to place an article on November 14, 1964, titled "Integrated Cast Cheered in South." It told of a standing-room-only crowd at St. John's Institutional Missionary Baptist Church in a black neighborhood of New Orleans applauding a production of Ossie Davis's *Purlie Victorious*.

Davis and Dee were Debuskey's frequent companions in various civil rights efforts. Like Levy, Dee had connected with Debuskey through *Sholom Aleichem*. "He had a great sensitivity to the people who suffered under McCarthyism at that time," said Dee, "who lost their jobs, who were on the spot and uncertain about their future. He was part of the time. He wasn't on the outside looking in. He was sympathetic."

Through Davis, Dee, and the Free Southern Theatre, Debuskey became familiar with the Student Nonviolent Coordinating Committee (SNCC). It had grown out of a spontaneous student sit-in movement at Shaw University in Raleigh, North Carolina, that began in February of 1960. At first it devoted itself to voter registration and direct action in southern communities. Led by John Lewis, SNCC played an important part in the 1963 March on Washington

and Freedom Summer, in which volunteers organized black Missis-
sippians to register to vote, and in 1965 Martin Luther King Jr. led
the dramatic march for voting rights from Selma to Montgomery,
Alabama. The march was catalyzed in part by the murder of a
SNCC member, Jimmie Lee Jackson, during the committee's voter
registration drive.

Without telling him, Debuskey adopted Ossie Davis as his tutor
and guide into this world. "One could not hope for a more honest,
decent, level-headed, perceptive, wise, humorous model to emulate,"
said Debuskey. "He and Ruby were strong, unwavering, and uncompromising in their convictions despite the costs that were inevitable
in those days."

At times Davis would readily accept his role as Debuskey's coach
in racial matters. Once, during the time of the Selma marches in
the spring of 1965, an emergency SNCC meeting was held in New
York. It was attended by Stokely Carmichael, a leader of the march,
who, said Debuskey, "instigated and personified the rallying cry
'Burn Baby Burn,' a distant creed from that of Dr. King, understood
by blacks but frightening to whites and used by the march's opponents to vilify its participants. So concerned were the New York
supporters that a meeting was called and Carmichael summoned
off the march to attend and explain himself."

Just before stepping into the meeting room, Davis whispered a
caution into Debuskey's ear: "Remember, Merle, you ain't black."

Debuskey became a member of SNCC's Committee of Communications Consultants, along with Robert Gottlieb, who would later
become editor of the *New Yorker*; the black journalist Elizabeth
Sutherland; and others. Each was given specific assignments for
securing coverage in major media outlets.

When a major event celebrating SNCC's fifth anniversary and
featuring a gaggle of Broadway stars was set for Town Hall in New
York on January 31, 1965, the committee recognized it as Debuskey's
natural territory and gave him the job of publicizing it. Scheduled
to appear were Alan Alda, Alan Arkin, John Henry Faulk, Gloria
Foster, Julie Harris, Rita Moreno, Diana Sands, Davis, and Dee.
Debuskey admits the task wasn't that difficult, given the personnel.

"There was ample, easily obtained advance publicity; the evening sold out, and many people were turned away." For his efforts Debuskey received simply a note of thanks.

After Carmichael defeated Lewis for the post of chairman in 1966, SNCC's character changed. It became more radical and more impatient in its demands, and it no longer eschewed violence. "This altered climate made me superfluous," said Debuskey, and his association with the group ended.

Debuskey remained in contact with Joanna Grant, a black reporter who wrote for the liberal journal the *National Guardian* and who was involved with SNCC. In November of 1966 Grant asked Debuskey if she could come to the office with Julian Bond.

Bond, a founding member of SNCC, had been elected to the Georgia house of representatives in the fall of 1965. The next January, just before taking office, he endorsed a SNCC statement criticizing the Vietnam War and opposing the draft. He said he "admired the courage" of draft-card burners. As a result, the house barred him, saying that because he had advocated violating the Selective Service Act, he could not conscientiously take an oath to support the United States and state constitutions. A special election was held to fill the vacancy, and Bond won again—and was barred again. He was chosen by the voters for the third time in the election of November 1966, defeating his opponent by 2,139 votes to 948.

Martin Luther King had joined Bond in a motion before the Federal District Court to force the legislature to seat him. That court had denied his motion, ruling in a two-to-one decision that the courts had no power to overrule the house's decision that he could not conscientiously take the oath.

The Supreme Court had heard the case on November 10, and a decision was expected the first week of December. Bond met with Grant and Debuskey a few days beforehand to discuss what his public reaction should be upon hearing the news—whether the vote was yea or nay. Said Debuskey, "We worked out two statements for Bond to have ready for release when the court's decision was handed out." The trio sweated over the idea that Bond might pull out the wrong speech at the moment of truth, so they painstakingly worked out a system.

> One [speech], if the court vindicated his right, was written on blue paper; the other, if his motion was denied, was written on white paper. He was to carry the blue in his left pocket and the white in his right. The paper's color and the pocket carrying it were differentiated so as to remove the possibility of confusion and error in the excitement and chaotic atmosphere that predictably would ensue with the decision, especially if he was upheld and the Georgia legislature forced to seat him.

To make certain the statements weren't confused, Debuskey even stored the statements in different drawers in different desks.

On December 5 the court unanimously ruled that Bond's constitutional rights had been violated. Bond drew out the statement on blue paper and read it. "For a day or two, I thought myself pretty grand," said Debuskey.

———

In January 1966 Debuskey once again met up with Jim Proctor and Joanna Grant. All three had been invited to be the press representatives for an event sponsored and set up by a group called the Committee of the Professions. The evening was called "Read-In for Peace in Vietnam" and was scheduled, as the SNCC event had been, to play at Town Hall. The date was Sunday, February 20, 1966. The committee formally described itself as

> a spontaneous association of individuals—artists, writers, scientists, doctors, professors, teachers, clergymen, social workers—who are dismayed at the increasingly dangerous course of the war in Vietnam. The unifying conviction of the Committee is that a peaceful solution is the most immediate necessity confronting mankind. We oppose a policy that is inexorably leading to the United States' involvement in a major land war in Asia and ultimately to nuclear destruction.

The list of writers scheduled to read sections of their work read like a who's who of contemporary literature: Hortense Calisher, Jules

Feiffer, William Gibson, Lillian Hellman, Alfred Kazin, Stanley Kunitz, Robert Lowell, Norman Mailer, Bernard Malamud, Arthur Miller, Joel Oppenheimer, Susan Sontag, William Styron, Louis Untermeyer, and Robert Penn Warren. Actors who volunteered either to read material from writers who could not be present or to perform their own material included Ossie Davis, Ruby Dee, Hal Holbrook, Viveca Lindfors, Elaine May, Tony Randall, and Maureen Stapleton.

"It became a powerful attraction," Debuskey recalled. The 1,500-seat auditorium was packed, and a crowd of people of all ages who were unable to get tickets gathered around the outside of the theater. Debuskey squeezed in the important domestic and international press while taking note of members of the opposition. "The house contained a substantial number of representatives of the various police agencies, both those who identified themselves—some in uniform, some not—and an unknown number of those from undercover agencies who we rightfully assumed would be there incognito. For them, this gathering was a veritable bouillabaisse of un-Americans."

The news coverage of the event, however, was upstaged almost entirely by an unscheduled, weirdly comic interruption in the proceeding.

Debuskey was in the green room, making sure that the order of speakers was being followed, when a messenger arrived and said there was a problem in the outer lobby. He sprinted upstairs to witness the doorman and a couple of ushers in an animated discussion with someone.

They turned him over to me, and he identified himself as Detective John Heslin of the city's bomb squad. He told me that the squad had received a bomb threat that afternoon during a concert by a Cuban singer. After the search came up negative, he had decided to relax with a drink or two at a bar across from the hall. He showed me his badge—and incidentally displayed his gun holstered at his waist. He was speaking in a friendly but insistent fashion, and he said he wanted only to continue his assignment inside the house.

Debuskey sized Heslin up. If his present state of inebriation was the result of one or two drinks, they must have been served in tankards.

Trying to prevent an incident, Debuskey walked him inside the hall and into the stage-door corridor, where he could keep him out of sight. He waylaid the drunken detective with chitchat and soon discovered that they had something in common: they had both taken part in the same invasions in the South Pacific. Heslin had been a frogman, an underwater demolition operator. He and Debuskey were now buddies.

But the press agent began to worry about the situation in the green room. He asked someone to find Proctor, a big man who was familiar with the behavior of drinkers; he'd serve as a good bodyguard for the policeman. Proctor arrived, and Debuskey briefed him and then went down to the green room. "Along with those assembled, I was listening to the people onstage when suddenly the speaker was interrupted by what we at first thought was someone delivering an impromptu comical improvisation." After about a minute, he recognized the voice: Detective Heslin. He had seized the mike and was waving his arms like a conductor (flashing glimpses of his gun), encouraging the audience to join him in a sing-along of "God Bless America!" Then another voice announced that he was the poet Joel Oppenheimer and was ordering the intruder off the stage. "I rushed up into the wings in time to nab my recently discovered Navy buddy as he exited the stage. I put my arm around him, congratulated him on his performance, and steered him out into the stage-door alley, where we were greeted by three or four uniformed police officers and a couple of unidentified men in suits."

The officers had been in the house and had seen Heslin's performance. Unsure of what to do next, one of them called the precinct; a captain would be there in a matter of minutes. Oscar Sachs, the chairman of the antiwar group, arrived on the scene while officers walked Heslin back and forth in the alley and gave him black coffee. The captain arrived, spoke with the cops, and apologized to Debuskey and the other organizers for the incident. He then asked if they wished to press charges. Recalled Debuskey:

He told us that Heslin had been cited three times for outstanding bravery, that he had an unblemished record, and that he was a good family man with two children. He explained that if we pressed charges there would have to be a departmental trial, with the possibility of a dishonorable discharge. We asked, "What if we did not?" The answer was a promise that the detective would receive proper disciplinary action, probably involving a loss of rank.

They agreed not to press charges.

The next morning, headlines in the conservative newspapers were almost gleeful. These were followed almost every other day by stories recounting the support given Heslin's "heroic" action by groups like the three-thousand-member Detectives Endowment Association, the Catholic War Veterans, and—his loudest admirers—the *Daily News*. On February 22 the *News* printed a story filed under the headline "Chorus Rallies for Cop Who Stole Pacifist Show." It included the sentence "Police of the W. 47th St. station, who had been summoned by Merle Debuskey of 246 E. 46th St., arrived and took Heslin into custody."

But 246 East Forty-sixth Street was not the address of Debuskey's office. "The address cited was my home address," observed Debuskey, "even though all the press material I had issued carried my 300 West Fifty-fifth Street office address. And I had not summoned the police—he was taken into custody by the officers who had been assigned to the event and had witnessed his action."

Debuskey soon began receiving threatening phone calls at his home, late-night ringing of his doorbell, and frightening, crudely written letters.

———

The year 1968 has frequently been cited as one of the most tumultuous in American history. The presidential race was first upended by the Minnesota Senator Eugene McCarthy, an unusually diffident, eccentric Democratic politician who did the unthinkable by entering the contest in direct opposition to a sitting president from his own Party. His aim was to influence the administration to curtail its aggressive course in Vietnam. The results of the March 12 New Hampshire primary shocked the nation: McCarthy came within a few hundred votes of beating President Lyndon B. Johnson. On March 31 Johnson chose not to run for reelection, and the race broke wide open. The Democratic presidential candidate Robert F. Kennedy was assassinated just weeks after the murder of Martin Luther King. The Democratic National Convention in Chicago was plagued by student riots and police brutality.

Debuskey, Jimmy Proctor, and their fellow press agent Harvey Sabinson were drafted to handle an August 15, 1968, rally at Madison Square Garden in support of McCarthy. McCarthy was running against the Party's nominee, Vice President Hubert H. Humphrey. "I had worked on political events before," recalled Debuskey, "but never in an attempt to elevate a candidate to the most powerful office in the world. I favored almost anyone who was against the war in Vietnam. I did not trust the machine candidate, Humphrey. And I had been impressed by positions taken by McCarthy."

Kermit Bloomgarden, who was running things, had commitments to appear from Colleen Dewhurst, Melvyn Douglas, Arlo Guthrie, Dustin Hoffman, Eartha Kitt, Garry Moore, Tony Randall, George C. Scott, and Dick Van Dyke. The senator had promised to throw out his standard campaign speech and instead make an important statement.

The evening would not go as planned. The first surprise to Debuskey was the absence of any McCarthy campaign publicists. "It was left to us to handle all the up-front and complicated arrangements for the press. And this was a keystone event in the campaign. It all was a bit beyond our everyday activity, so it was on-the-job training."

The evening was a huge, sold-out event. The Garden held twenty thousand people, including hundreds of journalists and camera crews. "The audience exuded excitement," Debuskey remembered. "The entertainment was delightful and the joint was jumping. We enjoyed talking with the political media and hearing their tales of the McCarthy staff's fuck-ups." But as the press deadlines approached and the entertainers continued to hold the stage, the reporters grew testy. Where was McCarthy? Why hadn't he spoken? "I located McCarthy's press secretary, who was fascinated by the crowd's enthusiasm. I tried to make him understand that if the media did not get McCarthy's remarks in time to make their deadlines, they would wrap up and leave. They were not drama or cabaret critics and could not care less about the entertainment. He was adamant about not wanting to cut it off and disappoint the crowd."

A CBS reporter with whom Debuskey had worked on several theater and civil rights events suggested that he take a shot at appealing to McCarthy directly. Debuskey, who had never met the senator, found the truant at the stage entrance, deep in conversation with Arthur Miller. Miller recognized the publicist and introduced him to McCarthy. "I explained the problem—but McCarthy did not seem to care."

"The twenty thousand people in the hall do not need any convincing to vote for you," Debuskey told the politician. "Their minds were made up when they bought their tickets. The media already had more of the celebrity performers than they could use. We are about to lose the opportunity to reach many millions of voters who had not yet made their decision, and this is a rare opportunity to tilt them in your direction."

"Listen to him," Miller told McCarthy. "These guys know their business."

McCarthy said that it was too late to give his full speech to the press—it was too long. "I suggested that since the press could not use more than a couple of minutes, why not give me a couple of attention-grabbing excerpts for them. He did, most likely to get rid of me and resume his conversation with Arthur. I ran his copy back up to the press room, and one of the reporters read the excerpts out loud, to the relief and satisfaction of all." One reporter from *Newsweek* commented, "With press agents like you, the theater will never die."

━━━

The oddest chapter in Debuskey's career as a political publicist, and the one that likely earned him the most black marks in his FBI file, began one day in late August of 1972, when Cora Weiss, an activist and the daughter of Sam Rubin and the stepdaughter of Rubin's new wife Cyma Rubin, called and asked to meet the publicist at noon the next day at a satellite building of the United Nations. The purpose of the confab she wouldn't reveal.

Debuskey's most recent contact with Weiss had been with Women Strike for Peace. She was focused on ending the Vietnam War and had fashioned close contacts with representatives of North Vietnam. Recalled Debuskey, "When I arrived at the United Nations, a raggedy press conference was wrapping up. I recognized those conducting the conference—the group was from the Committee of Liaison, co-chaired by Cora and by David Dellinger. It was an organization devoted to the families of American servicemen imprisoned in North Vietnam."

When the room cleared, Debuskey sat down with Cora, Dellinger, and another member, Vincent McGee. Dellinger was a longtime pacifist with a history of confronting the government. He had been imprisoned as a draft resister during World War II and had been the leader of the Chicago Seven, whose disruption of the 1968 Democratic National Convention had resulted in a notorious five-month trial in which all were convicted of "inciting to riot." He had also become the most famous individual to use a fast as a pacifist weapon since Mahatma Gandhi, and his daily progress had been faithfully reported by the media.

Debuskey asked questions. Their replies were strange and unin-formative. Seeing confusion on Debuskey's face, they pointed to the lamps and overhead lights. "I grasped that they were worried that the room might be bugged." Someone suggested they write their words on pieces of paper, then tear them up, and chew and swallow them. "No," Dellinger hollered. "I cannot. I'm on a peace fast." So the group moved to a coffee shop that was presumed clean.

"The story that unfolded might have delighted John le Carré or Graham Greene," recalled Debuskey. "Somehow the committee had arranged with North Vietnam to permit them to invite a parent or wife of each of three prisoners of war to accompany them on a trip to Hanoi and bring back the prisoners." Debuskey was to work on press relations with McGee, who worked out of the committee's office. Debuskey enlisted the subordinates in his office, instructing them that no one was to talk to the press without the approval of either him or McGee.

There were no commercial U.S. flights into Hanoi. The American Air Force patrolled air access to the capital, and any unscheduled flights would be turned away or shot down. The airport security at Kennedy Airport would have to be contacted and arrangements made to secure both the departure and the return and to provide contained press access. One of the mission's most delicate decisions was to select a pool reporter to accompany the committee and file daily reports. "It had to be someone who was a prime journalist, one who had experience in covering the war and would be neutral if not sympathetic to the committee's position. We were to try to have the trip shot from beginning to end by a TV camera."

The choice of reporter was narrowed to two: Peter Arnett of the Associated Press and Mike Wallace of CBS News. "We elected to take along Arnett," said Debuskey, "who had been in Vietnam reporting the war honestly. I had to tell Wallace that he was not to go. We trusted him, but not CBS. I don't think he held it against me, as he later included me in a tennis doubles game booked by the *60 Minutes* gang."

Weiss and Dellinger coordinated the plan with the North Vietnamese. They found a travel agent willing to book the tickets for the flight to Vientiane, Laos, and then by Aeroflot, the Soviet airline, to Hanoi. Cora Weiss's husband, a lawyer, and Debuskey went to Kennedy Airport and met with the captain in charge of airport security. "Surprisingly, we were greeted with cordiality and cooperation in making sensible and satisfactory security and press arrangements."

Debuskey was left on American ground to arrange for television coverage and to find some money to help cover the cost of the tickets. The sum had not yet been raised, and the wealthy media outlets he had approached—*Life*, *Time*, and *Newsweek*—had all turned him down. On the day of the flight, the final payment for the tickets still not in hand, Debuskey met with CBS-TV News and made a deal. "We would give them exclusive television coverage for a price—enough to cover the shortage for the tickets—but they could not send a crew. A couple of committee members were experienced and could handle a camera, and if they had trouble could get help when they arrived in Vientiane."

A technician was sent to get a camera and show Debuskey how to use it. Then it was discovered that there was not enough film on hand at CBS to go along with the camera. Someone ran to a photo supply shop to buy some. Debuskey began to sweat. "Time was flying, and I had yet to pocket the cash and get it to airport in time. When the film arrived and a check was drawn, the bank had closed. I was almost traumatized by the thought of my not getting to the airport with the money and having the entire carefully constructed plan crash down on my head."

An artful CBS News producer persuaded someone in CBS's financial department to call the bank, which agreed to get the money ready, let Debuskey in, and give him the cash if he had the check in hand. After a hectic limo ride to Kennedy, Debuskey arrived just in time and turned over the cash. The group was given the tickets and finally boarded the plane. "Off it went. The action was launched. The scheme was in place."

The committee members on the trip were Weiss, Dellinger (both familiar with Hanoi), William Sloane Coffin Jr. (the chaplain at Yale University), and Richard Falk, a professor of international law at Princeton. There also were the mother of one prisoner and the wife of another. The father of the third had been unable to get away and canceled at the last minute.

On Sunday, September 17, the *Times* broke the story of the group's arrival in Hanoi and included the report that "the immediate Hanoi area was placed off limits to United States fighter bombers today for the arrival of Americans to pick up three captured pilots. . . . There was no word how long the off-limits order would remain in effect." The article was accompanied by a three-column picture of the former prisoners in civilian clothes. The next day all the papers front-paged the AP story: the *Times* headline read, "Hanoi Frees 3 P.O.W.'s; Wife and Mother Greet 2." The story was picked up and played similarly by journals around the country and abroad. On September 20 the *New York Post* informed its readers that "there was increasing evidence today that a Soviet Aeroflot airliner expected to carry three released prisoners of war out of North Vietnam Saturday may bypass Vientiane and make its first landing in Burma or India. This would deny U.S. officials the opportunity to take control of the three men in the Laotian capital and get them away from the American antiwar activists who are escorting them."

This is where the preplanned intention to slightly deceive CBS came into play. Explained Debuskey:

> Before leaving Hanoi, the TV film would be given to someone who would fly it back to Vientiane and turn it over to CBS reporter John Hart, who was coming from Japan to receive it. The only difference with the original deal with CBS was who would carry it from Hanoi. The assumption was that the committee would bring it when they returned to Vientiane. I did not think the slight change was a violation of the trust and the financial arrangement. As a matter of fact it was better, because this way the military was denied the opportunity to seize the group and their belongings, including the film.

On September 23 the *Daily News* reported, "American officials have been staked out at all stop-offs along the homeward bound route of the three United States pilots freed by North Vietnam, to remind them they are still U.S. military officers and should avail themselves of government medical and travel facilities." The *New York Post* located the travelers with the September 26 front-page headline, "PWs Out, Land in Peking." From Beijing they flew to Moscow and then to Copenhagen (instead of the planned-for Sweden), where they transferred to a Scandinavian Airlines plane. It was immediately boarded by American military officials, who ordered the former prisoners to change into the military uniforms that the officials had brought with them. In Copenhagen they had been offered the chance to fly home on an Air Force jet, but they had chosen to remain with the group that had freed them.

McGee and Debuskey kept track of the plane's scheduled arrival at Kennedy Airport and arranged to get there an hour before it was to land. But the airport was besieged by just about every police agency: federal officers, military police, the shore patrol, the New York City police. The arrivals building had been cordoned off.

Recalled Debuskey:

I went to the entrance and was blocked by heavily armed soldiers and several men in street clothes with identifying lapel pins who had transmitters in their hands and receivers in their ears. My importuning and pleading went for naught. Their expressionless faces did not even register my being there. Just then I spotted a commotion and discovered that the father of one of the former prisoners had arrived with two beautiful young women and was informing everyone, including the delighted photographers, that he had brought a welcoming gift for his son and insisted on being admitted. He was volubly angry at being refused.

The comely ladies also began to attract the attention of the media.

Debuskey shouted to one of the officials that he knew the man and could quiet things down if they let him in. The press agent and the others were then taken to a corridor outside the glass-walled press room, which was jammed with reporters, camera crews, and photographers. Still, Debuskey was not able to communicate with anyone in the room or on the arrival ramp. The atmosphere inside was developing into a sauna, and the crowd awaiting the appearance of the former prisoners grew impatient and testy. Said Debuskey:

I spotted Gabe Pressman of NBC and waved to him. He recognized me, knew that I was handling the press, and came to the door; he opened it a crack and asked me why there was a long delay. I told him that I was being prevented from coming in and that the committee and the former prisoners had been instructed not to come up to the press room until McGee or I came down to accompany them.

Pressman and a couple of other reporters rushed the door and argued with the officers. McGee and Debuskey were then admitted, and McGee went down to get the former prisoners of war. Soon Weiss, Dellinger, and the other committee members arrived in the press room. Dellinger informed the reporters that the former prisoners "had been promised that they would be free to speak to the press" upon landing and could also "go to a private room where they could talk to other prisoner-of-war families," but the military had reneged on the promise.

When the melee subsided, the committee, the men's families and the committee staff reassembled in the bar of a nearby motel "to tell their tales." Said Debuskey, "We were pleasantly astonished when the former prisoners entered the room, free and easy, to join in celebrating their return. For reasons of its own, the military (and, we suspected, Washington) had decided, after taking them to the hospital, to give them restricted travel liberty for a couple of days."

For Debuskey, the circumstances "exceeded that of all but a few theatrical adventures. The only discernible untoward effects were the confused fouling up of my phone system and, I would hazard, the addition of a few of the blacked-out lines on the report I obtained under the Freedom of Information Act."

———

Given Debuskey's love of causes involving the rights of the downtrodden and abused, it's no surprise that he was a fervent advocate of labor. In 1978 he was elected president of ATPAM. He would be reelected again and again, eventually serving continuously for twenty-five years, longer than any president in the union's history.

Debuskey bordered on the blindly romantic when it came to the subject of organized labor. It was nearly impossible to convince him that unions were fallible. He'd formed this viewpoint when he was still a teenager.

> My attitudes about unions was developed early on when I was in high school and the period between it and college when I worked in a whiskey bottling plant, in a clothing factory, and in a cardboard box–manufacturing business. All were non-union and strongly anti-union enterprises wherein the workers were at the mercy of their employers and suffered for it. I had read, somewhat romantically, about Samuel Gompers, Clarence Darrow, John L. Lewis, John Reed, Big Bill Haywood, Sacco and Vanzetti, the Pullman Strike, and John Steinbeck's moving *Grapes of Wrath*.

Once he arrived in New York, there was no avoiding unions, for though the professional New York theater is primarily a bastion of art, it is also a fierce beehive of labor strongholds. Stagehands, actors, ushers, musicians, playwrights, directors—each group has its union or guild.

ATPAM's majordomo was the secretary-treasurer, a post filled in Debuskey's young years as a press agent by Milton Weintraub, whom Debuskey described as a

> tiny, tough, spare, fiery, highly emotional, committed trade unionist born of the Socialist-leaning Yiddish theater. Uncle Miltie was a beloved and respected figure in the theater by management as well as other union leaders. He was a consummate actor, a tummler, demanding that both employee and employer fulfill the terms of the minimum basic agreement, and in contract negotiations his performance would have been envied by Maurice Schwartz and John L. Lewis.

Debuskey learned a lot about negotiating from Weintraub, who also assisted Debuskey professionally on a couple of important occasions. "He allowed me to work for nothing in the first years of Free Shakespeare in the Park, and when it had grown in importance he created a special contract paying me a nominal $75 a week when shows were playing."

Debuskey remembered how a membership meeting was once such an event that it would temporarily stop business on Broadway: "A half hour before it was to begin, Times Square was dotted with a couple hundred members finishing lunch and ambling and gossiping along their routes funneling into the Newspaper Guild's meeting hall."

Being president of ATPAM often put Debuskey in the uncomfortable position of having to be purposely contentious with producers, employers with whom he hoped to retain friendly relations. Typically, union negotiations were spearheaded on the management side by Gerald Schoenfeld and Bernard Jacobs, of the Shubert Organization.

During one contract negotiation management was stubbornly and ignorantly insisting on eliminating the multiplicity condition for press agents, maintaining that a press agent could only serve one show at a time. Recalled Debuskey:

> The union negotiating team was headed by its president, me, the former ATPAM secretary-treasurer Dick Weaver, and our chief counsel, Jerry Lurie; Gerald Schoenfeld was the head of management's team. I pointed out that the condition did not cost management one penny, so cost could not be a factor in their reluctance to continue a condition that had been in play since the very first negotiated contract. Further did I point out that if I was working on a Feuer and Martin production and the Shubert Organization wanted to hire me to represent a show they were to produce, they would not be able to. If they were to succeed in eliminating multiplicity, producers would not be able to hire the press agent of their choice, an extreme disabling of the producer's right to assemble the staff of their choosing.

Schoenfeld would not see reason and held firm. Debuskey made more points: because of the union's self-imposed requirement of requiring the senior to add associates on a prescribed schedule, there would always be several on hand to cover the needs of multiple shows. But nothing cut any ice with the Shuberts.

Finally, remembering Uncle Miltie's tactics, Debuskey stood up, assumed an angry stance, pounded the table, proclaimed that they were insisting on staking out a position that was injurious to themselves and absolutely unacceptable to the union, offered up demeaning descriptions of each of the management team, refused to participate further, and left the meeting. "To my surprise and chagrin," recalled Debuskey, "no one else joined me in my walkout. One day later, Weaver called Schoenfeld and asked if he would meet with him and me. He agreed, and we met and concluded the contract amicably in one hour. Schoenfeld stated that he was making the case for eliminating multiplicity to satisfy a few minor members of the League [of Theatre Owners and Producers] who had proposed it and had to go through the motions. Understood."

Schoenfeld always introduced Debuskey to friends by smiling and saying, "This is a great labor leader."

—

Debuskey's connection to the political fights of the 1950s and '60s was not forgotten as he got older. In 1994 the New York Public Library gathered a group of artists and show-business professionals to discuss their experiences with the blacklist. Among them were Madeline Lee Gilford, Kim Hunter, Ring Lardner Jr., and Debuskey.

A couple of years later, a Debuskey comment in a *New York Times* article about the conference caught the attention of a group backing a new Freedom Museum to be housed inside the downtown Chicago's Tribune Tower. The museum had held an international competition for a central sculpture. The winning design was a metal tree that had two hundred leaves, each inscribed with a quote from an American, some notable, some not, about the nature of freedom. The museum collected thousands of quotes and whittled them down to a final couple of hundred. The quote from Debuskey, former "New York State subversive" and threat to national security, was among those selected:

> There was absolutely nothing that came out of this [blacklisting] except exploitation. No plot was unfolded. It was a hollow drum that was being beat, and beat loudly, which gave rise to headlines. Nothing happened. And the First Amendment, which had been in existence since the creation of the government and was one of the great documents in the history of man, was diminished. And the right of people to have their political convictions and not have to reveal them if they didn't want to do so was destroyed.

Chapter 8

JOE PAPP/HENRY V

It wasn't Shakespeare who brought Merle Debuskey together with Joseph Papp, the founder of the New York Shakespeare Festival. It was Sean O'Casey. Joseph Papirofsky—a CBS stage manager who was the ambitious son of a hardscrabble, Yiddish-speaking family from Williamsburg, Brooklyn—thought he could jump-start his career as a director by staging three of the Irish playwright's one-acts. The *New York Times* drama critic Brooks Atkinson was an O'Casey devotee, and Papirofsky, politically savvy even at that early date, thought such a bill stood a good chance of attracting the all-powerful critic's attention.

Papirofsky gathered three friends: Bernard Gersten and Charles Cooper, with whom he had worked at the Actors' Laboratory in Los Angeles in the late 1940s, and Peter Lawrence, who had been an assistant director at CBS and was now a Broadway producer. They raised $800 and in 1952 rented space in the Yugoslav-American Hall at Forty-first Street and Tenth Avenue.

Lawrence and Papirofsky were both in the Communist Party. So were half of the actors in the play. They needed a good, politically progressive publicist, so they called Debuskey, who had been making a name for himself on and Off-Broadway. Debuskey was another Atkinson: O'Casey was a god to him. So he said yes and met with the lion-maned, wild-eyed Papirofksy. Papirofsky talked fast, Debuskey slowly; the director was excitable, the press agent subdued; Joe was charismatic, Merle dignified. But the two men liked each other right away. Strangely enough, for two such high-minded men, their first bond was a love of bad puns. Nearly everyone of their acquaintance remembered, with accompanying winces, the constant barrage of wordplay, though no one can recall any specific pun. "We used to sit and exchange them for hours," recalled Debuskey. "He was very bright and very engaging, very personable. I had no indication at that time of what his inner strength was, a strength that was essential to the man he became and to what he managed to achieve."

Though O'Casey was the project at hand, Debuskey remembered Papirofsky talking endlessly about Shakespeare.

> He wanted to evolve a method of performance, a style of acting, that would be American, that would handle the classic language beautifully, that would not try to ape the British. And above all, that would not submerge the production in that method school of acting, which was ever-present on Broadway. Joe always maintained that everyone could relate to Shakespeare's works, that you didn't have to be a college graduate, you didn't have to be lettered in any way; your formal education could be minimal. Joe felt that Shakespeare wrote for the masses, for plebeians as well as for nobility, and that his work was universal.

Debuskey was paid for his work on the O'Casey evening. It would be years before he would be paid again for anything he did in connection with the future Joe Papp.

Papirofsky's plan worked; Atkinson showed. But the visit did nothing to boost the director's career. Atkinson called him and the actors amateurs, out of their depth. The review knocked Papirofsky back for a while, but it wasn't long before Debuskey heard from him again. The scrappy would-be impresario had asked the minister of Emmanuel Presbyterian Church, in the no-man's block of East Sixth Street between Avenues C and D, for permission to use the basement of the church as his own theater. He amassed a whopping budget of $160, shortened his name to the punchy Joe Papp, and asked Debuskey to come down and take a look at what he called the Shakespearean Theatre Workshop. The workshop was small in means but large in ambition. There was even a charter, which listed five goals:

To study Shakespeare and his Elizabethan contemporaries;

To train actors in an appropriate style to give expression to poetic verse and drama;

To put on plays from time to time;

To engage in educational programs for the dissemination of Shakespeare;

To create a replica of Shakespeare's Globe Theatre.

One day, not long after the workshop had started, Papp asked Debuskey to come down and take a look. Debuskey—not too far removed from his beginnings with the Interplayers in Greenwich Village—obliged. Papp had remodeled the space, replacing the rotting wooden pews with seats from an old movie theater in the Bronx that was being torn down. A few days later Papp sent Debuskey a plaintive note scribbled on the back of a Playbill: "Think you could help us get some attention for this? We'd like to ask the public in, not just invited audiences." There would be no pay, but Debuskey, always attracted by pluck and idealism, agreed.

At first, and for a while, the workshop did only excerpts from plays. There was no money for advertising, and the actors would give out handbills in the neighborhood to publicize the performances. Finally, in early 1955, they decided they were ready for a full production, and Papp chose *Much Ado about Nothing*. Louis Calta, a theater reporter and third-string critic for the *New York Times*, attended an October production of *As You Like It*. Between acts Papp, always willing to seize an opportunity, got up to explain the workshop's mission to the audience. Calta got the message. His review on October 20, 1955, said that he liked what he had seen, that the performance was "spirited," and that the actors possessed "enthusiasm, self-assurance and boldness...they bowl over the viewer with their infectious exuberance."

Thus began Debuskey's thirty-two-year relationship with the irrepressible, impetuous, capricious self-crowned prince of populist theater. Papp would become, through equal parts raw ambition, barnstorming idealism, skilled self-marketing, and sheer dumb luck, a major figure in American and world theater. At the time, however, neither Debuskey nor anybody else would have guessed it.

"The beauty of this story is that Joe was the least likely person to be ordained the high priest of the American theater," observed Debuskey.

> His formal education was limited to high school. He came from a background of poverty, growing up in the Williamsburg section of Brooklyn with his immigrant parents and moving from apartment to apartment during the Depression because they couldn't pay the rent. Until he became known, his social orbit did not include anyone with money. He was not, to begin with, well connected to politicians or to people of importance in the industry. No one connected with him in those early days had any ambitions beyond "what can we do next?" And Joe was very relaxed about it all. The enormity of the problem of getting all this done never fazed him. That was a characteristic that continued all through his life. He was one of the most magnetic men of his age, the kind of person of whom you said to yourself, "If he's going to do something, I want to go along, because we're going to have one hell of a good time."

Papp was not altogether unlike other flamboyant producers Debuskey had worked with before. He waved around fat cigars, quoted Shakespeare at length, and in later years would affect lavish sartorial dashes like a cape and a top hat without the slightest sense of irony. But the difference between Papp and such showboating, self-promoting fantastiques as Jed Harris and Mike Todd was the focus of their energies. Harris and Todd were commercial producers. They wanted to make a buck. If their efforts burnished their profile in the process, so much the better. But the buck came first. Papp was simultaneously selfish and altruistic. It was all about his dream by his rules, but the dream was there to serve the people. He wanted to bring high art to the huddled masses, a member of which group he'd only recently been. To his mind, they—he—deserved the classics as much as, or even more than, the swells in the box seats up in Times Square. Furthermore, he wanted to foster new artists— American artists, of all colors and ethnicities. In short, he wanted a democratic theater that would mirror the true face of the city.

Debuskey didn't have to manufacture enthusiasm for that kind of a vision. He had it in his bones. He may not have had to fight gangs and pluck chickens on the grimy streets of Williamsburg—grandiose claims of abject destitution that Papp later made with glee—but, growing up in segregated Baltimore, he knew the United States was a world of divisions, of differences that were currently shunned but ought to be celebrated.

It wasn't long before Papp grew dissatisfied with performing in a church. He wanted that larger audience he had spoken of, the people for whom he felt Shakespeare had been written. They were easily found, of course; they were just outside, on the streets of the East Village and the Lower East Side. In 1956 he told Debuskey that he wanted to do full-fledged productions out of doors, with free admission. Everyone would be welcome. All they would have to do is stumble in, and they would see the best production of Shakespeare that he could do.

"Joe, you're crazy," said Debuskey. "What are you talking about? You can't do that. It's going to cost money. And where the hell are you going to do it?"

"We're going to do it in the public parks," said Papp.

"You can *want* to do it in the public parks, but getting permission is something else again," argued Debuskey. "There's a whole bureaucracy you'll have to crack."

But Papp wouldn't be discouraged.

He had either read or remembered everything that had taken place in the theater during the Depression, in the Works Progress Administration days. There were outdoor performances all over the country in those days, and there were still some remnants of that around. And he went ahead and talked the city into allowing him to use an amphitheater between the East River Drive and the East River that had been constructed in the 1930s. The shell was still there, backed right up to the river bank.

The East River Amphitheater was in a small park called East River Park at the foot of Grand Street. In 1936 Robert Moses, New York's master builder and head of the Department of Parks and

Recreation, decided it would be appropriate to build an amphitheater there. His goal—surprisingly like Papp's two decades later—was to bring culture to the residents of the almost entirely working-class immigrant neighborhood. His reasoning was that the people never got to see theater since they could not afford to go to the luxurious and expensive Broadway playhouses farther uptown, so why not bring a proper arena directly to them? But Moses's idea did not pan out, and the 2,000-seat amphitheater sat unused much of the time.

Getting approval to use the amphitheater was relatively easy. No one much cared about the Lower East Side anyway. Papp said he would provide his own sound equipment, his own lighting, and his own staff to hand out programs, though he had no idea where he would get such things. Now he needed money. So he and his actor friends went to the better-known performers with whom they had worked at times and persuaded them to join a committee Papp had created.

Debuskey was summoned to get the project some ink. The first article announcing the summer performances appeared in the *Times* on March 28, 1956. "Open-Air Theater to do Bard Here," the headline read; "4 Shakespeare Works to Be Given Free June 20–Sept 7 in East River Park." The article promised that "over a two-week period, the following plays will be performed: 'As You Like It,' 'Much Ado about Nothing,' 'The Taming of the Shrew' and 'Twelfth Night.' They will be repeated during the remainder of the 12-week stand." It also said $15,000 was being raised.

The article was the first in a cart-before-the-horse con that Papp and Debuskey would deploy again and again over the history of the New York Shakespeare Festival. They would announce in the press as factual an ambitious project and fantasy budget in hopes that the publicity would inspire an influx of funds and assistance that would actually make the thing a reality. The theory was not far from one Moses himself employed many times, in which he would begin construction on an as-yet-unapproved project to ensure that it would be completed. The team happily abused the Paper of Record in this respect. "We worked from the conviction that if the *Times* printed it, it was a reality," said Debuskey. "There was a high percentage of the stories becoming true."

In later years Debuskey's associates would recall him taking relish in plotting out the course of a Festival news story once the initial press release was issued. "If we do this," Debuskey would explain, "then the press will do that, then we'll do this, and then we'll get what we want!"

The *Times* eventually realized that it was regularly being taken in but, recognizing the worthiness of the cause, went along with the ruse. Herbert Mitgang, who edited the drama pages at the *Times* in the 1950s and '60s and later was elevated to the op-ed page, recalled, "I would get the annual call from Merle saying Joe Papp needs an editorial very badly about continuing Shakespeare in the Park. In his extravagant way he would say that unless he gets support from the public and the *New York Times*, Joe threatened to shut down Shakespeare in the Park. That was the annual message. It became a kind of joke between Merle and me."

No matter how much space the *Times* gave the Festival, Papp always wanted—even felt he deserved—more. He once fired off a note to Sy Peck: "Merle Debuskey informed me of the reasons you gave him for burying our season's opening in last Sunday's *Times*. I can only say that I feel the treatment was not justified and that I am sorely disappointed." Peck forwarded the letter to Debuskey, with a note: "Funny, I can't recall Mr. Papp ever writing to express pleasure at the huge breaks we have given him and you in the past." Yet the *Times* continued to take Papp's guff and hyperbole, partly because it was filtered through Debuskey's reliable voice. "Merle was the guy who guided us through the Joe Papp material," said Mitgang. "He knew the plays themselves, so if you asked him 'What is this about?,' he was familiar with the content. We supported it because it was obviously a good thing to widen the influence of theater in New York and bring in new audiences for free."

In 1956 not enough money was forthcoming to support four plays and nearly three months of Shakespeare by the river. The budget for the entire year, including the plays at the church, turned out to be $7,447. Papp decided to limit the Festival to three plays:

Julius Caesar, The Taming of the Shrew, and *Twelfth Night*. Papp hired the young director Stuart Vaughn to stage *Julius Caesar*. The cast rehearsed under the blistering sun, wearing little clothing and bearing bottles of suntan lotion and thermos jugs filled with cold drinks. For the technical aspects of the production, Papp depended on the kindness of CBS, his friends, and their donations. He still needed more funds, however. And there was no money for advertising; for that, Debuskey was responsible. Debuskey persuaded Meyer Berger, the legendary *Times* reporter and essayist, to visit the amphitheater for a dress rehearsal. And on June 29, 1956, Berger devoted one of his widely read and vastly praised "About New York" columns to a description of the workshop's delights.

"Somehow we got a production on," Debuskey recalled,

> and it was incredible. We had to walk across a bridge to get over to the East River Drive, and people would come walking in. We had tried to inform people with flyers, and we had people walking around various communities, and we tried to involve community organizations. Every language but Shakespearean English was spoken until the symbolic curtain went up. The rest of the time you were hearing a lot of Spanish, Yiddish, and some Chinese. And it was really quite marvelous. And as the play began and the sun began to sink and the light in the sky changed from dusk to darkness, with an occasional ship going by with red and green lights on the mast, it was quite beautiful. It really was. And we were kind of in awe of what we had done.

But there was no review in the *Times*. The critic for the *Village Voice* came, but none of the citywide newspapers sent reviewers. Papp's *Julius Caesar* was looked on as a spectacle for the masses, a charming and well-intentioned idea, worthy of a smile on a summer night; it was not theater to be meaningfully reviewed. And, as always, the money was running out. On July 10 Papp announced that unless he found $850 for costumes, sound equipment, and props, he would have to delay the opening of *The Taming of the Shrew*. Henry Hewes, the critic for the *Saturday Review*, had attended the dress rehearsal and liked the production, and although he had reservations about Shakespeare on such a large scale, he helped Papp get $500 more from ANTA. The opening was put off from July 27 to August 3. The third production, *Twelfth Night*, was dropped. J. D. Cannon was to play Petruchio. A young actress named Colleen Dewhurst, barely known at the time, had agreed to play Kate.

Despite the financial difficulties, the show went on. The audiences continued to come, but not the critics. Without additional funds, $750 or so, he would have to close things down; he would not be able to finish the summer. Debuskey got on the phone with the *Times* and managed to get Papp an appointment to see someone in the theater department.

On August 10, 1956, Debuskey got on the subway and took Papp to the Times Building on West Forty-third Street. "Joe never knew where the *New York Times* was," recalled Debuskey. "I ushered him." They got off at the third floor, where the newsroom was guarded by a man with a walrus mustache. The guard knew Debuskey and waved the two men in. They had been hoping to accost Brooks Atkinson and ask him why *Shrew* had not been reviewed. But it was August, and Atkinson was on vacation, as was Lewis Funke, the drama editor. Arthur Gelb, then a reporter and second-string critic in the paper's drama department, was left in charge.

Papp excitably walked over to Gelb and introduced himself. He told Gelb he *had* to see his Shakespeare production. Gelb, somewhat affronted, told Papp he couldn't possibly come that night. Maybe sometime next week. But Papp was adamant. "He said, 'No, no, no.'" Gelb recalled. "'You can't do it next week, because unless we get some financial support we'll have to close by then. And the only way we'll get the financial support is if we're recognized by the *Times*.'" Gelb repeated that there was no way he could come. So Papp, childishly and ingeniously, said he was going to sit there and not move until Gelb agreed to see the play that night. Debuskey overheard the outrageous demand and remained at his station, a couple of desks away, to witness the result. Sure enough, Gelb changed his mind. That night he went downtown.

"Everybody thought that actors getting together to do Shakespeare by the East River would be awful," Debuskey recalled. "But it wasn't awful at all. It may have been a bit raw on occasions, and I mean the style and the performances. But there was a kind of energy there that had not been seen in classical performances. They were reasonably young people, many of whom were talented. And it was glorious. And Gelb was somehow infected with this activity."

During the first act, however, a light rain had begun to fall. Papp had insisted that the production continue—after all, the man from the *Times* was finally in the audience. But just before the intermission, the heavens opened and rain came pouring down. Papp had no choice; there was no way the show could go on. Gelb told Papp he was going home and would return another night. Again, Papp browbeat the critic. He liked the show; why couldn't he review it anyway? Gelb sniffed that it was impossible. But on the taxi ride uptown, the critic changed his mind. He went to the *Times* and wrote a few hundred words about the show, mentioning they needed money. It worked. The producer Herman Levin read the review, phoned Gelb, and messengered $750 down to Papp. What's more, Atkinson had read the notice and, after questioning Gelb, took in the show himself. He wrote his own account in the Sunday paper.

Encouragement was oxygen to Papp's ambition. His mission grew. He would not wait for the city's congested neighborhoods to find his productions; he would bring the shows to them. The summer in the amphitheater had proved there was a hungry audience out there. Most of them, he reasoned, were basically the same types as the groundlings who'd crowded the pit of the Globe in Shakespeare's day.

"When the summer in the amphitheater ended," Debuskey recalled,

> Joe told me that he wanted to have a mobile theater tour the five boroughs and give free performances of Shakespeare in the parks. My immediate reaction was: "Joe, you're nuts. How the hell are you going to pull this off? We have no money, no equipment, no permissions." But Joe had truly remarkable and singular qualities—not only obsession and persistence, but imagination, initiative, and street smarts. He was fearless. He would approach anybody he thought would make his project flourish.

This time he again approached New York City's Department of Parks and Recreation to expand the 1956 program, to bring Shakespeare to all five boroughs, and to perform in Central Park as well as in the East River Amphitheater. He decided to abandon the church productions and focused on the next summer. There were to be fifty performers and technicians, presenting fifty-two performances. At roughly 2,000 people per performance, Papp anticipated an audience of more than 100,000, five times the number that had seen his Shakespeare in 1956. Papp prepared a budget and decided that he would need a minimum of $30,000 to present a season of three plays. He began writing letters to philanthropic foundations, visiting offices, and beleaguering every wealthy individual and every foundation he could find. Early on the Doris Duke Foundation came to his aid with a grant of $10,000. Then the New York Foundation said it would provide $10,000 more if Papp could raise $5,000 from other sources by June 1.

Papp got permission from Robert F. Wagner's administration and immediately penned a letter to the mayor. Dated April 6, 1957, it itemized his needs:

A tractor, to pull the thirty-five-foot-long portable stage he had planned to build on a trailer

A driver for the tractor

A pickup truck to haul the lights, sound equipment, and lighting board

A portable generator

An attachment on the back of the pickup to haul the generator

A sound system, perhaps donated from the city-owned radio station, WNYC: ten microphones, twelve horns, amplifiers, mixers, and booms

An electrician

Debuskey got the news announced publicly in the *Times* on April 12. The Summer Shakespeare Festival would perform in the East River Amphitheater and the Belvedere Tower area of Central Park,

Brooklyn's War Memorial Park, Williamsbridge Oval Park in the Bronx, Clove Lakes Park in Staten Island, and King Park in Queens.

Three plays would be presented: *Romeo and Juliet*, *Two Gentlemen of Verona*, and *Othello* (*Othello* was later dropped and *Macbeth* substituted). Stuart Vaughan would direct all three. "A thirty-five-foot trailer truck opening up into a 'Renaissance-style' stage 35 by 30 feet will be used," the article said. "The Parks Department, according to Mr. Papp, will provide the seating arrangement, which will be either bleachers or regular benches. Altogether, including the grass areas that will be available to spectators, it is expected that an average of 2,000 persons can be accommodated in each of the locations." At the time Debuskey distributed the news of this around to the various news outlets, Papp has none of these elements in hand.

Central Park, unlike the amphitheater, was in the middle of town. There would be little trouble getting publicity for the productions staged there. The performances would be presented smack in the center of the greenery, off West Eighty-first Street, beside a gentle lake and below an appropriately enchanting Renaissance-style castle, just south of the Great Lawn—on the exact spot where five years later the Festival's permanent Shakespeare theater would be built.

Opening night was Thursday, June 27, 1957, the first evening ever of Joseph Papp's productions of Shakespeare in Central Park. The weather was perfect, Debuskey recalled. The members of the audience had begun to enter the park early, many of them bringing picnic baskets and setting out blankets to dine before the performance. "The audience was not what is going there now, not the Manhattan intellectual elite," recalled Lee Silver, at the time a critic for the *New York Daily News*. "The audience was what Joe wanted. It was people who might be hanging out in the park. The people were working class. There were a lot of young people. The audience was racially mixed."

Half an hour before the 8:30 p.m. curtain, Papp and Vaughan were speaking to reporters from NBC and CBS Television who had arrived to record the event. Getting them to cover "the crowds in

the sylvan abundance of the park being seduced by the poetic work-
ings of Shakespeare" was not difficult, Debuskey recalled. It made
for a good TV news spot. There was a brief crisis when someone
noticed that the production's chief electrician, who had been having
problems ever since rehearsals began, had disappeared, taking the
lighting plot with him. It was an extreme case of backstage fright;
he would never return. Papp and Vaughan, still giving interviews
and pretending that nothing was wrong, arranged for the assistant
electrician, who had been on the job for only one day, to take over.
The critics rewarded the whole effort with kind words.

When it came to touring the boroughs, the cleverly created stage
turned out to be awkward and bulky, and it immediately began to
fall apart. As the *Romeo* tour came to an end with the final performances back in Central Park, Papp and the Parks Department
decided that it would be necessary to forgo the other boroughs for
the rest of the summer and present all the performances of both the
other plays beside Belvedere Lake.

Papp would return to the idea of a mobile theater in 1963, after
the Festival's future in Central Park had been secured. He still wanted
people in the outer boroughs to have access to free theater. Getting
crowds was not a problem. Attracted by a circus-come-to-town
motorcade of two white station wagons and four large brown trailers,
all festooned with balloons, making the trip uptown, followed by
actors in costume, kids and parents drinking soda and eating pop-
corn filled up the performances fast enough. But getting critics to
come out to locations like Mount Morris Park, near 118th Street in
the middle of Harlem, was next to impossible. "It was my job to get
the critics up there, and they just wouldn't go," Debuskey recalled.
"I literally had to pick the newspaper people up in my car, either in
their offices or somewhere, and I personally would drive them up
and into the park and pick them up after to escort them out safely."

Sometimes the neighborhood locals were hostile to the combination of Shakespeare and local parks. "We were going to a playground
in Brooklyn that was surrounded by a chain-link fence," Debuskey
recalled. "At night, the gates to the playground would be closed and
the youths would be locked out, so nothing untoward could happen.

At least that was the theory. But a gang had declared the playground its turf and had cut holes in the fence so they could sneak in at night."

The Festival's security people patched up the holes. But that afternoon the Festival got a frantic phone call from a youth worker who worked with the gangs. "He said we had a big problem; we had to get our asses out there, because the gang members were about to demolish the stage. So we went out and had a meeting with the gang. These guys came on very strong; they could be very frightening. 'Who the fuck did we think we were,' they said, 'taking over their turf?'"

Papp, a kid of the streets himself, wasn't about to back down, certainly not in his native Brooklyn. "He listened to them and he looked them right in the eye. 'What the fuck do you mean, your turf?' he said. 'Do you know where I was born? I was born right over in Williamsburg. Don't tell me about whose turf this is.'" The gang leader pointed to one of his members, calling him his war minister. Papp countered. "See this guy?" he said, pointing to the tall Jewish lacrosse player at his side. "He's my information minister."

Papp then hatched a golden compromise, converting the hostile gangsters into empowered allies. "He told them that if they wanted to do something, they could take charge of the playground, to police it, to make sure nobody interfered with the performance," said Debuskey. "That way, he said, their sisters, their brothers, everybody they knew could come and see the performance. 'Take over,' he said. And the leader and the war minister had a consultation, and that's just what they did. And everything went beautifully. That was...the kind of man Joe was. He was never intimidated."

New York City may have begun to love Joe Papp, but Washington did not. In 1958 Papp's Communist roots caught up with him. He was called to testify before the House Un-American Activities Committee—coincidentally, on the same day that Jimmy Proctor and Bernie Gersten were to testify.

By that time Papp had quit the Communist Party. When he received his subpoena, he called Debuskey and asked what he should do. "I said first thing you have to do is to get a lawyer," the press agent recalled. "Joe said he didn't know anybody. I said I would make a phone call." Debuskey called Ephraim London, a noted Brooklyn-born civil liberties attorney and First Amendment expert who had worked with Proctor and had experience before the committee. Over the course of his career, London would argue nine cases before the Supreme Court and win them all.

> London knew of Joe and knew what he had been doing. London said to me, "Is he a good fellow?" That was a code—is he politically correct? I said, "Yes, he's terrific. I don't know whether he's a member of the Party or not. You'll have to ask him that. But all of his philosophies of life are things with which I am totally in agreement, and I support him, and I'm sure you will too." So London said, "Tell him to call me, and we'll arrange things." I said, "Ephraim, he doesn't have any money." And London said, "Don't worry about it."

Debuskey worked with Papp the evening before the testimony, going over questions and answers, preparing him for the ordeal. Despite Papp's concerns, there was never really any doubt in his mind over what he would do: he would not name names, and when asked about his Communist past, he would refuse to answer, citing the Fifth Amendment. There was, for him, no other choice. Not apologizing for anything was one of Papp's lifelong creeds.

Debuskey supplied Papp with a modus operandi to use before the committee: try to bury the Communist thing under other information. "He was going to give them so much information about himself that had nothing to do with what they were after," explained Debuskey,

> that at some point the committee counsel would ask the chairman to direct the witness to answer. So we rounded up everything we could, all the magazine pieces, a film that had been made about Joe; there was a cover of a magazine the State Department made and sent over to Russia, and Joe was on it, to show how marvelous the Shakespeare Festival was and what a great American Joe was. We kept throwing this stuff at them, how this was a great American institution, and the best spirit of what America is. And at the end, one of the questioners

walked over to Joe and congratulated him, told him how much he appreciated all the good work he had done.

He had held his ground with the committee. But it didn't matter. The damage had been done. Later that day CBS dismissed Papp from his job as a TV stage manager. The next morning a report of the testimony and the dismissal appeared on page 1 of the *New York Times*. It was, perhaps, the one *New York Times* page 1 story Papp would gladly have done without.

Papp's union didn't react at first. But the members, who were angered by his dismissal, soon pressured the board to do something about it. The union, the Radio and Television Directors Guild, announced on July 10 that it would hold a referendum of its members to determine whether it should take the case to arbitration. The question, the union said, "is whether the guild should recognize the invocation of his constitutional privileges by a witness before a Congressional investigating committee as constituting 'good and sufficient cause' for discharge or 'gross misconduct' within the applicable provisions of collective agreements between the guild and the networks."

"I went to Jack Gould, the radio and television critic at the *Times*," said Debuskey, "and told him all about it. He didn't like blacklisting, and he thought that what was happening was atrocious and that this was a good time to get involved. He wrote a big article describing what these duplicitous acts were, and he got everybody in the TV industry excited and upset."

On July 29 the union decided to submit Papp's case to an arbitrator, and on November 13 the arbitrator ordered that Papp be reinstated. This made him the first person ever fired from a television network for refusing to testify about his Communist past to be reinstated in his job.

"When Joe was asked about his Communist background in later years," Debuskey said, "he would never apologize. He would always say he felt at the time that he was doing the right thing. In those years, he would say, he felt it was the only way to seek social justice in this country."

—

Debuskey now realized he was aligned with a man who possessed the energy and charisma to fight against powerful institutions and win. This was to be proved over and over again the next year, when Joe Papp took on Robert Moses regarding his desire to build a permanent outdoor theater in Central Park in the shadow of the Belvedere Castle.

Debuskey called the episode the best time a press agent could hope to have.

Papp first offered free Shakespeare on that patch of civic grass in 1957 when the mobile theater truck broke down near the Great Lawn. He continued his new tradition in the summer of 1958. Plans for 1959 were being made, and Papp was considering asking Moses about making the tradition a permanent one. If Moses agreed, it would be so, no questions asked; Moses was, and had been for nearly a quarter of a century, the most powerful man in New York. His name was a household word, not only in New York but through-out the United States, as a battler for parks and a champion of large-scale urban renewal. He raised bridges, dug tunnels, created beaches, and opened countless vest-pocket parks, all with very little oversight from either City Hall or Albany. Among his projects were the Bronx-Whitestone, Triborough, and Verrazano-Narrows Bridges; Jones Beach State Park; the West Side Highway; the Gowanus, Grand Central, Henry Hudson, Interborough, Laurelton, Northern State, and Southern State Parkways; the Brooklyn Battery Tunnel; and the Cross Bronx and Long Island Expressways. He was great and fearsome, and even his severest critics acknowledged his over-whelming influence.

Moses's top Parks Department aide, Stuart Constable, did not like Papp. An ultraconservative, both politically and socially, he was furious that this up-from-the-streets impresario, whom he per-ceived as a Red demon trying to destroy American society, had been given free rein by Moses in Constable's leafy fiefdom. Ever since the HUAC testimony, Constable had been looking for a way to scuttle Papp's plans, and he was confident that, if he managed to make the first move, his boss would back him, because Moses always supported his aides.

The previous June, after Papp's testimony had been reported in the press, Constable had said that no plans were afoot to drop the park productions. But the parks aide had simply been waiting for the proper time.

Early in March 1959—with Moses vacationing in Barbados—Constable abruptly announced to Papp that there would be no more free Shakespeare in Central Park. Admission would have to be charged. And what's more, the Parks Department would get 5 percent of the income to help pay for upkeep of the grounds and other expenses supposedly incurred by the city because of the Festival. Apparently, the high heels of female theatergoers were digging up the lawn. Constable figured that to Papp, the idea of a fee was anathema. He was right. When Moses returned a few days later, he acted as Constable had expected: he supported his executive officer unflinchingly.

A desperate Papp began a series of meetings with Constable in Parks Department headquarters, in a building called the Arsenal, just inside Central Park at Fifth Avenue and Sixty-fourth Street, next to the Central Park Zoo. But the antagonistic Constable refused to budge. It was now an edict: charge money or get out.

"They supported their demand with several justifications," recalled Debuskey. "We were cluttering the park, destroying the grass and so on. Which, if you take it to its logical extreme, you would exclude any human being from the park and let the blades of grass survive in their most pristine form. It would be great for squirrels. And one does not object to that, but it was not what its original purpose was. That park only had a life when people were alive in it."

Constable was a supercilious sort, with a reddish British-army-officer's waxed moustache. He reminded Debuskey of a "remittance man"—"from Sri Lanka or someplace, the youngest son of a family, who was a no-gooder, so they sent him down to the Bahamas or India." Debuskey recalled one unproductive meeting. "Constable had a Band-Aid on his finger. He wouldn't look us in the eye and kept picking at this Band-Aid, and finally he said thank you for coming and goodbye. He ushered us out and he *still* wouldn't look at us."

Papp, stymied, began to vacillate. Would a small fee be so terrible? At about the same time Walter Kerr, the theater critic of the *New York Herald Tribune*, had written a column imploring Papp to appease Moses and charge 25 cents. "Joe had to consider that he was faced with utter elimination," said Debuskey.

Debuskey hated the idea of charging a fee for the outdoor Shakespeare productions. As the Festival's press agent, he had predicated the enterprise's worthiness on Papp's selfless, tireless contribution to the city's cultural scene and the project's overall altruistic spirit. Exchanging money, however small an amount, for admission upset the equation. It endangered the Festival's future as a unique and pure—and *pressworthy*—endeavor. Madeleine Gilford recalled Debuskey complaining to her and Jack about the dilemma. "He brought us the *Times* and asked, '*Where is the free Shakespeare?*' And it was on the front page. He said, 'I got it there because it's *free*. Joe wants to charge a quarter. If they charge a quarter, it will be in the back of the arts section.'"

Gene Wolsk, then the general manager for the Festival, also attended the Parks Department meetings. He considered Constable "a pompous English type. After Joe's tenth meeting the message was the same: you can't come in unless you charge admission."

The three men left one particular meeting at the Arsenal in low spirits and began walking dejectedly down Fifth Avenue.

"We were all very discouraged," Wolsk recalled years later.

We were on the park side, on the cobblestones. And Joe said: "Well, so we'll charge. It's not the end of the world. What are we gonna do? It's the only way we're going to perform." And Merle said: "Joe, I've worked for you since the beginning. I've worked for you a long time. I've knocked myself out for you. I've worked for nothing. I don't mind. I'll do anything in the world for free Shakespeare. But I can't work for *cheap* Shakespeare."

The short protest moved Papp. After a few more phone conversations with Debuskey, he reconsidered.

"I really felt that this thing had to continue on in the fashion in which it was begun," recalled Debuskey.

> We worked close together on this—fourteen hours a day. The conversation went on to the wee hours of the morning, where we established the position that they should not charge. My argument was, Joe, the difference between nothing and twenty-five cents isn't two bits. Joe, your armor and your spear is "free." You can win battles if you're free. You could lose them if you charge a quarter. You have the world on your side. You can get all kinds of concessions on stagehands, ushers, musicians, treasurers. Once you start charging money, you have union conditions you're going to have to accept.

Papp convened his board and sent a letter to Moses. "The whole idea of charging came up for re-examination yesterday by members of our Board of Directors," Papp wrote. "It was resolved that the concept of paid admissions is utterly inconsistent with the stated objectives of the New York Shakespeare Festival—'to introduce classical theater to the vast uncommitted audiences through the free presentation of Shakespeare.'"

Debuskey's campaign began. He rallied the city's newspapers to their side, drawing on some of the fundamental rules Bernays had taught him a decade back at the New School: "Find important or well placed individuals to advocate your positions, individuals who had no inherent connections with your client which would, as they were independent authorities, lend great credence to your intent; and never underrate the power of working from the bottom up."

Bernays, in fact, was watching the Moses-Papp fight closely. One day the grand old man of PR called Papp to ask which public relations company he was using. He told the stunned Bernays, "My public relations is my press agent."

Sometimes Debuskey wrote impassioned letters defending the park program, had Papp sign them, and then dispatched them to the press; at other times Papp wrote the letters and sent them to Debuskey for his comments. He had a graphic artist make up a map of the playing area in the park showing the existing walks and suggestions for additional paths to the building, illustrating an orderly

Debuskey in his brown velvet tuxedo.
"He looked so good in a tuxedo, he
could model for bourbon ads," joked
the journalist Harry Haun.

Merle and Pearl on their wedding day.

Debuskey during the 1982 Times Square "Save the Theaters" protest against a plan
to tear down three old Broadway theaters to make way for a Marriott hotel.

Debuskey, in his "impresario coat," with Pearl Somner at Debuskey's surprise fiftieth-birthday party.

Debuskey admires the collage prepared by Pearl for his surprise fiftieth-birthday party.

Ossie Davis at Debuskey's fiftieth-birthday party.

Producer Joe Papp at Debuskey's fiftieth-birthday party. His and Debuskey's thirty-year professional relationship would be the longest of Papp's career.

Merle with the cast of *Sarafina!*

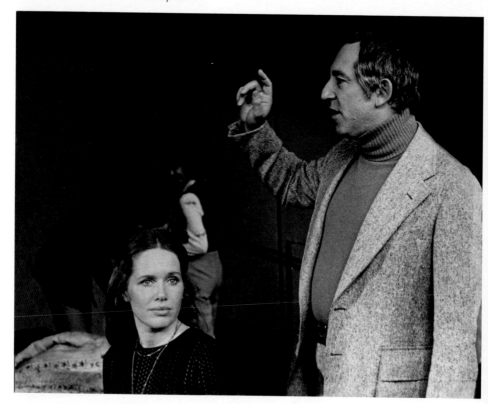

Debuskey working with Liv Ullman on a 1975 New York Shakespeare Festival production of *A Doll's House*, during the Festival's short-lived and tumultuous tenure at Lincoln Center.

The New York Shakespeare Festival's Shakespeare in the Park.

Debuskey with the producer Cy Feuer. A Debuskey outburst saved the title of Feuer's show *How to Succeed in Business Without Really Trying*.

PLAYBILL®

A TRIBUTE TO MERLE DEBUSKEY

Top: Debuskey with John Lindsay. After the former New York City mayor became the new chairman of Lincoln Center Theater, he consulted with the press agent on how best to revive the luckless theater. Eventually Debuskey would be hired as Lincoln Center Theater's press agent.

Left: The James McMullan portrait on the Playbill at Debuskey's farewell dinner on May 8, 1996.

Mac West,
Summer Stock, 1951

Liv Ullmann at
A Doll's House picture call

Priscilla Lopez & Donna McKechnie, closing
night *A Chorus Line*

Liz Smith at yet another opening.

with Mike Nichols

Larry Gelbart, opening night
Mastergate

PROGRAM

Opening & Closing Night
May 8, 1996
The Supper Club

The Perpetrators of this evening are:
Joe Benincasa/Alexander H. Cohen/Arthur Gelb
Madeline Lee Gilford/Jane Gullong/Shirley Herz
Sally Campbell Morse/Hildy Parks/Frank Rich
Lee Silver/Pearl Somner/Marilyn Stasio/Eugene Wolsk

INTRODUCTIONS
Alexander H. Cohen

BRIEF REMARKS BY

GENE SAKS

EUGENE WOLSK

CY FEUER

MADELINE LEE GILFORD &
MARY CLEERE HARAN

ROBERT KAMLOT

PAUL LIBIN

SALLY CAMPBELL MORSE

GEFFREY HOROWITZ

FRANK RICH

BERNARD GERSTEN

TOM DILLON

PETER HOWARD *AT THE PIANO*

The Perpetrators wish to thank
James McMullan, Jim Russek, Janice Brunell, Kristi Moore,
Playbill and The Actors' Fund

Pages from
the Playbill
distributed at
Debuskey's
retirement
dinner.

Debuskey at the Freedom Museum in Chicago.

Pearl and Merle.

flow of traffic that avoided the grass. It was sent out to the Parks Department as well as to the press.

"Joe was not afforded the protection or assistance of important personages when the argument commenced," recalled Debuskey.

> In the beginning, our only weapon and mercenaries were the press. Their participation led to the voluntary contributions from all levels of the community, quite a varied conglomerate. After a healthy dose of media support we were deluged with offers of help—some genuine and some smelling to me of being self-serving. I had to fend them off. The press had to be kept in sharp focus and control. There were some well-wishers who were offended by my shouldering them aside.

Moses fumed. Accustomed to praise in the press, he unexpectedly found himself attacked in the most bald-faced manner by everyone from Eleanor Roosevelt to Hedda Hopper. "All of a sudden," said Debuskey, "he was being confronted by this little ragamuffin [Papp]." What made the turn of the tide all the more surprising was that Moses had an entire political machine behind him, built up over decades, while Papp was backed by a single flack with an old Underwood typewriter. Debuskey and Papp scored hit after hit. They didn't know it at the time, but every day they bloodied Moses's motivations and intentions, they were cementing the Festival's civic significance, both present and future. Said Debuskey:

> There was one event after another, with everyone coming aboard, and after something happened we used it, whether it was an elementary Catholic school in deepest Brooklyn who had put their pennies and nickels together along with the sisters who helped support the thing, or something else. Help came from all sides, and every time something happened it was exploited fully. And it was known as the battle of David and Goliath—little Joe Papp and big Robert Moses. And all the Shakespeare Festival had on it side was its absolutely untarnished purity of purpose. And it fended off all kinds of weaponry. I think it tortured the shit out of Moses.

Papp sought the support of City Hall, but when Mayor Robert Wagner knuckled under to the unfireable Moses, they went to court with the help of the law firm of Paul, Weiss, which worked pro bono. The case was heard quickly to try to save the summer season. Moses took the first round. However, the Festival appealed, and Papp won the appeal. Moses could still have demurred and taken the fight to the next highest court. But he gave in. Papp was victorious.

"Joe was a terrific general," Debuskey said.

> The day the court decided in our favor, Papp sent a telegram to Moses inviting Moses to be his partner in producing an improved arena for Shakespeare in the Park. When Moses got the telegram, he immediately went to work on Joe's side. Joe had said, and was absolutely convinced, that Moses was a supporter of culture and would understand and appreciate what Joe was doing—that Moses had been misled, had gone out on a limb and couldn't get back. Joe said he would give Moses the opportunity to get back, and at that moment, when Joe could have rubbed Moses's nose in Joe's victory, he didn't do that. It was part of Joe's genius, his ability to seize the moment. He was still a modest fellow and had not become suffused with himself.

Before long, Moses would even agree to build a theater for Papp: the Delacorte.

The fight over Central Park had been harrowing, but it had also arguably made the Festival's reputation. "The Shakespeare Festival had an identity in the theater," said Debuskey, "largely because we made all our problems public. It was the nature of it. We were able to get a lot of help that way. It was almost a pure activity. What the battle with Moses did was make Joe a veritable household name, and make the Festival significant."

For years afterward, from time to time someone would put forth the bright idea of charging for admission for Shakespeare in the Park, and Debuskey and Papp would have to make their argument all over again. "I remember Merle making arguments that were very idealistic and purist in respect to the park," recalled Gail Papp, Joe's last wife. "There'd always be a board member who would say, 'Why don't you charge?' They'd have to be reeducated."

—

In those early days Joseph Papp was fun to work for, but he was never easy to work for. Debuskey might have been an unpaid volunteer, but that did not stop the producer from insisting on unending labor and unflagging devotion.

By the early 1960s Debuskey had left the small-time. He was a principal press agent in partnership with Seymour Krawitz, with clients that included Feuer and Martin. He was doing well and could easily have left the non-paying Papp behind. The Festival's mission, however, continued to appeal to his socialist heart. And so the phone under the eaves of the Forty-eighth Street Playhouse would continually ring with calls from the Man Who Slew Moses.

"Papp was very demanding," recalled Larry Belling. "I remember Papp calling Merle and saying, 'Why aren't I on the front page of the *New York Times* today instead of so-and-so?'"

Judy Davidson recalled instigating a mini-tempest when she sent out a Festival press release using the wrong language.

> Joe was very volatile. He said he wanted a release sent out because he was going to do *Much Ado about Nothing* with J. D. Cannon and Nan Martin. I wrote a release saying, "Joe Papp announced that J. D. Cannon and Nan Martin are going to star in 'Much Ado.'" Joe called and he was screaming. "I don't have *stars* in my shows! How could you send out something that says I have a star! I don't have stars!" I could hear him screaming. Merle said, "You know, Joe, I've worked for you for nothing for God knows how many years and you're going to make such big deal out of this? I quit." And Joe said, "You can't quit. I fire you." I said, "Merle, for God's sake, why didn't you tell him it was me?" He said, "Anything that goes out of this office is my responsibility." Joe called back several hours later and rehired him.

In May 1960 Robert Moses resigned as parks commissioner to head up preparations for the 1964–65 World's Fair in Queens' Flushing Meadow Park. But before he left, it was clear that Papp had the full backing of both Moses and Mayor Wagner in building a permanent theater in Central Park for the Shakespeare Festival. Moses's successor, Newbold Morris, appointed by Wagner, was both pro-Shakespeare and pro-Papp. The necessary $250,000 was approved by the Board of Estimate. When costs for the outdoor theater ran over, George T. Delacorte Jr., the founder and president of the Dell Publishing Company, provided an additional $150,000.

With the Delacorte built and established, Papp grew restless. He announced his 1963 season, starting with *Antony and Cleopatra*. Colleen Dewhurst, by then an established stage and screen presence, was to return to the Festival for the first time since 1957 to play the Egyptian queen. *Antony* would be televised locally on CBS, as *The Merchant of Venice* had been the previous year. But Papp had more than a small screen in mind for *Antony*: he boldly announced plans to send the play, with an integrated company of forty-five actors, on a tour of twenty southern cities beginning in January 1964. He also declared that the state department was considering a plan to sponsor the company on a later tour of Africa and Asia.

The plan, typically for Papp, was an audacious one given that the nation was in the thick of the civil rights struggle. And of course Papp had no money to fund it. But Papp and Debuskey didn't tell the press that. They never did. This time around, though, the ploy didn't work. Despite the backing of President Kennedy, by August 1963 only 17 bookings had been obtained out of the 285 schools and colleges contacted in twelve southern and border states and the District of Columbia. And only two of them had acknowledged in writing that the integrated company and nonsegregated seating were the reasons they were refusing to book the play. More important, though, Papp simply couldn't raise the money. His five-and-a-half-month campaign had brought in only $11,250 of the $50,000 he needed, and so with a one-page press release and a five-paragraph note in the *Times*, the plan was canceled.

The New York Shakespeare Festival won a permanent home in the late 1960s in a place that was fittingly improbable for such an improbably successful enterprise. The Astor Library on Lafayette Street had opened in January 1854 as the first free public library—built with a $400,000 gift by John Jacob Astor. After the library moved to Fifth Avenue and Forty-second Street in the early 1900s, the building was taken over by the Hebrew Immigration Aid Society

(H.I.A.S.), which provided temporary shelter for new refugees; now, in 1965, the society was giving it up. Preservationists considered the red-brick and brownstone library, with its facade of Italian Renaissance columns, one of the best early Victorian buildings left in the city. And following the controversial destruction of Pennsylvania Station—an event that birthed the city's landmarking movement—they were intent on preserving the structure.

Papp had become more and more convinced that he required a permanent indoor theater, and that he needed to present modern works as well as the classics. "He began to feel that he wasn't fulfilling his mission," said Debuskey. "He really wanted to establish his own theater. And he felt that a classical theater can't stand isolated from contemporary theater and contemporary times—a true theater would have both things simultaneously." Papp traveled all over Manhattan, along with Bernie Gersten, who had by then joined the company. But none of the buildings they inspected seemed right.

At the same time, the city's Landmarks Preservation Commission was trying to find a buyer for the Astor Library willing to consider preservation. At the September hearing both H.I.A.S. and the buyer, a real-estate development company named Lithos Properties, spoke against landmarking. But the next month the commission voted overwhelmingly to create its first official landmark. On September 29 Papp had phoned the commission chairman, Geoffrey Platt, asking for his help. He then sent a follow-up letter the same day. "The New York Shakespeare Festival is most interested in obtaining a structure to house its Winter Theater operation," Papp wrote. "The idea of collaborating with the Landmarks Commission of the City stems from our devout concern for the preservation of significant historical buildings as well as our present need for a theater."

On October 13 Platt phoned Papp and named some suitable properties, among them the library. Papp suggested that they immediately go look at it.

The building was practically abandoned. It wasn't heated, and it was very cold inside. There was an elderly caretaker with a Central European accent who lived in the hall. One room was the old synagogue. There were prayer books and prayer shawls everywhere. On the balconies were posters; on each poster was a picture, and under the picture was a description of it in English, so that immigrants could learn the first phrases of their new language. Debuskey, who joined Papp and Bernard Gersten on a second tour of the library, recalled that one poster showed George Washington; underneath it was written Washington's name and the phrase "Father of our Country."

"We really enjoyed wandering around it," Debuskey said. "There were marvelous kitchens down in the basement—one was for meat dishes and the other for dairy dishes, to respect and honor Orthodox Jews by not making them mix the two." For the three Jewish men, however irreligious, the décor and trappings of the old hall must have looked like favorable signs. Papp fell in love with the place, and arrangements were made with Lithos.

It was Debuskey's job to keep the press apprised of this odd fairy tale and to make sure it was on Papp's side—which, as ever, it was. He went beyond the newspapers' theater departments and talked to journalists such as Ada Louise Huxtable, the *Times*'s renowned architecture critic, persuading them to write about the possibility. On January 5, 1966, a news conference was held across the street from the library at the Cooper Union School of Science and Engineering. At Papp's side in the ornate nineteenth-century brownstone—a fitting neighbor to his new home—were the actress Julie Harris and August Heckscher, the executive director of the Twentieth-Century Fund and a former consultant on the arts to President Kennedy. Beside the school's aging columns, Debuskey handed out press releases with old drawings and photos, hundred-year-old depictions of what would become the experimental abode of contemporary American drama.

Before a score or so of reporters and a large number of onlookers, an excited Papp formally announced that he planned to build two theaters inside his new acquisition, one seating 200 and the other, 800. (The plans would change, and eventually Papp would have six theaters. The largest would hold 299 patrons; there would never be an 800-seat playhouse on the site.) He planned to have a children's stage, rehearsal halls, shops, classrooms, administrative facilities, escalators, and air conditioning. He would depart from Shakespeare, he said, charging an admission of between $2.50 and $3 and presenting modern plays and classics. A member of the Festival's board, Florence Anspacher (Papp referred to her only as an anonymous donor), had given a gift of $250,000, but he estimated that over the next three years he would need $2.375 million to both purchase the library and convert it to a complex of new theaters. Heckscher would head a committee to assist in fund-raising for what he described as "a new theater for a new audience that will belong to the people and to the city." The city's parks commissioner, Thomas P. Hoving, acting on behalf of Mayor John V. Lindsay, who had been elected two months earlier, sent a congratulatory message pledging his boss's support.

Preservationists were thrilled. Huxtable wrote that as far as she was concerned, the rescue of the library deserved a formal title: "The Miracle on Lafayette Street."

A visitor to the Public Theater (as it was called) at the start of the 1970s would have experienced a building throbbing with excitement day and night. It was "soul-fulfilling," in Debuskey's words, filled with creativity and vitality, with unceasing activity behind and before every door—even though getting the money to make all that happen was an ever-present problem. Throughout the 1970s Papp's footprint in the American theater only grew larger. At the start of the decade, the Public became home to its first Pulitzer Prize: the black playwright Charles Gordone's *No Place to Be Somebody* was based on his experiences in a Greenwich Village bar. In addition to the Astor Place productions and the free Shakespeare in the Park, Papp began to send shows to Broadway, a development Debuskey found amusing. "It was kind of funny. Papp was the guy who used to call Broadway 'the Fleshpot.' But he always had answers."

Around this time Debuskey finally began to receive a salary. Early on the press agents' union had intervened and cut a deal whereby he received $75 a week during the Festival's playing weeks. That, however, went primarily toward covering office expenses. Fed by his Broadway contracts, Debuskey wasn't hurting for money, but with the Festival becoming more powerful each day and his press responsibilities growing, it didn't make sense for him to continue working almost gratis. Additionally, as the new president of ATPAM, Debuskey was responsible for fashioning contracts that applied to its members' employment. To preach fair pay for the union while working below scale for his friend Joe was a position that Debuskey thought could be perceived as unethical. He needed a contract with the Public. He broached the topic with a typically garrulous letter to Papp; it opened with Debuskey comparing himself to Bert Lahr, that is, the Cowardly Lion. "How does a believer speak of finances to a continuous deficit operation?," he asked. He added that he himself was, as a result of his Festival expenditures, "in the deficit spending operations."

"I didn't get paid a salary until the late 1960s, after the opening of the Public Theater and the success of *Hair*," recalled Debuskey. "And even then I got just the Off-Broadway minimum scale. I never, in the history of my connection with the Festival, got more than scale. In other words, if someone had been plucked off the street, the union would have demanded that he get paid the same amount I got. Even thirty years later."

Hair was the first Public show to make it to Broadway. A groundbreaking countercultural rock musical by a couple of actors, Gerome Ragni and James Rado, about young people, hippies, and Vietnam protest, the work was in chrysalis; they had written the book and the lyrics and roughed out some music—some dummy tunes to go with the lyrics—but they had not worked with a composer. It was the kind of loosely formed, ambitious project that, at that time, could have been nurtured into being only by the Festival.

The music publisher Nat Shapiro introduced the two men to a composer he knew named Galt MacDermot. MacDermot, a writer of rock and jazz songs, a dance-band pianist, and a sometime church organist, had been looking for a show for which he could supply the music. It was an unlikely marriage. Rado and Ragni were quintessential hippies whose look and demeanor screamed East Village, Washington Square Park, and Sheep Meadow. MacDermot, as one interviewer remarked, looked as if he sold insurance. A native of Montreal who had resided in South Africa for four years and taken a degree in music at the University of Cape Town, he lived with his wife and his four children on a quiet, middle-American street in very unchic, very Establishment Staten Island.

The reviews were generally good, but the reviews really didn't matter. The public was coming to the theater to see it. *Hair* was a product of its time and spoke to the people who were living through it. It became a phenomenon, one that would make a lot of money for the producer moved it to Broadway. (But that producer, unfortunately, would not be Joseph Papp.) Though the Festival gained a few million in royalties, it lost out on many more. Papp never forgot it, and he would never again let an opportunity like that slip away from him.

The Festival would be in full control of the Broadway productions that followed. First came another McDermot show, a musical adaptation of *Two Gentlemen of Verona* that began in Central Park, and then *Sticks and Bones*, a Vietnam-drama by a young writer named David Rabe whom Papp had taken under his wing. Papp embraced wild ideas left and right. The Festival became a haven for artists looking for a producer-father figure, and Papp was happy to play the part.

Verona had been a surprise smash at the Park; critics called it an evening of unbridled joy. Debuskey and Bernard Gersten partly helped to pull *Verona*'s fat out of the fire during its move from the Park to Broadway by convincing Papp to hire the choreographer Dennis Naha to shape the production, which needed a firmer hand to meet Broadway standards. Recalled Debuskey:

> Bernie and I were convinced that the Park and Broadway were very different animals, and that while the musical didn't have a choreographer in the Park, on Broadway it needed a choreographer's fine hand. So we made the suggestion to Joe, but he said we didn't need a choreographer. He wouldn't hear of it. One preview evening, Bernie and I gathered up Joe in the inside lobby of the St. James Theatre, and we were talking, and Joe said, "I think we should look into a choreographer." And we said, "Hey, that's an idea." But Joe didn't know where to turn. So Bernie said, "Well, I think the perfect choice

for this would be a former dancer turned choreographer named Dennis Naha." Joe asked where we could find him. And Bernie said he was right there in the theater. And Joe spoke with him, and decided it would be a good move.

It was a prime example of what became Debuskey and Gersten's modus operandi: the two men acted as a tag team to steer their changeable and volatile boss in the right direction. "We would conspire," recalled Gersten. "That's what cronies would do. We had Joe's ear and knew how you approach the ears of those who are arbitrary, capricious, unreasonable, fruitcakes, all those things."

"We had a very effective relationship in maneuvering Joe," said Debuskey.

> Very often we would come up with an idea that we thought significant and positive. But because we knew that if anyone came to Joe with an idea that wasn't Joe's, the first response would be cool. So we knew how to present an idea and walk away from it—to plot how we could put Joe in a position where he could come up with a brilliant idea. It was a tactic we used frequently. And we knew that in a later conversation, Joe would say, "Listen, I have an idea."

Gersten and Debuskey has first met in the early 1950s, when Gersten was working as a stage manager on a Philadelphia show that Debuskey was flacking. Debuskey recalled his first impression. "We had similar backgrounds. He's very open, very garrulous, he has a good sense of humor, very bright, good company. Bernie was characterized by the marvelous joyful exuberance about being alive and working."

The two made an easy connection. "Merle and I are of similar age and we're both Jewish," said Gersten. "Politics bound us. I was a leftie and he was a less-leftie." The men had also both served in the war, Debuskey on a ship in the South Pacific, Gersten with the Army's Special Services assisting with Maurice Evan's touring production of *Hamlet*. They had also collaborated on the hit Off-Broadway production of *The World of Sholom Aleichem*.

Gersten had first connected with Papp in 1948 at the Actor's Lab in Los Angeles. He got his first paid job at the NYSF in the summer of 1960 as associate producer. The bonhomie between the three men—so like-minded, yet with such different temperaments—was infectious. "There was a lot of joking, playing, riffing off each other's lines," recalled Gail Papp. "Very convivial. There was a lot of camaraderie. And Joe was a very funny person. There was always a party atmosphere."

Joe and Merle made for a particularly enjoyable double act, given their sharply contrasting personalities. Nothing in Papp's rushed, manic nature could make the press agent give up his leisurely massaging of lingering elocutions. "Joe used to kid Merle about his speechifying and the florid vocabulary that he employed," said Gail. "I loved the way Merle talked. He was the only person I knew who talked in Edwardian phrases. It seemed to be quite natural with him."

Many Festival decisions were made at weekly staff meetings attended by Papp, Gersten, Debuskey, and Bob Kamlot, who was the company's first general manager in the early 1970s (later replaced by Jason Steven Cohen). "What I always remembered is Merle Debuskey a lot of time sitting, but a lot of time standing," said Cohen. "He was always in a jacket. He always looked great. He looked like he came out of *Gentleman's Quarterly*. And he had this extraordinary air about him. Confidence. Assuredness about what he was saying. A calm, almost comforting voice. It just smacked of knowledge of his craft."

Of course, it was Papp who would dominate these confabs, and listening to Papp hold forth was not always easy. His many flights of fancy were difficult for more pragmatic minds to hear. "People are frequently and customarily appalled by what they hear these very brilliant people say," recalled Gersten. "Joe Papp was brilliant in many ways, but there was much eye-rolling going on." Debuskey, however, had known Papp too long not to voice his opinion on an idea gone astray. "One thing I learned from Merle is you have to be honest and you have to speak your mind," said Kamlot. "If I was going to be fired, so be it."

Meanwhile, Papp was getting more press attention than ever. Magazine after magazine wanted to interview him. *Time, Saturday*

Review, and *Show* did major articles about him. *Time* called him a "populist and imperialist"; *New York* magazine, in an eight-page profile, announced that he was "the hottest show in town." *Newsweek* put him on its cover and declared that he and he alone was responsible for putting "new life in the American theater." The "brilliant and stormy producer," it said, "has emerged as the single most creative and controversial figure in American theater. At a time of esthetic and financial crisis, Papp is finding brilliant new writers, building audiences, winning prizes and telling off the critics."

"The media coverage of Joe was quite unusual in its volume, breadth, and tone," remembered Debuskey. "I think that it was rooted in the romantic image of this academically unlettered, untutored street guy becoming the self-anointed promoter of arguably the world's greatest dramatist. He was able to stride along his path with occasional foot-in-mouth. He even looked romantic. He was a perfect module for media attention, encouraging and reveling in it."

Debuskey never had to worry about the outcome when he set up a meeting between a Papp and journalist, because a lovefest was sure to ensue. "Joe was an eminently witty interviewee. A very colorful character, and on television he had a marvelous demeanor. He looked like an impresario, he spoke very well and was able to express himself very emphatically—and he had a sense of humor, so he could undercut his pomposity with a remark that would put everything right again."

This was all according to plan. Debuskey had convinced Papp early on that, in the press agent's words, "the Festival needed a human body and voice in order to appeal to the press and the masses, and Papp was to be that public face."

———

Rejiggered and partially recast for Broadway, the reviews for *Two Gentlemen from Verona* were again superb. Notices were also good for *Sticks and Bones*, but the audiences were not coming to the drama, or at least not coming in large enough numbers to allow the play to break even; the Festival was losing $10,000 or more a week on it. But Papp was making money on *Two Gentlemen*, and he decided to take $10,000 a week from the proceeds of the musical and use it to make up the deficit of the Vietnam play in order to keep it running.

In early spring, when the Tony Award nominations were announced, *Two Gentlemen* received nine nods and *Sticks and Bones* got four: Papp's first two Broadway productions had been honored thirteen times. At the ceremony Debuskey was purposefully seated next to the shy, lanky Rabe. "I think he found it somewhat difficult," said Debuskey. "When he won the Tony for Best Play, I had to shove him out of his seat and on to the stage." On an evening of overly long acceptance speeches, he gave one of the shortest: "I really didn't think it was possible. I mean I really didn't. So thank you very much." Some minutes later, the award for Best Book of a Musical went to a young, pudgy, and mustachioed John Guare. And then *Two Gentlemen* won for Best Musical. Papp had done what no one had done before. His first two Broadway shows, a play and musical, had both been selected the best of the season. He was the first Off-Broadway producer to win the Broadway Tonys.

Papp was a purist who eschewed Broadway as a den of commercial corruption. But Debuskey, who had tasted the excitement of a Times Square opening many times before, sensed his boss relished his new arena.

> There's nothing like Broadway. That was Joe's first taste of what Broadway was and the power of Broadway in contrast with everything else. He was disdainful of it, he was disdainful of the people on it. At the same time, he knew and kind of lusted for the notoriety that could come only from Broadway. And successful as he was and as successful as anyone might be away from this arena, you are not in the National or American League. You ain't gonna play any World Series down there.

Furthermore, one had to consider that Broadway success meant financial stability—something that had always eluded the Festival, despite its many critical successes and the support of the press and public.

With the enormous successes of *Two Gentlemen of Verona* and *Sticks and Bones*, as well as of *That Championship Season*, another

Broadway transfer, and a hit Broadway production of *Much Ado about Nothing* set in the period just before World War I and starring a young Sam Waterston, Papp became the undisputed king of Broadway as well as the champion of Off-Broadway. But Broadway and Off-Broadway weren't enough. Papp wanted a national audience; television was national.

Papp had hired an agent, Sol Leon of the William Morris Agency, who had begun discussions with CBS about presenting some of his client's work. The irony was thick: Papp was seeking to go back to work with the network that had fired him and then been forced to rehire him. In those early days he had been a mere floor manager; now he was a vaunted producer, negotiating with the top executives. Leon's timing could not have been better. CBS had a paucity of drama; its golden age was long gone, and the network was looking to renew its cultural status.

On July 31, 1972, Papp and Robert D. Wood, president of CBS Television, held a news conference at the network's Sixth Avenue headquarters announcing that the Shakespeare Festival would present thirteen productions, both classical and modern, in the next four years, at a cost of more than $7 million. It was an unprecedented deal. The works would run from ninety minutes to three hours during prime time. Reporters immediately raised the problem of censorship. Television standards were quite different from theatrical ones; how would Papp be able to translate some of the plays, especially ones like Rabe's, with their proliferation of profanities, for a national family audience?

"We'll have to go through the CBS continuity department," Papp said, "which is a euphemism for censorship department. There's no question that CBS will have the right to approve whatever I suggest. That's the way it is. My premise is that there will be areas of disagreement. I accept that." He and Debuskey prepared a press release on the subject. "Our aim," it said, "is to engage the audience, not alienate it. We are interested in family viewing as well as controversial adult material. We will try not to offend gratuitously, but we will risk offending if the theme is meaningful and serious."

CBS very much wanted *Romeo and Juliet* as its first production. It was popular, it had young lovers and poignant tragedy, and it would probably go over well with an unsophisticated audience. But Papp's heart wasn't in it. He wanted to present his best work. His production of *Much Ado* was in great shape. Light, clever, and funny, it would do perfectly. Papp called Wood, who was on the West Coast. Wood was upset; two hundred affiliates had been promised *Romeo and Juliet*, he said, and Papp had to deliver what was promised. On hearing that, Papp simply asked Wood if he wanted a bad show or a good show. Papp also pressed for approval of *Sticks and Bones* as the second play. Surprisingly, the CBS executives were interested in *Sticks and Bones*, despite its thematic assault on middle-class American values.

After a successful run in the Park, *Much Ado* opened on Broadway in November for what was announced as a limited ten-week run. The idea was that it would continue until two weeks after the scheduled January 14 telecast. But the play again received excellent reviews, and business was great—shows were selling out—so the decision was made to keep it running. The telecast was postponed until February 2. But the prospect of the telecast had a disastrous effect on the Broadway run. In the week before the broadcast, when CBS filled the airwaves with promotions for the show, the Broadway box-office take dropped to $9,000, compared with $25,000 the previous week. People who had bought tickets would show up at the box office trying—unsuccessfully—to return them, saying that if they had known the show was going to be on television they would never have paid to see it. The Broadway production closed on February 11.

For CBS, if not for Broadway, the broadcast of *Much Ado* had been good, despite some bumps; but *Sticks and Bones* was downright disastrous. It was scheduled for a Friday night in early March. There was no concern about its effect on ticket sales, because the play had closed at the end of September. But suddenly reports began circulating that CBS was going to cancel the broadcast. It turned out that many of the network's affiliates were refusing to carry it. Only two months earlier the United States had signed a peace accord with North Vietnam, and the feeling was that with so many soldiers and prisoners of war returning, the airing of a play that treated that subject with such cynicism and bitterness would not be in tune with the national mood.

That week Lincoln Center announced that Papp had been chosen to take over the Lincoln Center Repertory Company, which had been plagued by failures since its Vivian Beaumont Theater had opened eight years earlier. Debuskey arranged a press conference at Lincoln Center—yet more historic ballyhoo for the unstoppable Papp. It went smoothly, and Papp and his party decided to go out for lunch to celebrate an even greater expansion of his influence. The next morning the front page of the *Times* declared solemnly that "such a concentration of power is unprecedented in modern theatrical history." By then, though, Debuskey was hardly in the mood to enjoy the coverage. The very day of the great press conference, the CBS deal came crashing down.

Debuskey was at the office, eating his lunch at his desk and catching up on work, when he got an urgent call from Papp. Debuskey sped to the Public Theatre. Papp, Gersten, Gersten's wife, Cora Cahan, and Gail Merrifield, Papp's personal assistant (and later his wife), had just abandoned a dinner at the Steak Casino in Greenwich Village, their favorite hangout. While they were waiting for their drinks, a phone call came in. It was Wood calling with the decision on *Sticks and Bones*: CBS was canceling the Friday telecast. Nearly seventy of the network's affiliates had so far refused to air the play, and only two minutes of commercial time had been sold. CBS had concluded that the viewing audience across the country would not be receptive to what he termed the "unnecessarily abrasive" drama.

Papp was livid. As always, he was quick to attack. He said that CBS had an obligation to put on the play, no matter how many affiliates rejected it. If the network didn't air *Sticks and Bones*, he said, it would be contributing to the whittling away of the First Amendment. He called Wood a coward. The network president replied that he was not canceling the show, just postponing it to what he termed a more "propitious" time. But Papp would not be appeased; he felt there could be no compromise. If CBS would not present *Sticks and Bones* that Friday night, he would cancel the deal, no matter the consequences. He would not produce the eleven shows remaining on his four-year, $7 million contract. And he hung up.

"Joe's reaction was immediate," Debuskey recalled. "The war was declared immediately. There was a very brief discussion when I got there in which I asked him if he was sure this was what he wanted to do, because once I got on the telephone we would be opening a very large Pandora's box. But he was determined. He just looked at me and said, 'Get to work.'"

Debuskey did. He devised a press campaign surrounding the idea of CBS as "The Cowardly Network." "I called Arthur Gelb at the *Times* immediately after I was alerted by Joe and within the hour they sent a reporter down to the Public to front-page the story the very next morning." Journalists from all over the country were calling. Papp sat down and told each in turn, his voice a model of tightly controlled fury, that the CBS executives, all of them, were cowards.

Debuskey was elated. Ever the moral purist, he heartily supported Papp's decision.

> I worked the phones, briefing the media and arranging interviews with Joe either by phone or in person. It was a very fecund moment for a press agent. That morning the drama desks had covered the interesting, important, and colorful news of the Festival and Lincoln Center. We had become familiar with another section of the media— TV and radio—when we entered into the agreement with CBS, and I was able to induce and add them into the rat race that ensued.

Wood took personal responsibility for the move, but it was revealed later in March that the ultimate decision had been made by William Paley, who had viewed the show and objected strenuously to it, even though Wood and his superiors, Frank M. Stanton and Arthur R. Taylor, the network's vice chairman and president, had approved it. Two days after the postponement the American Civil Liberties Union came to Papp's aid, calling the CBS decision "corporate cowardice." Papp kept up the battle, noting that all of CBS's top executives had approved the script before production began. But Wood pointed out that when they had approved the play the previous August, there had been no way to predict the declaration of peace in Vietnam and the return of prisoners.

Debuskey remembered that while the dispute was still raging, Wood called Papp and pleaded, "'For Christ's sake, get off my back. You're killing me. If you keep it up there's nothing I can do.' I remember that. I put a little merit badge on my shoulder that we'd really done it. There was no pussyfooting. Papp was quick to make up his mind, and that was it. He usually did not suffer from after-the-fact concerns about whether the decision he had made was correct or incorrect. Self-doubt was not in his makeup."

Papp tried briefly to reconcile with the network. Two weeks after the telephone call, he wrote Wood to note that the last of the Vietnam prisoners were scheduled to be released by March 28 and asked when the telecast might be rescheduled. He said that if *Sticks and Bones* were shown, he would reverse himself and continue to produce plays for CBS. But it was too late. Papp's attitude had permanently alienated the network. In June he and CBS agreed that the contract had lapsed. The next month CBS finally decided that it would telecast the production on August 17, a Friday, from 9 to 11 p.m., in the heat of summer, when few people were watching television, in a period when the ratings were essentially meaningless, and long after the Emmy deadline. The play was presented without commercial interruption—only because no sponsor was willing to be associated with it.

Papp never produced again for CBS. In November he signed an agreement with ABC, but that deal was for two dramas and $1 million, not thirteen plays and $7 million, and it couldn't possibly provide Papp with the audience he had sought.

Debuskey never condemned Papp for his rashness. To him, it was extraordinary that Papp was willing to give up such an enormous power base for a principle.

> This was an amazing position for him to take. Anyone else might have said, "So what, so it's not getting on before the Emmy cutoff. What

the hell. We're getting it on, they're doing it, we have so many more to do. They're not the nicest guys in the world but what did you expect, they are what they are. This kind of decision on their part is understandable if you understand the world in which they live. We can handle that. We'll just absorb it and go on." But no. Joe couldn't do that.

Chapter 9

JOE PAPP/KING LEAR

Despite the problems *Sticks and Bones* had caused him, Papp stayed loyal to David Rabe, choosing his *In the Boom Boom Room* to open the director's new reign over the seemingly cursed Lincoln Center Theatre program. This time Debuskey and Gersten couldn't use their powers of indirect persuasion to change Papp's mind. As for Rabe, he felt from the start that the august and austere Beaumont wasn't the proper arena for the play's subject matter. From almost the moment rehearsals began, "everything fell apart," Rabe said, "and it seemed like I had known all along that it would."

In the Boom Boom Room is the story of Chrissy (portrayed by Madeline Kahn), a go-go dancer, one of those battered, displaced people who live on the fringes of American society. Chrissy spends much of her life in a sleazy strip joint, wonders how she wound up there, and aspires, sort of, to better things. Meanwhile, she meets the kinds of people one would expect to meet in such a place, the type one would not necessarily expect to encounter at Lincoln Center, on or off the stage.

Partly because the main character was a woman, and partly because Papp consistently desired to be in the forefront of theatrical progress, he hired a female director, Julie Bovasso. From the beginning, however, she and Rabe disagreed, and Papp always sided with his playwright. Bovasso felt Joe and David were threatened by a strong woman. Papp, with Rabe's backing and over Bovasso's objections, removed the $65,000 multilayered set Santo Loquasto had designed for the production and had Loquasto create another. He had Theoni Aldredge design three sets of costumes before he found ones he approved.

There were also problems with the actress Julie Newmar, who was portraying a bisexual go-go dance captain: she was not memorizing her lines and was feuding with Bovasso. Soon she was fired. Papp was constantly being told of the problems and coming to the theater to witness the troubled rehearsals. Bovasso wanted to cut the play, which was running three hours, and Papp agreed that the cuts would help. But Rabe absolutely refused to make them, and Papp again took his writer's part over his director.

Rabe at the time was Papp's golden boy. Papp had discovered him, which meant that the writer could do no wrong. The director had many of these anointed artistic children over the years, and each was as special as the first. Debuskey remembered that the director Stuart Vaughn, back in the days of the East River amphitheater, was the very first genius-elect. "He became one of Joe's successions of designated genies. It was cyclical. It was like a salad bowl. A tomato would turn up, you would stir, and it would disappear and an anchovy would come up. And he had his convictions that this was the greatest artist for the moment. And Stuart was the first." Others would include the composer Elizabeth Swados and the directors Kim Friedman, Gerald Freedman, and Wilford Leach.

During previews of *In the Boom Boom Room*, many audience members voted with their feet and left. Finally, on October 30, 1973, a week before the scheduled opening, Papp fired Bovasso and made himself the director. He restaged the play in one day. Opening night was November 8. After the performance, everyone headed over to O'Neal's Balloon, a restaurant across from Lincoln Center, for a party. Trailing Papp was Patricia Bosworth, a freelance reporter assigned by the *New York Times* to write about the opening for the Sunday Arts and Leisure section. Debuskey knew Bosworth as a good writer and a decent person, but he had argued against the arrangement.

"I didn't recommend that you allow anybody to follow you around, because you are placing an incendiary instrument right up your ass," said Debuskey. He had been overruled by increasingly vainglorious Papp, however, who believed by then that the press would never turn on him.

Less than an hour into the party, Papp and Gail Merrifield went back to the Beaumont to listen to the television reviews. Bosworth followed. Gersten, Debuskey, and several others were already at the theater, although a nervous Rabe had decided to wait at the restaurant. The first television review, from CBS, was a rave. The next, from ABC, was mixed. Later on, other reviewers would call the play a "near masterpiece" and "affectingly powerful." But the reviewer who meant the most was, as always, the New York Times's Clive Barnes.

Papp had been concerned about Barnes because the critic had written frequently since March that he was opposed to Papp's plan for the Beaumont. Barnes had not taken kindly to the idea of emphasizing new American plays at Lincoln Center; he favored a repertory theater, perhaps a national theater, and a devotion to the classics. Papp had even taken Barnes to lunch to try to get him to change his mind but had not succeeded.

"I spoke with Joe about this differing opinion and how it may have been reflected in Clive's reviews," recalled Debuskey, "and that I thought a conversation might be of subsequent value. I always thought Clive to be a decent fellow who—even as the New York Times drama critic—thought of himself as 'of the theater.' This, in a positive, even sweet, attitude."

"My relationship with Joe ran very hot and cold, and it was part of Merle's job to keep us both lukewarm," remembered Barnes. But the meeting, as it would turn out, did not affect Barnes's opinion of In the Boom Boom Room.

In those years, the practice with Times reviews was to have someone in the newspaper's composing room call up and read the notice to the eager producer or press agent. At the Beaumont, a loudspeaker had been attached to the telephone so everyone in the room could find out immediately whether the word was bad or good. And in this case, it was not good.

"The play is full of chic filth and a desperate Archie Bunker style of racism," Barnes wrote. "The dialogue aspires too frequently to the comforting jargon of TV serials.... The jokes are usually corny....The curious thing is how a playwright of Mr. Rabe's unquestioned promise should turn out such an empty and poorly crafted play....Mr. Papp must take the rap....Let us hope that the Shakespeare Festival will have better luck next time. There is nowhere to go but up."

Papp was furious. "That fuck!" he shouted. "That son of a bitch." He asked Debuskey for Barnes's home telephone number, stormed to the telephone, and, at 11:30 p.m., called the critic. "Hello, Clive?" he said. The loudspeaker was still on, so everyone in the room, including Bosworth, could hear what he was saying. "This is Joe Papp. I just heard your review. And you are a shit. You think you're going to get me? Well, I am going to get you. I am going to get you."

Debuskey was upset by the review, too, but he hadn't expected Papp's response. "I didn't know what Joe was going to say to him—except that I knew that he would say he [Barnes] was dumb or that his perceptions were dim and it was a poor review that didn't reflect the show. It turns out that he says to him that he was going to have his job—which was recorded and reported."

When asked why he handed over the home phone number of the city's most powerful drama critic to a livid producer widely known for his volatility, the press agent replied, "I didn't know Joe was going to attack him to that degree. If we were back in the sword and lance combat era, and Joe had said, 'Hey, have you got a spare lance?,' I would have given it to him. We were shoulder to shoulder."

Still, Debuskey recognized the moment as "one of the first tactical mistakes" of Papp's career. With Bosworth present, it was certain the story would become widespread. After hanging up the phone, Papp told anyone who would listen that he considered the unfavorable review part of a personal vendetta: Barnes was attacking him because he would not take the critic's advice on what to do with the Beaumont.

The next day, a letter from Barnes was hand-delivered to Papp's office. It read in part:

> Our telephone conversation (or rather your monologue) last night disturbed me. Not merely because I am unaccustomed to receiving

obscene telephone calls, and certainly not because of your violently phrased defense of Rabe's play—I would expect no less—but because in your anger at our difference of opinion, you questioned my integrity. You told me that "You are out to get me." This is transparent nonsense. I admire you as one of the major forces in our theater— and I imagine you have kept the press clippings to prove it.

But Papp was having none of it. "I don't accept it," he told Bosworth. "I'm at a crucial period with my theaters and Clive is out to destroy me for personal reasons. But he won't get away with it."

In the end, Papp had as little luck with Lincoln Center as had his predecessors. Though he enjoyed some late successes with *The Cherry Orchard* and *The Threepenny Opera* in 1977, he left the Center after three years of increasing controversy and declining audiences, saying that it wasn't the right place for him. He suddenly declared that he felt "trapped in an institutional structure both artistically and fiscally."

"Joe's decision to take over at Lincoln Center had been prompted by his opinion that moving into that venue would enhance his potential for raising funds for his downtown and outdoor Shakespeare Festival," said Debuskey.

He was also determined to shatter the monolithic aging upper-middle-class audience that all the Lincoln Center constituents were attracting. His choice of plays was geared in that direction—and they were very successful in destroying that audience. But he never managed to come up with another kind of *audience*, despite some earnest attempts. In truth, it had been too much for him to handle—the two theaters up there and his rabbit warren of theaters at the Public, and the outdoor free Shakespeare, and the shows we moved to Broadway and then duplicated for road tours.

If little could go right uptown, magic was still possible downtown. The roots of *A Chorus Line* were established when Papp got the idea to revive the Kurt Weill musical *Knickerbocker Holiday*, with Michael Bennett directing.

Bennett was a Broadway gypsy who had graduated to choreographer and then director. He had left high school just before graduating to join a European touring company of *West Side Story* (on which he worked with Jerome Robbins) and went on to Broadway in 1961 to dance in the choruses of *Subways Are for Sleeping*, *Here's Love*, and *Bajour*. In the mid-1960s, he began choreographing shows, working as an uncredited assistant. His first four official stints as a Broadway choreographer all led to Tony Award nominations, although three (*A Joyful Noise*, *Henry, Sweet Henry*, and *Coco*, with Katharine Hepburn) were financial failures. The fourth, however, was *Promises, Promises*, which ran for almost three years. His breakthrough came in 1970 with Stephen Sondheim, George Furth, and Harold Prince's *Company*, a musical about marriage and commitment. The success led to another collaboration with Prince and Sondheim, and Bennett's first Broadway directing job. On *Follies* (1971), in addition to his choreography, he received co-directing credit with Prince and won his first two Tony Awards. And then he was called upon to take over the troubled production of *Seesaw*; he changed every aspect of the production and won his second Tony as a choreographer.

Papp has been told about Bennett by Gersten. "Joe was not too knowledgeable about Broadway choreographers or Broadway musicals," Debuskey recalled. "He didn't go to ballet or dance presentations. He didn't see too many Broadway shows, and he wasn't that familiar with Michael."

Bennett passed on *Knickerbocker Holiday*, saying it wasn't his kind of thing. But Bennett said there was something else he wanted to talk to Papp about. He had been making these tapes, and he had a crazy idea for a musical. The next day he came down to the theater with the tapes, hours and hours of interviews with dancers just like him, the kind who would journey from show to show, never become stars, never even get speaking roles. They talked about their lives, their careers, their doubts, their hopes, their frustrations, their desires, their fears, their love of the theater. He played some of the tapes for Joe and said he thought they could be the basis for a musical.

But Bennett needed time to create it and shape the work, and wanted to use the Public Theater as a home for a workshop. He had not thought of Papp before the phone call, he said, because he had never worked Off-Broadway or in noncommercial theater. But when Papp had called, Bennett had decided to try and interest him. The method he was suggesting—experimentation, trial and error, hopefully learning from the mistakes, and trying again, without definite plans for a full-scale production—had never before been used for a Broadway show. He dubbed the process the workshop, and it would become for decades afterward accepted practice on Broadway and off.

Gersten strongly urged his boss to go along with the idea, and Papp was won over by Bennett's, and Gersten's, enthusiasm. There were two workshops, the first in the fall of 1974 and the second in the winter of 1975. Papp and Bennett clashed repeatedly. Bennett would ask for more money for further work, and Papp would balk. Papp would press for the show to open at the Beaumont, and Bennett would resist, saying the show was meant to be intimate—he wanted the smaller Newman Theater. To bring Papp around, Bennett shopped the show to the Shuberts, who were interested. Papp gave in.

Bennett often turned to Gersten and Debuskey for support when he reached impasses with the headstrong Papp. After one breaking-point meeting at Lincoln Center in which Papp refused to hand over money for yet another workshop, Gersten and Debuskey took Papp into an adjoining room and went to work on him. "Joe said that it wouldn't be fair to his other shows and writers if he gave more money," Debuskey recalled. "Michael said that he wanted to do the show at the Public—that it had advanced to a point where they could get a Broadway producer, but they didn't want to do that, they wanted to do it with Joe. Things weren't going anywhere. Joe wasn't giving any ground. Bernie and I tried to persuade Joe that if he really respected creativity, he had to give this another shot. Finally he agreed."

"I felt it would be a terrible mistake if we abandoned this—it would be calamitous," he added. "None of us projected the enormous [commercial] success. Our interest was in the work and the quality of it."

One of Papp's prime benefactors, his board chairwoman, LuEsther Mertz, supplied money. So did the Shubert Organization. A seven-week rehearsal period was agreed to, during which the show began to take its ultimate form. There were extensive trims and rewrites, with Bennett and his writing and composing team—Nicholas Dante, Marvin Hamlisch, James Kirkwood, and Ed Kleban—finding the solutions that had previously eluded them.

Previews began in April, and the word on *A Chorus Line* was immediate and strong: it was a hit—in fact, a seminal event in the history of the theater. Lafayette Street, just outside the Public, became limo heaven as practically every celebrity in town vied for tickets. Opening night at the Newman Theater was May 21, 1975. The raves were more than unanimous: they declared that *A Chorus Line* would find its place with the landmarks of musical Broadway, classics such as *Show Boat* and *Oklahoma!*.

There was never any doubt the show, produced by Joseph Papp and the New York Shakespeare Festival, would move to Broadway, and that summer that's just what it did, to the Shubert Theatre. *A Chorus Line* ran for almost fifteen years, winning nine Tony Awards, including Best Musical. Its profits kept the Festival going for years.

Debuskey did press for Bennett's last three shows, which included *Ballroom* and *Dreamgirls*, and the press agent credits the director with giving him one of the greatest experiences of his life. Soon after *A Chorus Line*'s success, it was decided to form an international company and a national company that would start in San Francisco. "Michael had to do two new companies, which actually were three, because the national company actually had to borrow people from the New York company. So he had to fill those spots. For him, the idea of doing a show three times, following the prior experience to get it in the first place, wasn't exciting." Bennett's solution was to work out the dates of the shows' openings so the companies could all could be rehearsed together. "The basement of City Center is where he did them. I used to come in and watch him rehearse three companies at once. It was an experience, and the fucker managed to do it."

Debuskey believes it was this experience that taught Bennett how to handle the now legendary September 29, 1983, performance of *A Chorus Line*, when the New York show set a record as longest-running musical in Broadway history. It was Bennett's plan to enlist every actor who had ever appeared in the show over the world. Supports were built under the Shubert Theatre stage to hold the additional weight from all those bodies, and Bennett directed from the top of a ladder. For the first time in his career, Debuskey operated from a base outside his office, erecting a construction shack in Shubert Alley for two days. "Everybody in the world wanted in. I mean literally. They wanted to see it." He managed to sneak away now and then from his sixteen-hour days to catch bits of the rehearsal period. "They had to come in from everywhere, they had to be gotten together, they had to be costumed, they had to be integrated. That was a glorious experience."

Everything at the Festival changed after *A Chorus Line*.

The initial changes were all for the better. The musical's many productions provided millions upon millions of dollars to Joseph Papp's New York Shakespeare Festival. Finally, Papp would not have to beg for money. The Festival would expand even more, add staff, and produce more and more plays. From 1976 until 1983 income from the various productions of *A Chorus Line* made up almost 70 percent of the Festival's operating costs.

But the great good fortune of being connected to a huge hit drained Papp of the fight that had caused him to strive so furiously. A man with both power and money had no need to scrap and complain. Neither could his claim to the artistic high ground go unchallenged any longer. The Public was now the Establishment, not a tradition-bucking upstart. Furthermore, the Festival and Papp's connection to Bennett and *A Chorus Line* indirectly led to the severing of the producer's relationship with his two closest associates, Debuskey and Gersten.

A Chorus Line generated endless press attention, while the Festival's programming grew by the season. Papp pressed Debuskey to move his offices from midtown to within the Lafayette complex. The press agent was by then the only important Festival staff member who did not work out of the Public. Debuskey resisted. "I couldn't," he said. His commercial shows were "what kept me alive to do" things for the Public.

"Merle always had his own office," recalled Bob Kamlot. "Joe would ask Merle to come down. That was one of the things that stuck in Joe's craw. He was going to give him office space and even let him work on outside assignments." Being one man's vassal, however, didn't appeal to the man who, then in his heyday, was in Gersten's words "king of the press agents."

"He was a servant to many different masters at the same time," said Kamlot. "Merle didn't want to work for just one person." To patch up the problem, Debuskey engaged Bob Ullman as an associate and installed him in the Public offices. Debuskey would remain the Festival's general press representative, and Ullman would do the day-to-day reporting to Papp. Soon afterward, Ullman asked for an apprentice, and Richard Kornberg, a college newspaper critic Debuskey knew, was installed. Later, said Debuskey, "when *Chorus Line* went to Broadway, I gave the contract to Ullman so he could make some money, and Richard became the downtown press agent." The situation would do for the moment, but the issue was to return years later, with disastrous results.

Gersten, meanwhile, had strengthened his bond with Bennett. More than anyone at the Festival, Gersten had made *A Chorus Line* possible, and he was anxious to have the Public produce Bennett's next work. Papp seemed interested. The producer and Bennett had gone so far as to take a melodramatic "blood oath" of friendship and mutual support on June 11, 1975, at a restaurant called Orsini's. Two days later the pact was drawn up as a written document, with Gail Merrifield as witness.

Three years later, when it was time for Bennett's next show, *Ballroom*, Papp simply ignored the oath. He disagreed with Gersten about the show, saying that it was too commercial for the Public—this despite *A Chorus Line* and all the money it had brought to Papp's theater. Gersten believed the musical—which starred Dorothy Loudon and Vincent Gardenia as a widow and a married man who meet and begin an affair at a dingy Bronx ballroom—was worthwhile. He also thought the Public owed a great debt to Bennett and should present his show.

The enterprise disturbed Papp on two fronts, Debuskey believed. "Whatever blood that had passed between Bennett and Papp had curdled. Michael had become too big. *Chorus Line* had become Michael, not Joe Papp, and Joe resented it. Joe was the Festival and the Festival was Joe. The fact that it couldn't exist without other people was irrelevant."

Bennett went to Papp and said that he wanted to do *Ballroom* directly on Broadway—it would be impossible to do at the Public. Papp said no. Even though he took shows to Broadway, he couldn't, he said, allow himself to be seen as a Broadway producer. Said Debuskey: "This was an overtly Broadway production, Joe said, and he didn't want to have to raise the money. Michael said that Joe wouldn't have to put up a cent, that Michael could get all the money, but that he wanted to do it with Joe and the Festival, and that the profits would accrue to the Festival as if it had raised the funds. There would be no financial risk, and the chance of a great profit." Papp still turned him down.

One likely motivation for Papp's stonewalling was Gersten, who had developed into a Festival player almost as significant as Papp. If the producer blew up at a funding meeting with the Board of Estimate, the level-headed, congenial Gersten was always there to pick up the pieces. And artists knew that. Even if Papp gave the go-ahead for a project, it was Gersten they had to go to if they wanted to make the thing actually happen.

A fateful symbol of Gersten's competence and ability came in June 1978, when Gersten successfully planned a titanic surprise birthday party for Joe at the Delacorte—all without the impresario's knowing about it.

Papp arrived at the party already upset. In order to get him to go, Gail had had to employ subterfuge and force him to abandon a respite with her and his children at their country home in Katonah, New York. But Papp was just as upset after the surprise was sprung: how could anyone, without his knowledge, plan an event at his theater involving all his stars and two thousand guests? Bob Kamlot recalled that, following the party, Papp wouldn't let him sign contracts or checks, "because all this money was allotted without him knowing it [was] for the party."

The entertainment didn't help. There was a skit, written by John Guare, that satirized Papp, Gersten, and Papp's wife, who still worked at the theater as his assistant. Its send-up of Papp's imperious ego and Gail's slavish subservience to her husband were, some thought, brutally and destructively exaggerated, though others found it delightful satire. But upstaging Joe Papp never did anyone any good.

When Gersten insisted on working on *Ballroom*, it looked to Papp like another power play, just like the surprise party, though he never characterized it in those terms. Said Debuskey:

> Bernie was adamant about doing it, and he and I tried to persuade Joe. We told him that he was interested in talent, that he wanted to nurture talent, and did he know anybody more talented than Michael? Look what happened before, we said—we're living off what Michael did for us. And he's offering it to us as no cost. But the more we pushed, the more his back stiffened. It turned out we were making a big mistake in talking to him that way.

Since Bennett wanted Gersten to supervise the producing of the show, someone suggested that Gersten take a leave of absence to do so. "We said to Joe, suppose Bernie said he was burned out," recalled Debuskey, "and wanted to go to the Fiji Islands for two months, you would let him go, wouldn't you? Bernie has earned your consideration for his wishes, and it's not going to damage the Festival. He won't go away. He'll be working from here. But Joe said no. That was it."

So Gersten told Papp he intended to work on *Ballroom* anyway. Papp fired him.

Steve Cohen was at their final argument. "I was actually sitting there when all that was going on. I had to walk out. It got more and more heated. And Joe looked at me and said, 'It's like you're watching your two older brothers having a fight.' I said, 'That's exactly what it looks like. I'm going to leave. This is uncomfortable.' By the end of that meeting, Bernie was fired."

Debuskey, hearing of the rupture, rushed down to the Public to try and get Papp to change his mind. "I knew how important Bernie was to keeping the Festival in a state of equilibrium," Debuskey said.

> The last meeting I had with Joe about Bernie, I said everything I could possibly think of, and we sat there crying. It was a teary meeting. We felt terrible. But the decision to fire Bernie had nothing to do with reason. I remember very distinctly Joe telling me sincerely, and I think he meant it—but it was one of the most convoluted lines of reasoning—that Bernie consciously or unconsciously forced Joe into this position where he had to fire him. I remember that, and I was a bit shaken by it.

Clive Barnes recalled the shock that ran through the theater community when they heard of Gersten's dismissal. "Joe was making the headlines, but it was in fact people like Bernie and Merle who were actually doing the hard slogging work," he said. "Joe really thought that the Public Theater was him, and to a certain extent it was."

Gail Papp saw the conflict differently.

> Joe didn't want Bernie to leave the Festival. So Bernie created a concept that there was a moral obligation to participate with Michael. Joe didn't see it that way. Bernie said, I'm going to do it anyway. The problem with that was a kind of blurring of boundaries. It was Joe's organization. He founded it. He was territorial and possessive. He was not a partner with anybody. That was not in his character—to be partners and share responsibility or authority and control. That's not how he was made. Bernie didn't realize that he was crossing a boundary that for Joe was just unacceptable. To say you're going to do it anyway is to say you're a co-partner in the organization.

Debuskey put the same thought in uncharacteristically concise terms: "Joe always hated it when, referring to the Festival, I said 'we.'"

After Gersten left, Papp took Bernie's name off his office door, recalled Kamlot. Gersten and Papp didn't speak for three years.

———

Debuskey, though disheartened and distraught over Gersten's dismissal, would stay on. Right up until Gersten's departure, the two men had remained close. People described them as brothers. On July 6, after the surprise birthday party, Gersten wrote Debuskey, "You are indeed the strong moral force and how your have sustained this posture these many years not only confounds me but continues to win my deep regard and love." Years later, however, Gersten would say that he held it against his old friend that he hadn't quit in protest—"I suspect I thought he should"—a contention that may have weighed on their future business interactions.

But even though he remained, the Festival had changed for Debuskey, because Papp had changed. "I think what happened is that if you take Janus, the two-headed god, and you remove one, what do you have on that opposite side of the face? Bernie had many qualities that Joe lacked, such as warmth, principally, but also humanness, genuine convivial vitality."

Journalists had always compared the theatrical Papp to various characters in the Shakespeare dramas he produced. Early on he was Henry V, leading a small band of warriors to unlikely victory. In his last decade, however, he more closely resembled King Lear, unwisely and capriciously dispensing of trusted family and associates. Staff meetings became lopsided affairs, dominated by Papp's far-ranging discourses. "He developed this autocratic approach, with an ego that exceeded all reasonable boundaries," remembered Debuskey. "Dialogue became an outmoded form. He used to deliver monologues that upset me terribly, because our whole relationship had been built on our talking together. I became an irritation to him."

Papp had a retinue now, a galaxy of people who would travel with him, including a sort of Boswell whose job it was to follow the producer and jot down any stray ideas he had. Debuskey was not part of this new circle of acolytes. "As he evolved, he demanded complete fealty," remembered the press agent. "Not loyalty, but fealty. And that was not me." And whereas he used to always have Papp's ear, he now found it difficult to dissuade him from any decision.

"Joe's trajectory—you could feel it happening as he became more of a megalomaniac," recalled Pearl Somner. "He was very difficult. But even when I first met him, he could be very doctrinaire, opinionated, and tough." (Pearl actually met the young Joseph Papirofsky—that is, Joe Papp—and Bernard Gersten years before Merle would encounter them, at the Actors Lab in Los Angeles. According to Pearl, Joe engaged in a brief flirtation with her, which she did not encourage, as he was married. "I was very principled. And he cut me dead for the rest of my life. We had very few words together thereafter.")

In the early years Debuskey had worked hard to make Papp the human face of the Festival. Now Papp was literally the face of the Festival, replacing none other than the Bard himself. For a musical version of *The Human Comedy* in the early 1980s, Papp arranged for a Broadway marquee that had him looking like Uncle Sam and saying, "Joe Papp wants you." "That 'I Want You' is a very interesting evolution," contended Debuskey. "The Shakespeare Festival logo was an old line drawing of William Shakespeare, which on occasion had been supplanted by an image of Joe Papp. This may have been funny as a one-shot, but embarrassing in a second shot, in my opinion." Soon Debuskey couldn't turn around without someone asking him why he had allowed Papp to do the poster. "I let him do it because I couldn't stop him if I wanted to; and . . . at that point, we weren't getting into those kinds of discussions."

When in the early 1980s the city approved a plan to tear down three old theaters and put up the Marriott Marquis Hotel, with one new theater inside, Papp led an uprising. Recalled Debuskey:

> He assumed he was all-powerful and could do anything he wanted, that people had to bend to his will. He jumped in and really extended himself to continue the demonstrations in the most highly visible fashion. He got a flatbed truck to sit on West Forty-fifth Street and got all kinds of people to perform, people like Plácido Domingo, trying to get the message across. But anybody who knew anything about operating theaters and the economics involved knew that these theaters were no longer practical, because they had second balconies,

where nobody wanted to sit, and the orchestra seating wasn't large enough to make the theaters profitable.

One Friday during the demonstrations, Debuskey was with Papp when the producer received a phone call from a lawyer in Washington who told him that an injunction had been obtained to hold off on the wrecking ball, but that the hotel's lawyers would be in court Monday to get the injunction lifted and there was no way to prevent it.

> And the next thing, Joe gets off the phone and I hear him holler, "Get me Thurgood Marshall." Now Marshall was a Justice of the United States Supreme Court, and there was no way Joe could get him or get him to lift the injunction. I said, "Joe, you'll never get him on a weekend." And Joe said, "I know what kind of guy he is, if you get him, he'll do it." That's when I thought, "That's right, Joe and his pal Thurgood." That's when I knew the ego was unstoppable.

There were sit-down demonstrations and mass arrests, but, of course, the three theaters came down.

Debuskey could now no longer count on Papp's coming off well in the press. "I remember one interview Jerry Tallmer did with him and Joe said, 'Power corrupts. Absolute power corrupts absolutely.' And Jerry said, 'But Joe, you're the absolute power,' and Joe said, 'Yeah, but that doesn't apply to me.'" In the late 1980s, when Merv Rothstein, a reporter from the *New York Times*, asked about the increasing agreement among critics, theatergoers, and others in the theater that the quality of the presentations at the Public was declining, Papp became infuriated and swore at the journalist, driving him away.

Papp even turned on Arthur Gelb, the earliest supporter of the Festival at the *New York Times* and the man Debuskey frequently turned to for coverage. Gelb and his wife, Barbara, had become prominent experts on Eugene O'Neill after their biography of the playwright was published. The couple formed the Eugene O'Neill Committee to plan annual celebrations of his birthday after his centenary in 1988. Many theater personalities were invited to be a part of the committee, including Papp and Debuskey. Each year the group would do something. Soon a Eugene O'Neill Birthday Medal was created for people important to O'Neill's resurgence; the first one was awarded to Brooks Atkinson.

At one such party, José Quintero directed Colleen Dewhurst and Jason Robards in a play written by Barbara Gelb. Performed for one night only at the Public, it was a big success. Barbara thought the piece should tour and pressed Papp about it. At a subsequent event at Martin Segal's home, Papp stormed out in high dudgeon, insisting that he would not be part of any exploitation meant to benefit the Gelbs. Debuskey called him about the incident.

> He told me that he didn't want to be part of it anymore. He was cutting out. And I said, "Joe, you know what this means? I can't pick up the phone and say, 'Artie, we have a front-page story for you.'" Joe said, "I don't need him. I can go right to [the publisher of the *New York Times*] Abe Rosenthal." I said, "Joe, number one, Abe has a lot to do. He is responsible for one of the most important newspapers in the world. And also, he and Artie are very close friends. And if Artie feels that he has been injured, your relationship with Abe is not going to override his relationship with Artie." It was this "Fuck 'em" attitude. And I thought that if he really thinks that he can live without them and can override them, then he is unreal. He is too smart not to understand this.

Debuskey and Papp's relationship grew more and more chilly. In 1985, in a long profile on Papp in the *New York Times Magazine*, Debuskey felt so unhappy about his boss and friend that he actually went on record about his disaffection. "All the people he was intimate with are gone now," he told the *Times*. "It's like he's one of those species of palm tree that grows very tall. All the lower leaves fall off, so only the leaves at the top are left. That tree trunk, when it grew, had to be alone—anyone that might challenge it had to be cut off. Joe can't stand there and be dragged down by anything—including people. Everything had to be discarded so you can move on."

Still, Debuskey stayed loyal to his old friend and client. "I never doubted that Joe and I had a relationship that wasn't going to be impaired by any of this. I was wrong."

Papp remained upset that Debuskey continued to represent other theatrical clients, that he did not devote his full efforts to publicizing the Public, and that Merle's office was not at the Public. He began to mull a change. "Joe kind of hinted that he wanted someone new there," Clive Barnes remembered. "He asked if I thought Merle was doing a good job, and I remember saying yes."

One day Laurel Ann Wilson, who had become general manager of the Public in 1983 and was not overly familiar with Debuskey's long history at the Festival, was discussing finances with Papp. "*A Chorus Line* had stopped being the giant money machine that it had been for so long," said Wilson. "Joe was not very good at belt-tightening. And it was always my job to say no. I was looking for ways to economize, and I pointed out that we had perfectly adequate press agents on the staff—and we could save money by getting rid of Merle."

The suggestion fed Papp's need to have all his minions at his immediate beck and call. "Joe was a person that you had to be there, you had to be on site," said Steve Cohen. "I had dinner with Joe once or twice a week. . . . It was always about business. Joe was about popping into your office and having a conversation with you. He functioned by 'Get me.' 'Get me this' or 'get me that person.' Everybody was there except for Merle."

To Cohen's thinking, the associates Debuskey had placed in the building had become Papp's de facto press agents. "They created the relationship with Joe because they were on site. In one hundred steps, Richard Kornberg was there. The fact that Merle sent the assistants down there may have actually sealed his own fate."

"He got a stipend whether he was on a show or not," recalled Gail Papp. "Everybody else was on premises. He was the only off-premises person. There was some unhappiness about that. Some people on the administrative staff, they expressed themselves about that. They felt it was unfair. "

Wilson, however, never thought her budgetary suggestion would have the painful denouement it had. "It was very badly handled," she said. "I thought Joe was going to tell Merle, which would have seemed only appropriate. Joe didn't. I was awfully naive to think that he would. He tended to avoid stuff like that unless he was in a towering rage, which he wasn't. So no one told Merle. He was, understandably, absolutely infuriated."

The way Papp handled the firing was to quietly stop paying Debuskey his $18,000 yearly salary for handling the Public Theater and supervising its various touring shows. Soon afterward Debuskey was going through his bookkeeping and noticed that he hadn't received a check for a couple of weeks. He called the Public and spoke to the comptroller. "He said it seemed odd and he would look into it," recalled Debuskey. "He called me back and said, 'You weren't supposed to get it.' Joe or the general manager had said to terminate the payment."

In a rage, Debuskey went downtown to the Public.

I asked to speak to the general manager and was told that she was busy, that I couldn't go into her office. And [the office staff] said, "Listen, Merle, we had nothing to do with this." I banged the door open and went in, and she literally cowered. And I said they had been cowards, and how could they do something like this without calling and alerting me? And she said she wasn't the one who did it. I told her that she should have called me and that I was going upstairs to see Joe. So I went up to see Joe. Gail, who sat outside, said I couldn't go in, that he was meeting with a city agency. I said I would wait. When they exited, I walked in. He was somewhat taken aback.

"I understand you've decided to terminate my payment," said Debuskey. "Why didn't you call me and tell me?"

Papp responded, "I thought you would understand."

"Understand what?"

"We have to cut back."

"If you want to cut back, you cut your lousy radio ads."

Then he talked about the fact that I wouldn't move down there. I told him that this was thirty years together, and you just discovered I wouldn't move down there? There's a phone we had that was a direct line between us, and all he had to do was pick it up and call me and I would be there in twenty minutes if he needed me.

Papp offered to give the relationship another three months, a tryout. "I'm not going to audition for you," Debuskey spat back in disgust. Things eased momentarily. Papp pulled a book off his shelves and gave it to Debuskey as a gift. They joked. They agreed that Debuskey would continue to handle the planned Broadway opening of the musical *The Mystery of Edwin Drood*. On opening night he and Joe stood outside the Majestic Theatre together to welcome the critics, as they had done for hundreds of previous openings at all the Public's theaters. But after that opening, Debuskey noticed that he was again no longer being paid, and he went down to see Papp again.

> I just opened the door to his office, and he was behind the desk, and he was startled at my bursting in on him. And we had at it. And this time he was adamant—from now on he wanted his press agent to be available to him in the building. If I wanted to do that, I was welcome to stay. But if not, that was too bad, and he had to economize, he couldn't afford the $18,000 any more. We got nowhere.

Richard Kornberg was made Papp's general press representative. "It may have satisfied Joe's deepest desire for ultimate control," said Wilson, "but it began as an economic thing."

And with that, the longest unbroken professional association of Joe Papp's career came to an end.

———

One could make the case that Debuskey never completely recovered from his break with the man whose vision and mission he had served devotedly for thirty years. A largely private man, he confided his feelings about the matter to almost no one. When people would ask about the rift, Debuskey would dismiss the topic with a "Fuck him, I'm through with all that." But friends and associates easily sensed his anguish.

"It was a very painful thing to endure," remembered Paul Libin, the managing director of Circle in the Square, another nonprofit Debuskey had long represented. "I think it hurt him to the quick. One of the hard things about that whole situation is in the world of

Joe Papp, it's Joe Papp. It was about Joe Papp. But Merle was instrumental in a lot of things that Joe accomplished. There's an aspect of architecture there."

"He was in pain," recalled Marilyn Stasio.

And he struck me as being baffled. He could not understand. Bafflement is a very important word. There is a way of thinking for people who are very high-minded and principled. They really believe that if they can make you see the truth, the scales will fall from your eyes and you will desist from this terrible behavior and all will be right again. I think it finally sank in that it wasn't going to happen— whether they saw it or not it was irrelevant. And that was the shocker.

Debuskey the idealistic pragmatist had run up against Papp the irrational fabulist and was stopped dead.

Papp was diagnosed with cancer in 1987 and fought the disease for the next four years. After the death of Colleen Dewhurst in late August of 1991, an open-house memorial was held at her farmhouse in Westchester County for an invited group of friends. Debuskey was asked by Dewhurst's sons for the names of people he thought she would have wished to be there. "I suggested Bernard Gersten, who had an estate a few miles away. When I arrived, I was told that Bernie had been there and had asked that I call him when I arrived." Gersten, after hearing of Papp's illness, had reconciled with his old boss, letting Papp live in his Manhattan apartment because Papp's son Tony, who was dying, was in hospice in the Papp apartment in Greenwich Village. As Gersten explained it, "I wished he would die, and he was dying, so I reconciled." Debuskey called Gersten, who said that Papp was at his house. He encouraged Debuskey to come over and make amends.

"I had not spoken with Joe since our acrimonious parting some years before," said Debuskey. "I was struggling with a decision when Joe came on the line and began with, 'Merle, we had some interesting times together, didn't we?' Tears came to my eyes. Then he continued: 'You should understand why I had to do what I did, and put it away.'"

It was a rare moment of reflection from a man who often boasted that he never looked back and regretted nothing. But Debuskey heard nothing resembling an apology in the words. Instead he may have heard an echo of the self-justifying abnegation of responsibility that Papp uttered after firing Gersten, when he claimed Gersten's actions had forced him to terminate his colleague.

"That did it. My anger and hurt returned as it became clear he was continuing to ignore his inconsiderate behavior as well as the immeasurable contributions I had made. Those feelings overrode my sadness at his fatal illness. I ended the call and returned to the palpable love for Colleen being exhibited by the mourners who had gathered to express their feelings."

A little more than two months later, on October 31, 1991, Papp died. The next day, the producer received his final page 1 story in the *Times*. "Joseph Papp, Theater's Champion, Dies," the headline read. Susan Chicoine, who joined Debuskey's office in 1990, remembered that her boss was "devastated" on that day.

Papp had rediscovered his faith in his final years. The Jewish religion called for burial of the body within twenty-four hours, so arrangements began immediately. Gersten and his wife drove to Papp's apartment upon hearing of his death. Gersten, Cohen, and Joe's brother Phil began organizing a memorial event at the Public Theatre. Many people were enlisted to speak or perform, including Joanne Akalaitis (who would succeed Papp as head of the Festival), Mayor David Dinkins, Gerald Freedman, Gersten, Kevin Kline, James Lapine, board member Stanley Lowell, Mandy Patinkin, Meryl Streep, and Liz Swados. Debuskey was not even called.

Though the service was confusingly advertised in the *Times* as private, it was in fact open to all. "No one was invited," said Cohen.

It was going to be a private ceremony for family and friends, with a public ceremony at a later date. The public ceremony never happened. We never did anything after. About fifteen people talked. Because we asked all these people to speak at the funeral, that really became the memorial service. We never called anyone, except the people who were to speak. I didn't invite Bobby DeNiro or Al

Pacino to come, but they came. They just showed up and so did everyone else.

Debuskey, too, went to the Newman Theater. He told the door-keepers, "Just try and stop me," and walked in and sat on the steps.

Some time later, at a naming ceremony in which the name of the Festival headquarters was changed to the Joseph Papp Public Theatre, Gail Papp recalled seeing Debuskey. "The mayor showed up to speak," Gail remembered. "I was standing there with Bernie. There was a kind of crowd on the street, a lot of actors and other people who had been instrumental with us. And I saw Merle there. I thought, he shouldn't be just standing in the crowd. I thought they should both [Gersten and Debuskey] have a part in the ceremony."

"Maybe I was wrong in not meeting with Joe at Bernie's that day," Debuskey reflected.

What a shame. What a shame. I would never diminish his accomplishments. There has been no one like him in the theater. Not only did he produce shows, he produced good shows, and so much talent came out of there. Others tried and couldn't do it. He did so much for minority actors. For me, just to go out to Central Park before the shows, and see so many people sitting around, many of them having picnic dinners, and then get up and enter the Delacorte to see Shakespeare performed on a summer night, was an amazing thing. It was one of the most civilized sights you could ever see. And Joe Papp made it possible.

Chapter 10

FINALE

Debuskey had one more important chapter in his career after leaving Papp. Ironically, and perhaps poetically, it was in teamship with Papp's other discarded colonel, Bernard Gersten.

It began with a call from former Mayor John V. Lindsay, who had been asked to take over as the Lincoln Center Theatre's chairman and try to resurrect the ill-fated enterprise, which had sat vacant since Joe Papp walked away from it in 1977.

"Lincoln Center Theater by 1985 was widely known as the abattoir of producing organizations," said Debuskey. "Even such experts as the director Elia Kazan and the producer Robert Whitehead had failed at making it a working proposition." Debuskey was one of the few people in the New York theater to have seen that the Beaumont stage could be the site of success. He had worked with Alex Cohen on Peter Brook's famed production of *Carmen*, one of the few triumphs ever visited on the theater. Furthermore, because of his experience with Papp, he knew the complex in and out. Lindsay and Debuskey arranged to meet. Remembered Debuskey:

> One of the shibboleths about the place was that there was no way you could present plays in that architectural structure. And I told Lindsay that the shibboleth was wrong—that if you knew how to use that theater, you could succeed. Which was somewhat reassuring for him. Later Lindsay asked if I would be interested in being the press agent for the project when it got going. I said it would depend on who was going to operate it.

Not long after, on March 20, 1985, it was announced that Gregory Mosher, who had been running the Goodman Theatre in Chicago and was known for directing such playwrights as David Mamet and John Guare, had been offered the position of Lincoln Center Theater's new artistic director. On June 13 Debuskey's old friend and colleague Bernie Gersten was named its executive producer.

"I called Lindsay's office and asked if the offer was still open," said Debuskey. "I didn't know Mosher, but Bernie and I of course had been through so many wars together. Lindsay said yes, but . . . I would have to talk to the producers. So I called Bernie, and he was somewhat reluctant. He said he was a bit concerned about my also representing Joe Papp. Would there not be some conflict? I told him that that was my problem, not his." (By the end of the year Debuskey was out of the Public, and Papp wasn't a problem for either man.) Remembered Mosher: "I think Merle was the person Bernie said he couldn't imagine doing this without."

The new management's responsibility included the larger Beaumont, a Broadway theater, and the smaller Mitzi E. Newhouse. They decided to start small, with a couple of productions in the 299-seat Newhouse. And they concluded that the customary practice of establishing subscriptions should be abandoned. Instead, a yearly membership plan was established, in which a $25 fee gave a member first opportunity to buy choice seats for $10, significantly less than what the general public would have to pay—$20 to $40, depending on the show.

The first production, in December, was an evening of 2 one-acts by David Mamet, *The Shawl* and *Prairie du Chien*, directed by Mosher. They were indifferently received. But a subsequent play put Lincoln Center Theater on the road to success. It was a revival in March 1986, directed by Jerry Zaks, of *The House of Blue Leaves* by John Guare, yet another of Debuskey's old Public pals. Critically praised, it moved upstairs to the Beaumont and then to the Plymouth Theatre on Broadway, and was nominated for a Tony Award as Best Play.

Zaks had another success in 1986 with a revival of *The Front Page*. The next year Lincoln Center Theater presented *Anything Goes*, starring Patti LuPone and also directed by Zaks; it won a Tony for Best Revival. And the Newhouse offered *Sarafina!*, by the African musician Mbongeni Ngema, a musical tale of the horrors of apartheid in South Africa performed not by professional actors, but by two dozen black youths, most of them in their late teens, who were residents of a black township. The *Times* praised it, and it was transferred to the Cort Theatre on Broadway.

Lincoln Center was exactly what Debuskey needed. It revived his excitement about working in the theater. "At the beginning, when we first started that thing out, that was as much fun for me as anything," recalled Debuskey. "That place had been vilified. It had been declared dead."

"Merle and I argued a lot," remembered Mosher. "It was an argumentative office. Bernie said we argued every day. Yeah, and we laughed every day, and we hugged every day. That's how we made the theater happen."

Then, in 1988, Mosher and Gersten decided to present a new Mamet play on Broadway. It was called *Speed-the-Plow*, a drama of the hypocrisies of the movie business, and it told of two Hollywood producers, portrayed by Ron Silver and Joe Mantegna, and an office temp—played by Madonna. "I was really quite surprised when they informed me that the female part was to be played by Madonna," Debuskey recalled.

> She had already achieved iconic status as a singer, but she was unknown to us as a stage actor. This was to be her official stage debut, but she had taken part in a workshop at the theater with her husband at the time, Sean Penn, of David Rabe's *Goose and Tomtom*. And it had been the observation of everyone that she had arrived in a highly professional way, prepared to work, and she had worked very hard, and it was a pleasure to have her around.

Mosher and Gersten had no doubt decided that however successful Mamet, Mantegna, and Silver were, it was Madonna who would sell tickets. And indeed she did. "It, of course, made the press agent's life miserable just trying to handle the publicity," Debuskey said. "Everybody wanted to interview her, but obviously that couldn't be done. She said she was determined to do the best she could as an actor, and she needed the rehearsal period to concentrate on everything. She didn't want the play to be a showcase for her—this, she said, was not going to be the Madonna show. She said she was serious—wanted to try to do this and let the chips fall where they may."

But she couldn't help being Madonna. Debuskey arranged for a reporter for the *New York Times* to visit her dressing room at the Royale Theater for an interview with all three stars, and when he entered he found Debuskey standing by a window, Mantegna sitting on a sofa, and Silver leaning back in a chair, with Madonna perched erotically on his lap. She was talking about a recently opened steamy movie called *White Mischief*, about the young wife of an elderly lord and her affair with a younger man. "It's the kind of movie," she told Silver (and everyone else), "that you want to see with someone you want to fuck." At the opening-night party, the press asked her how it felt to be acting alongside Silver and Mantegna. "She said," Debuskey recalled, "that it was like having great sex." Madonna had her limited range of notes, and she struck them regularly.

In the first three years of the Mosher-Gersten reign, Lincoln Center took in $35 million at the box office, and membership shot from zero to 36,000. Recalled Debuskey, "No one saddled us with a kind of theater that we had to be. Nobody said, 'Well, you better be a repertory company or you fail,' or 'You better do all the classic plays of the eighteenth century or you fail,' or 'You better do the work of every new, promising American playwright or you fail,' or 'You better address every problem in America or you fail.'"

The team couldn't seem to fail. Perhaps the most important hit of all was Guare's *Six Degrees of Separation*, which opened at the Newhouse in June 1990, directed by Zaks and starring Stockard Channing. Based on a real event—the tale of a young black man who managed to move into the homes of rich white Upper East Siders by convincing them that he was their children's Ivy League college friend and the son of Sidney Poitier—it moved to the Beaumont and won a Tony nomination for Best Play. It also brought more attention to David Hampton, the con artist who inspired the play. He ate up the notoriety. "This guy was around and nobody knew how dangerous he was," Debuskey recalled. "He wanted to sue for rights to the piece. He would call the office and offer himself for interviews every other day. He came around the theater and was eventually barred somehow."

But within the success of *Six Degrees* lay the seeds of the end of the Mosher-Gersten partnership and, five years later, of Debuskey's unhappy departure from Lincoln Center.

"The theater had become a success for a number of reasons," Debuskey said.

> One was Bernie, who was the apogee of what an executive producer should be. He was born to the task. He was a well-grounded stage person, having started as a stagehand and a stage manager. He really knew the life inside a theater and was very knowledgeable about its physical aspects. I also don't know anyone who handled a board better than Bernie did. He was personable, affable, highly intelligent, and he related well to all kinds of people. Gregory was an experienced administrator and an accomplished director. He, too, was very knowledgeable about the theater, and was ambitious in a good way.

But with *Six Degrees*, Mosher's ambition suddenly looked as though it would become a liability for the theater's goals. "Jerry Zaks was our institutional director," said Debuskey. "He had directed *Blue Leaves* and *Front Page* and *Anything Goes*. He had directed our first successes and had gotten us out of the starting gate. But when *Six Degrees* came in, and Gregory realized that it was Guare's best play, he asserted that he, as artistic director, was going to direct it.

"Both Bernie and I had immediate twitching of our noses and flapping of our ears," recalled Debuskey. "Our senses roared impending danger. The artistic community we were constantly wooing would be the first to reach for their cudgels upon receipt of that news. Zaks had so gloriously directed the previous Guare play; he was the prime creative force of our productions." Debuskey thought Mosher's seizing of the play for himself would erase the goodwill the theater had built and replace it with "a viewing of selfish opportunism and disregard for the contribution made by Zaks."

Bernie told me that he had introduced the subject to Gregory and suggested my speaking with him. I made an appointment with Gregory and I told him what I honestly felt. He listened, promised to consider my opinion, and subsequently stepped down and properly gave the directing assignment to Zaks. I do believe this incident was the cause of Jerry's severing his bridle to the Lincoln Center Theater.

Zaks left Lincoln Center Theater shortly after *Six Degrees* opened, entering into a contract with Jujamcyn Theaters. Not long after, in March 1991, Mosher decided to leave. "It had to do with two things," he said. "I did what I was hired to do. Somehow, we had done what Joe Papp and Elia Kazan had failed to do. And I was exhausted."

———

Debuskey still had one more big nonprofit in his roster of clients. Debuskey handled the Circle in the Square for twenty-five years, from the day its managing director Paul Libin, attracted by Debuskey's track record with the New York Shakespeare Festival, sought him out to manage publicity for what was then an Off-Broadway troupe. When Debuskey arrived at the company's small theater in Greenwich Village, he found Libin on the roof, "displaying one of the myriad talents he was to exhibit over the several decades of our working together—repairing the air-conditioning." When the press agent agreed to represent the company, Libin handed him a pipe wrench and suggested that he begin then and there with the air conditioning. "That's the way it was Off-Broadway at that time— you simply pitched in where needed."

Debuskey would remain closer to Libin than to anyone else during his Circle tenure. As for Libin's partner and Circle's artistic director, Ted Mann, Debuskey admired the man "and how he had valiantly towed the Circle through its peaks and valleys over a turbulent decade and a half," but the two, while friendly, never developed a warm and trusting rapport.

Debuskey, firmly established on Broadway and laboring under the unrelieved load provided by the New York Shakespeare Festival, did not need the extra work. But he jumped in, attracted, as he always was, by the kind of valiant artistic mission the Circle exemplified.

"I thought his outstanding virtue was understanding the big story as opposed to small, little stories, which don't take a lot of skill getting," said Libin. "It does take skill to get the big story, to get the *Times* to write about you. In those days, he had a good rapport with the *Times*. He didn't care too much about getting you on every little radio show. Some people live by that stuff."

Furthermore, in some ways—perhaps because the roots of his career were Off-Broadway—Debuskey always seemed more at home downtown than up. "I felt more at ease, more belonging, more contributing, and more significant. Not too many people are fortunate enough to have their labors amount to something beyond an ephemeral nine-to-five labor. Hooking up to Circle and the others allowed me that satisfaction."

Circle, in the 1960s, was about as Off-Broadway as you could get. Some history books have the company basically inventing Off-Broadway with its 1951 production of Tennessee Williams's *Summer and Smoke*, though certainly theatrical ventures had thrived in the lower part of Manhattan Island for some years before that. ("Our official story," Libin chuckled, "is there was no Off-Broadway before Circle.") The company was founded in 1950 by the native New Yorker Mann and the Panamanian-born José Quintero. Mann, with the help of his father, took over a former nightclub on Sheridan Square in Greenwich Village whose dance-floor configuration dictated that the theater would have a circular shape—hence, Circle in the Square.

In the mid-1950s the theater struck gold by convincing Eugene O'Neill's mysterious and reclusive widow to let them have the rights to *The Iceman Cometh*. With an unknown actor, Jason Robards Jr., cast in the lead role of Hickey, the disillusioned salesman, Quintero directed the epic play into the pantheon of great dramatic works. Robards achieved instant fame, and Quintero became known as the quintessential O'Neill director. This led to Circle's getting the rights for the American premiere of O'Neill's *Long Day's Journey into Night*, which it presented on Broadway, starring Fredric March, Florence Eldridge, and Robards. It won Tonys for Best Play as well as a Pulitzer Prize. Few events in American theater history have been as important. But despite that huge success, and a large infusion of money, Circle almost died in 1959 when the landlord of their Sheridan Square theater decide to tear it down for a high-rise apartment building. The company moved to the old Amato Opera House on Bleecker Street. Quintero soon left, and Libin joined Mann in 1963; they stayed together for nearly thirty years.

Libin, a native of Chicago, had tried his hand at acting, a talent he soon recognized he did not possess, so he continued his theatrical education working in the office of the renowned scenic designer Jo Mielziner. "To keep shows afloat, he became a proficient electrician, carpenter, plumber, and box-office operator, doing things himself to save money," said Debuskey.

> He became an expert in all union rules and regulations, enabling him to properly hold down costs. In addition to choosing, with Mann, the plays to produce and assembling the appropriate creative team, casts, and staff, he was not above pushing a broom, wiring a light, fixing a dripping faucet, or hanging a drape. Libin was a complete theater person. He and Bernard Gersten were two of the most able people I met in a half century of working in the theater.

Like the Festival, Circle attracted and nurtured the great actors its generation: Philip Bosco, Ruby Dee, Colleen Dewhurst, Dustin Hoffman, James Earl Jones, Frank Langella, Al Pacino, Geraldine Page, Robards, and George C. Scott. And like the Festival in its early days, it was always in financial distress. Recalled Debuskey:

> Circle in those days didn't have the money, the rich board of directors, the professional grant writers, the interested foundations, and the government subsidies that came into play in later years. Its production and operating costs were largely financed by ticket sales, which became a determining factor in programming. When Circle came up with a success, it would extend the run, accumulating operating profits that would be used to mount the next play. This made advance planning of a three- or four-play season impossible. It survived on the talents it attracted, the remarkable financial legerdemain and technical expertise of Libin, and the tight-jawed tenacity of

Mann. With each production, the feet were put to the fire. Libin was the master wielder. He was Blackstone, Houdini. His machinations to keep the place alive over the years were beyond belief.

In 1972 Circle had the opportunity to change its destiny. A New York real estate development company, the Uris Organization, was planning to put up a large office building on West Fiftieth Street near Eighth Avenue, in the heart of the Broadway theater district. That theater district itself was experiencing a significant decline. New York City and the administration of Mayor Lindsay, eager to try to reverse the drop, were offering substantial zoning and tax benefits to Uris if it would include a new Broadway musical theater in its design—what would become the 1,900-seat Uris Theatre and is now the Gershwin. The developers would be given additional benefits if they added a smaller theater to the design. To their surprise, Libin and Mann received a phone call from the New York City Planning Commission inviting their interest in taking over and operating the smaller venue. Before anyone in the administration could come up with a better idea, they said yes.

The developer readily acceded to Circle's request to replicate the company's original unusual arena shape, which had worked so well downtown. No structure like it existed on Broadway. But the producers had found that the arena design enhanced the audience's intimacy with the performers and the play, and they wished to retain it. Circle in the Square began its new life on Broadway on November 15, 1972, with O'Neill's play *Mourning Becomes Electra*.

The news coverage lavished on the New York Shakespeare Festival and Joe Papp would be enough to make any theater jealous, and Mann occasionally complained to Debuskey asking why Circle didn't get equal play. "He was envious of the New York Shakespeare Festival," said Debuskey. "He'd ask, 'Why can't you do it for us?' Ted thought I was working harder for the Public. It wasn't true. They just weren't equal. Joe had many shows going on down there at one time. Circle did one at a time."

Debuskey did make at least one special effort on behalf of Circle in the Square. In 1976 the Tony Awards were being produced by his old friend Alex Cohen. While the producer sat at a bar and sipped at his glass of Absolut, the press agent made the case that Circle deserved a special prize. "I prevailed upon Alex to give them a special Tony," recalled Debuskey. "I asked him to do it and argued and told him why. He listened and said, 'You're right.'" Circle's Tony was granted in recognition of twenty-five years of service to the American theater. "He was the architect of that award, absolutely," said Libin.

In 1990 Debuskey lost his main advocate at Circle when Paul Libin joined Jujamcyn Theaters, which owned five Broadway theaters and produced as well. This left the press agent alone with Ted Mann, a figure described by many of his colleagues as difficult to know and hard to get along with. "I think Ted felt that I never thought him the equal of Paul in the operation," observed Debuskey. "To me, Ted wasn't as likable as Paul. And Ted had ambitions of an artistic nature that I never seconded. Paul and I were very close. When Paul left, I think Ted felt he was going to assert himself."

Mann hired the Broadway general manager Robert Buckley as Circle's new managing director. Debuskey must have felt a strong sense of déjà vu when Buckley and Mann began to suggest that the press agent move one of his associates into the Circle building as an in-house publicist. It was Joe Papp's ownership skirmish all over again. Said Buckley:

> We had enough activity going on. I felt there needed to be some real work on an institutional level in terms of branding. We needed to be out there as an institution, and not just show-to-show. We asked Merle if he could put one of the associates in house, and their main concentration of work would be on Circle. He felt that the way they had been doing it was fine. I said, OK, what if we just hired somebody and keep you as a consultant? He sort of dug his heels in.

"I thought, holy cow, thirty years and the relationship worked pretty well," said Debuskey. "Why change it now? We had a meeting and Ted said, 'Bob tells me that in the regional theaters, the press agent is in the office with the producer and they do all the marketing out of the producer's office.' I said, 'Ted, has it ever occurred to you that Circle in the Square is not a regional theater? It's a Broadway theater.'" The insistence on proximity seemed particularly amusing to Debuskey since Circle was on Fiftieth Street and his office was on Fifty-fourth.

A little later, Debuskey learned that a young woman named Maria Somma had been installed at the Circle offices with a desk and telephone. Buckley insists Debuskey was apprised of the change; the press agent denies it. Either way, after twenty-six years, Debuskey was out. Circle would struggle along through two more brief artistic directorships, under Josephine Abady and Gregory Mosher, before succumbing in 1997.

———

After André Bishop assumed the position vacated by Mosher at Lincoln Center Theater, Debuskey was free to devote his entire attention to the nonprofit. After decades of juggling myriad concerns, he now chose to handle a single client, albeit an extremely high-profile one. And he was content to be through with the commercial theater. Debuskey always gravitated toward the high concept, and those were only to be found in the Off-Broadway and nonprofit worlds. "I think it's some sort of inverted snobbery," he admitted.

Whether Bishop wanted Debuskey's full attention, however, was another matter. Bishop, a bookish-looking man with a drawling, quasi-British accent, had earned the theater world's respect as the head of the Off-Broadway theater company Playwrights Horizons, which had achieved much success in a smaller theater. Bishop had fostered the work of many new playwrights and presented three Pulitzer Prize winners: Stephen Sondheim's *Sunday in the Park with George*, Alfred Uhry's *Driving Miss Daisy*, and Wendy Wasserstein's *Heidi Chronicles*. By the late 1980s no artistic director in town had more cachet.

"I didn't know him," Debuskey recalled. "There was a certain coolness in the very beginning between us, which I did not recognize at the time. But several years later, Bernie told me that part of the deal when they were negotiating with André to come over was that he would bring his Playwrights Horizons press agent, Philip Rinaldi. But that part of the deal was denied him. So he was stuck with a press agent not of his choice."

The relationship would never jell. Debuskey began to believe that Bishop couldn't even stand to be in his presence. Part of the reason, the publicist thought, was that his long connection with Gersten, in Bishop's view, upset the balance of power at Lincoln Center. "It was liking having a stone in your shoe for André. His experience had been that he was the dominant figure at Playwrights Horizons. Now he was co-master with Bernie. And one of his tools, the press agent, was in Bernie's room, figuratively."

Susan Chicoine thought the division was a generational gap— not just in age, but in the divergent ways Bishop and Debuskey approached the producer—press agent relationship.

> André's approach to everything was much quicker. He knew exactly what he wanted, and there wasn't a conversation about 'Well, this might work better.' The press things were changing so much, in terms of the way we were approaching the media, with the Internet. Everything was moving much faster and that was something that Merle wasn't exactly staying on top of. It was much more of a collaboration in the old days.

Debuskey could be stubborn in his insistence on the old ways. For instance, he still had a manual typewriter. When the newly hired Chicoine arrived in the office with a computer, Debuskey scolded, "Oh, no, no. We use typewriters here." However, Debuskey eventually equipped his office with the latest technology.

The theater's success had continued under Bishop's watch, with shows such as Wendy Wasserstein's *Sisters Rosensweig*, which opened at the Newhouse and moved to Broadway; Tom Stoppard's *Arcadia*; and a stunning revival of Rodgers and Hammerstein's *Carousel*, directed by Nicholas Hytner and featuring a young actress named Audra Ann McDonald (soon to be multiple Tony winner Audra McDonald). All received copious amounts of positive ink. It would be hard to argue that Lincoln Center hadn't been represented well in the press.

Having been excluded from the Lincoln Center conversation by Bishop, and still smarting from his breaks with Joe Papp and Circle and the Square, Debuskey became somewhat jaded about the theater. "By the end, many... of my intimates had disappeared. Bernie was the only principal left. The only obligation I felt was to the people who were working with me." Chicoine said he often talked of retiring—"but he did not expect to be *asked* to retire." Gersten, in the opinion of the producer Emanuel Azenberg, who knew both men, sheltered Debuskey from Bishop's growing displeasure for some months. But two weeks before Christmas of 1995, that protection ended.

Debuskey was summoned to Gersten's office. "It was after lunch, and I ambled up there," Debuskey recalled. "I went through the reception area and a slew of offices and cubicles, and I stopped to talk to everybody on the way. Bernie wasn't waiting for me in his office. He was looking flushed and very disturbed. I thought, 'Oh Jesus, I wonder what's happening. Something's really got to him.'"

When Debuskey entered the office, he noticed that Gersten did not stay seated behind his desk, as was his usual habit, but pulled up two chairs and sat opposite his friend, knee to knee.

> I kept wondering what was going on. He said to me, with no elaboration, "You're handling three shows. They all close soon. You can work up to the end of those contracts and that's it." I said, "What are you talking about?" He said, "That's all you're contracted for."
>
> I thought, Holy shit, this is a man I've known for more than forty years, we've worked together on hundreds of contracts. I said, "Bernie, don't you think I'm entitled to some explanation?" He said, "Well, we've had this problem ever since André came over. And it's reached the point that he feels he can no longer work with you." I said, "What about you?" He said it wasn't him, that it was just his responsibility to give me the news.

Years later Gersten would deny this, saying it was his and Bishop's joint decision to dismiss Debuskey—which he actually characterized as "[asking] Merle to retire." Gersten added, "He'd been a press agent too long."

Debuskey asked Gersten why he had not come to him with the problem beforehand. According to the press agent, Gersten said, "Listen, whenever I had a problem, personal or professional, who would I call? I would call you. And now I had this problem and I couldn't call you."

They agreed that Debuskey would handle shows at the Newhouse for the rest of the season and that would be the end. Debuskey, always insistent upon straight shooting from his colleagues, demanded that Bishop talk to him face to face. When that happened, Debuskey said, Bishop told him simply that he didn't think the artistic director should have to be uncomfortable with the press agent.

If his break with Papp had hurt Debuskey, this crushed him. For the third time in ten years, he had been cast away by men he had known and worked with for decades.

"He was devastated," recalled Jeffrey Horowitz, the artistic director of Theatre for a New Audience, who in the mid-1990s courted and finally convinced a reluctant Debuskey to take on his theater as a client. "What Merle told me is that André wanted to work with someone else. He understood that. It was painful, but it was how it was done—so suddenly, in the middle of a season, just calling him down, handing him his walking papers, rather than giving him the time to do this in a dignified way. He was so devastated by it that he didn't want to practice anymore. It was 'Et tu, Brute?' for him."

Debuskey's wife was furious with Gersten and refused to speak to him. Gersten's wife, Cora Cahan, was equally furious with Pearl for being furious. The two met at Alexander H. Cohen's house and, according to Pearl, Cahan said, "How dare you be angry at Bernie?!" Somner replied, "I have nothing to say to you." "Yes," retorted Cahan, "well, where was Merle when Bernie got fired?"

But while many of Debuskey's friends were furious with Gersten, others were not surprised by the event. "There was a borderline entitlement," offered Azenberg. "In this business, you have new beginnings every year. You're not your last show, you're your next show. There's no great security, so you've got to pour it on."

Gersten and Debuskey never saw completely eye to eye on the split. Following Debuskey's departure, the two men did not speak for ten years.

———

Perhaps the break with Lincoln Center was inevitable. Times had changed in the theater since Debuskey first joined it, and his values and those of the twenty-first-century theater community were now worlds apart. It was more industry than artistry, more corporate than collaborative. Moreover, theater publicity was handled piecemeal, show by show, with little thought to the historical continuum or social impact of the art. "When he was really in his prime," said Horowitz, "before producing a play, you developed ideas with the producer; thinking through ideas was very much part of his work. It wasn't just 'What's the angle for the show?' It started way longer before. I'm not saying he developed a theater's mission, but he understood a theater's mission and how that connected to a choice for a play. It was something he was very interested in."

"The Broadway and Off-Broadway theater had undergone a radical alteration," observed Debuskey.

> It no longer was primarily theater—it was big business, adopting a corporate mentality. Absolutely, shows would be produced and some would be of a high level of creative accomplishment, but there no longer would be the same community of individuals who lived in and for the theater. No longer did one qualify as a producer by having toiled and garnered the necessary experience and know-how in lesser venues of the trade. They were major investors, more often than not selecting projects that had a previous life elsewhere. True, the clan of credited producers on a show usually had at its hub a true producer, someone with theater experience, a creative talent, but one very short on money.

In a different respect, however, things hadn't changed much for press agents at all. Before and after World War II, independent producers had dedicated press agents who slaved and sweated only for *their* shows. Toward the end of the century, producers still liked it best when a press agent was in their pocket, at their beck and call—a live-in servant. Independence of thought wasn't prized.

Debuskey resisted having a single employer throughout his career, and in the end it worked against him. Both Joe Papp and Ted Mann had wanted him on site. Debuskey refused, and eventually that refusal led to the dissolution of the partnerships. Lincoln Center was Debuskey's sole client toward the end, but even then he persisted in working out of his messy, cluttered Eighth Avenue office, rather than at the arts center. And so Debuskey left the industry as he had entered it—on his own terms.

And when he left the business, some felt it was the end of an era. "There is no press agent at the moment who has Merle's position," said Barnes, just before he died in 2008. "They don't have the gravitas."

"To me, he was the last of the gentleman press agents," said Chicoine. "Part of working with Merle was being able to meet the great showmen, the men who knew what they wanted and had a vision and made it happen. It was a different era. It was an era where you weren't expected to cover things up as much. There wasn't as much to hide from. It was a different universe. Saying no was a lot easier when artists weren't out there being crazy."

One of the things every associate who worked under Debuskey remembered was that ever-present sign on the wall—"No is also an answer." Every one of Merle's associates seemed to interpret the sign differently. Some interpretations were simplistic: when people call for tickets, you don't always have to say yes. For Chicoine, who has the same sign on her own office wall, it meant that you can't always accomplish everything you want to, that sometimes the powers that be in the media are going to turn you down.

For Debuskey, it could have meant a myriad of things depending on the circumstances. No, you didn't have to take on a show or a company if you didn't like it or didn't want to. You didn't have to agree with an opinion or course of action just because it happened to come from the mind of your producer. You needn't sit back and accept the verdicts rendered by the critics. You could say no to the blacklisters, no to the bigots, no to the labor busters, no to Robert Moses. You could even say no to your friends and colleagues while in heated discussion and still keep them as friends and colleagues.

———

Merle Debuskey was feted at a retirement party held on May 8, 1996. Several hundred people gathered to honor him at the Supper Club nightclub on West Forty-seventh Street. Among the speakers were the producer Alexander H. Cohen; the actress Madeline Lee Gilford, widow of Jack Gilford; Bob Kamlot, a general manager for four decades; Paul Libin, the producer of Circle in the Square from the 1960s to the 1990s and now the number 2 at Jujamcyn Theaters; the director the former *New York Times* chief critic, Frank Rich; Gene Saks; the Shubert executive Lee Silver; the Broadway producer and general manager Eugene Wolsk; and Bernard Gersten. (Cohen had persuaded Debuskey that Gersten should take part in the event.) All paid $75 a head.

Cohen spoke first. Debuskey, he said, fits "the modern definition of a curmudgeon—anyone who hates hypocrisy and pretense and has the temerity to say so; anyone in the habit of pointing out unpleasant facts in an engaging and humorous manner."

Gersten spoke last. "Merle was the strategist of the inevitable wars of the theater, the tactician of the day-to-day battles," he said. Debuskey was a "nonpareil of the species. Merle has been the guy who whispers in the ears—shouting when necessary—of the guys who run the theaters."

Debuskey was presented with a heavy glass award. It was inscribed, "May 8, 1996. To Merle, with great appreciation and gratitude for your wise and loving ministrations to sixty shows that put Lincoln Center Theater on its feet and the map. The Board and the Staff." The same day he was presented with the Actors Fund Medal of Honor and a portrait by James McMullan, the resident poster artist at Lincoln Center Theater.

During the years since that night, Debuskey has watched his profession and former stomping ground transform itself into something he can scarcely recognize. "The incredibly swift development of electronic media has pushed print and broadcast news almost to the point of extinction," he observed,

> and those that have survived had to create another means of exis-
> tence, both in terms of their financial structure and how it handled
> news. It shrunk, in numbers, areas of coverage and style of reporting.
> When I slid into the field, New York City had a dozen dailies, two in
> Newark, two in Westchester, three wire services, seven TV stations,
> eight "gossip" columnists, [and] a dozen magazines and major dailies
> in cities across the country. All of them had a keen interest in the the-
> ater, offering news of it on a daily basis, and were serviced regularly.
> Press agents and newsmen were very close, even intimate. We were
> sharing or competing for information, elbow room in saloons, and
> sometimes amours. We needed one another, and the competition was
> rife among all. There was an incessant intermingling.
>
> Today there is virtually no space in the dailies, and it has been
> replaced by an enormous outbreak of Web sites to wrestle with. The
> former traditional modus and style of critics has also experienced a
> radical change, not necessarily for the better. An opening night can now
> be a week. Today's press agents are certainly as expert and as dedicated
> as ever they were, but their qualities, characteristics, and mode of work
> have also changed to fit the new forms of media. Whereas contact
> with the press was once maintained by frequent visits to the welcoming
> offices of the media, lunches, telephone conversations, exchanging
> letters, meetings in the specific *boîtes* and restaurants known to be
> the homes-away-from-home for journalists and columnists, it now is
> largely confined to e-mails with few or no personal exchanges.
>
> Broadway's theaters still light up brightly for matinee and evening
> performances, and most of the theaters are offering audiences a sig-
> nificant night out. But what are the attractions, and whence did they
> originate? Today the Playbill of a show can note as many as twenty-
> four producers. Can you imagine that covey gathering to make the
> choices of the elements that go into a production? I can—and the
> thought frightens and amuses me.

Perhaps curiously, in the years since his retirement, when Debuskey has been asked what part of his life he is most proud of, he has not mentioned any part of his fifty years in the theater, but has harked back to his days on the playing field in high school and college, and to his tour aboard a Navy vessel, fighting the Japanese during World War II.

> We had been part of an effort we deemed noble—strangers working together in a common cause for the common good. I came away with the belief that with purpose, sacrifice, [and] willingness to work diligently, respecting the efforts and choices of others, almost anything was within one's grasp. This attitude had been ingested into the persona of World War II veterans for some years after the war. The insemination, conceiving, and nursing of the Off-Broadway movement in the late 1940s and '50s was heavily influenced by that quality.
>
> Today materialism, individualism, distrust of others, [and] political divisiveness have replaced that brief moment of nobleness. How this country had unselfishly pulled together during the war was remarkable and exemplified its potential for extraordinary accomplishments. And we had played a small part, not unlike the singers and dancers in the chorus of a Broadway musical—generally not distinguishable, but without whom the musical would not be complete.

BROADWAY CREDITS

Racing Demon	November 20, 1995–December 31, 1995
Sacrilege	November 2, 1995–November 19, 1995
Chronicle of a Death Foretold	June 15, 1995–July 16, 1995
Arcadia	March 31, 1995–August 27, 1995
The Heiress	March 9, 1995–December 31, 1995
Comedy Tonight	December 18, 1994–December 25, 1994
Gray's Anatomy	June 5, 1994–June 27, 1994
Carousel (Revival)	March 24, 1994–January 15, 1995
Abe Lincoln in Illinois (Revival)	November 29, 1993–January 2, 1994
Gray's Anatomy	November 28, 1993–January 3, 1994
In the Summer House (Revival)	August 1, 1993–August 22, 1993
The Sisters Rosensweig	March 18, 1993–July 16, 1994
My Favorite Year	December 10, 1992–January 10, 1993
Four Baboons Adoring the Sun	March 18, 1992–April 19, 1992
The Most Happy Fella (Revival,)	February 13, 1992–August 30, 1992
Two Shakespearean Actors	January 16, 1992–February 9, 1992
Taking Steps	February 20, 1991–April 28, 1991
Mule Bone	February 14, 1991–April 14, 1991
Monster in a Box	January 21, 1991–[unknown]
Six Degrees of Separation	November 8, 1990–January 5, 1992
The Miser	October 11, 1990–December 30, 1990
Zoya's Apartment	May 10, 1990–June 17, 1990
Some Americans Abroad	May 2, 1990–June 17, 1990
The Tenth Man	December 10, 1989–January 14, 1990
Mastergate	October 12, 1989–December 10, 1989
Sweeney Todd (Revival)	September 14, 1989–February 25, 1990
Ghetto	April 30, 1989–May 28, 1989
The Devil's Disciple (Revival)	November 13, 1988–February 19, 1989
The Night of the Iguana (Revival)	June 26, 1988–September 4, 1988

Juneo and the Paycock (Revival)	June 21, 1988–July 2, 1988
Speed-the-Plow	May 3, 1988–December 31, 1988
A Streetcar Named Desire (Revival)	March 10, 1988–May 22, 1988
Sarafina!	January 28, 1988–July 2, 1989
Anything Goes (Revival)	October 19, 1987–September 3, 1989
The Comedy of Errors	May 31, 1987–July 26, 1987
The Regard of Flight	April 12, 1987–April 26, 1987
Coastal Disturbances	March 4, 1987–January 3, 1988
Death and the King's Horseman	March 1, 1987–March 29, 1987
The Front Page (Revival)	November 23, 1986–January 11, 1987
You Never Can Tell (Revival)	October 9, 1986–January 25, 1987
The Boys in Autumn	April 30, 1986–June 29, 1986
The House of Blue Leaves	April 29, 1986–March 15, 1987
The Flying Karamazov Brothers "Juggling and Cheap Theatrics"	April 1, 1986–April 20, 1986
The Caretaker (Revival)	January 30, 1986–March 9, 1986
The Robert Klein Show!	December 20, 1985–January 4, 1986
The Mystery of Edwin Drood	December 2, 1985–May 16, 1987
The Marchriage of Figaro	October 10, 1985–December 15, 1985
Arms and the Man (Revival)	May 30, 1985–September 1, 1985
The Loves of Anatol	March 6, 1985–April 14, 1985
Accidental Death of an Anarchist	November 15, 1984–December 1, 1984
Design For Living (Revival)	June 20, 1984–January 20, 1985
The Human Comedy	April 5, 1984–April 15, 1984
Awake and Sing! (Revival)	March 8, 1984–April 29, 1984
The Rink	February 9, 1984–August 4, 1984
Heartbreak House (Revival)	December 7, 1983–February 5, 1984
La Tragedie de Carmen	November 17, 1983–April 28, 1984
Edmund Kean	September 27, 1983–October 29, 1983
The Caine Mutiny Court-Martial (Revival)	May 5, 1983–November 6, 1983
The Misanthrope (Revival)	January 27, 1983–March 27, 1983
Plenty	January 6, 1983–March 27, 1983
84 Charing Cross Road	December 7, 1982–February 27, 1983
The Queen and the Rebels	September 30, 1982–November 7, 1982
Present Laughter (Revival)	July 15, 1982–January 2, 1983
Eminent Domain	March 28, 1982–May 23, 1982
The World of Sholom Aleichem	February 11, 1982–February 28, 1982
Macbeth (Revival)	January 28, 1982–February 14, 1982
The Little Prince and the Aviator (never offically opened)	January 17, 1982

Dreamgirls	December 20, 1981–August 11, 1985
Candida (Revival)	October 15, 1981–January 3, 1982
Scenes and Revelations	June 25, 1981–July 19, 1981
The Father (Revival)	April 2, 1981–April 26, 1981
Woman of the Year	March 29, 1981–March 13, 1983
The Pirates of Penzance (Revival)	January 8, 1981–November 28, 1982
Frankenstein	January 4, 1981–January 4, 1981
John Gabriel Borkman (Revival)	December 18, 1980–February 8, 1981
Amadeus	December 17, 1980–October 16, 1983
Tricks of the Trade	November 6, 1980–November 6, 1980
The Bacchae	October 2, 1980–November 23, 1980
The Man Who Came to Dinner (Revival)	June 26, 1980–September 7, 1980
Past Tense	April 24, 1980–June 1, 1980
Charlotte	February 27, 1980–March 1, 1980
Major Barbara (Revival)	February 26, 1980–March 30, 1980
Comin' Uptown	December 20, 1979–January 27, 1980
Loose Ends	June 6, 1979–January 27, 1980
Bosoms and Neglect	May 3, 1979–May 5, 1979
Zoot Suit	March 25, 1979–April 29, 1979
Spokesong	March 15, 1979–May 20, 1979
Man and Superman (Revival)	December 14, 1978–February 18, 1979
Ballroom	December 14, 1978–March 24, 1979
The Inspector (Revival)	September 21, 1978–November 19, 1978
Once in a Lifetime (Revival)	June 15, 1978–August 27, 1978
Runaways	May 13, 1978–December 31, 1978
Angel	May 10, 1978–May 13, 1978
Dancin'	March 27, 1978–June 27, 1982
13 Rue de l'Amour	March 16, 1978–May 21, 1978
The Water Engine/Mr. Happiness	February 28, 1978–March 19, 1978
Saint Joan (Revival)	December 15, 1977–February 19, 1978
The Merchant	November 16, 1977–November 20, 1977
The Act	October 29, 1977–July 1, 1978
Miss Marchgarida's Way	September 27, 1977–January 1, 1978
Tartuffe (Revival)	September 25, 1977–November 20, 1977
The Cherry Orchard (Revival)	June 29, 1977–August 7, 1977
The Importance of Being Earnest (Revival)	June 16, 1977–August 28, 1977
Agamemnon (Revival)	May 18, 1977–June 19, 1977
Romeo and Julyiet (Revival)	March 17, 1977–May 22, 1977
The Cherry Orchard (Revival)	February 17, 1977–April 10, 1977
The Trip Back Down	January 4, 1977–March 5, 1977

The Night of the Iguana (Revival)	December 16, 1976–February 20, 1977
Sly Fox	December 14, 1976–February 19, 1978
Days in the Trees (Revival)	September 26, 1976–November 21, 1976
for colored girls who have considered suicide/when the rainbow is enuf	September 15, 1976–July 16, 1978
Pal Joey (Revival)	June 27, 1976–August 29, 1976
Threepenny Opera (Revival)	May 1, 1976–January 23, 1977
Streamers	April 21, 1976–June 5, 1977
The Lady from the Sea (Revival)	March 18, 1976–May 23, 1976
Mrs. Warren's Profession (Revival)	February 18, 1976–April 4, 1976
The Poison Tree	January 8, 1976–January 11, 1976
The Glass Menagerie (Revival)	December 18, 1975–February 22, 1976
Hamlet (Revival)	December 17, 1975–January 25, 1976
The Leaf People	October 20, 1975–October 26, 1975
Trelawny of the "Wells" (Revival)	October 15, 1975–November 23, 1975
Ah, Wilderness! (Revival)	September 18, 1975–November 23, 1975
A Chorus Line	July 25, 1975–April 28, 1990
Death of a Salesman (Revival)	June 26, 1975–August 24, 1975
Little Black Sheep	May 7, 1975–June 1, 1975
A Doll's House (Revival)	March 5, 1975–April 20, 1975
Hughie / Duet	February 11, 1975–March 8, 1975
Shenandoah	January 7, 1975–August 7, 1977
Black Picture Show	January 6, 1975–February 9, 1975
Mert & Phil	October 30, 1974–December 8, 1974
The National Health	October 10, 1974–November 23, 1974
Scapino (Revival)	September 27, 1974–March 2, 1975
Short Eyes	May 23, 1974–August 4, 1974
Scapino	May 18, 1974–August 31, 1974
An American Millionaire	April 20, 1974–May 5, 1974
Thieves	April 7, 1974–January 4, 1975
Dance of Death (Revival)	April 4, 1974–May 5, 1974
What the Wine-Sellers Buy	February 14, 1974–March 17, 1974
The au Pair Man	December 27, 1973–January 27, 1974
The Good Doctor	November 27, 1973–May 25, 1974
Boom Boom Room	November 8, 1973–December 9, 1973
The Waltz of the Toreadors (Revival)	September 13, 1973–November 25, 1973
Uncle Vanya (Revival)	June 4, 1973–July 28, 1973
Medea (Revival)	January 17, 1973–March 18, 1973

Purlie (Revival)	December 27, 1972–January 7, 1973
Mourning Becomes Electra (Revival)	November 15, 1972–December 31, 1972
Much Ado About Nothing (Revival)	November 11, 1972–February 11, 1973
That Championship Season	September 14, 1972–April 21, 1974
Sticks and Bones	March 1, 1972–October 1, 1972
Two Gentlemen of Verona	December 1, 1971–May 20, 1973
Unlikely Heroes	October 26, 1971–November 13, 1971
– Defender of the Faith	
– Epstein	
– Eli, the Fanatic	
Ain't Supposed to Die a Natural Death	October 20, 1971–July 30, 1972
Jesus Christ Superstar	October 12, 1971–June 30, 1973
No, No, Nanette (Revival)	January 19, 1971–February 3, 1973
Purlie	March 15, 1970–November 6, 1971
No Place to Be Somebody	December 30, 1969–January 10, 1970
Love Is a Time of Day	December 22, 1969–December 27, 1969
Trumpets of the Lord	April 29, 1969–May 3, 1969
Come Summer	March 18, 1969–March 22, 1969
But, Seriously.	February 27, 1969–March 1, 1969
Does a Tiger Wear a Necktie?	February 25, 1969–March 29, 1969
The Goodbye People	December 3, 1968–December 7, 1968
Morning, Noon and Night	November 28, 1968–January 11, 1969
– Morning	
– Noon	
– Night	
Lovers and Other Strangers	September 18, 1968–November 16, 1968
Portrait of a Queen	February 28, 1968–April 20, 1968
The Ninety Day Mistress	November 6, 1967–November 25, 1967
Hallelujah, Baby!	April 26, 1967–January 13, 1968
Walking Happy	November 26, 1966–April 22, 1967
The Investigation	October 4, 1966–December 31, 1966
Nathan Weinstein, Mystic, Connecticut	February 25, 1966–February 26, 1966
Man of La Mancha	November 22, 1965–June 26, 1971
Skyscraper	November 13, 1965–June 11, 1966
The Zulu and the Zayda	November 10, 1965–April 16, 1966
The Royal Hunt of the Sun	October 26, 1965–June 11, 1966
And Things That Go Bump in the Night	April 26, 1965–May 8, 1965

Peterpat	January 6, 1965–January 23, 1965
Bajour	November 23, 1964–June 12, 1965
The Owl and the Pussycat	November 18, 1964–November 27, 1965
The Sign in Sidney Brustein's Window	October 15, 1964–January 10, 1965
Absence of a Cello	September 21, 1964–January 4, 1965
Traveller Without Luggage	September 17, 1964–October 24, 1964
Cafe Crown	April 17, 1964–April 18, 1964
Abraham Cochrane	February 17, 1964–February 17, 1964
Nobody Loves an Albatross	December 19, 1963–June 20, 1964
Semi-Detached (Revival)	October 7, 1963–October 19, 1963
The Riot Act	March 7, 1963–April 13, 1963
On an Open Roof	January 28, 1963–January 28, 1963
Little Me	November 17, 1962–June 27, 1963
How to Succeed in Business Without Really Trying	October 14, 1961–March 6, 1965
A Far Country	April 4, 1961–November 25, 1961
Marchy, Marchy	March 8, 1961–December 12, 1964
Come Blow Your Horn	February 22, 1961–October 6, 1962
The Wall	October 11, 1960–March 4, 1961
Semi-Detached	March 10, 1960–March 12, 1960
The Good Soup	March 2, 1960–March 19, 1960
Toys in the Attic	February 25, 1960–April 8, 1961
A Raisin in the Sun	March 11, 1959–June 25, 1960
The World of Suzie Wong	October 14, 1958–January 2, 1960
Cloud 7	February 14, 1958–February 22, 1958
Look Homeward, Angel	November 28, 1957–April 4, 1959
The Diary of Anne Frank	October 5, 1955–June 22, 1957
A View From the Bridge	September 29, 1955–February 4, 1956
– A View From the Bridge	
– A Memory of Two Mondays	
Inherit the Wind	April 21, 1955–June 22, 1957
The Saint of Bleecker Street	December 27, 1954–April 2, 1955
Mrs. Patterson	December 1, 1954–February 26, 1955
The Crucible	January 22, 1953–July 11, 1953
Paint Your Wagon	November 12, 1951–July 19, 1952
The Rose Tattoo	February 3, 1951–October 27, 1951

INDEX